# CHOOSING NAIA

# Choosing Naia

## A FAMILY'S JOURNEY

Mitchell Zuckoff

BEACON
150

Beacon Press
Boston

BEACON PRESS
25 Beacon Street
Boston, Massachusetts 02108-2892
www.beacon.org

Beacon Press books are published under the auspices of
the Unitarian Universalist Association of Congregations.

Printed in the United States of America

"Never My Love" by Don Addrisi and Richard Addrisi,
© 1967 Careers-BMG Music Publishing, Inc.
(BMI) / Warner-Tamerlane Publishing. All rights reserved. Used by permission.

07  06  05  04  03   8 7 6 5 4 3 2 1

This book is printed on acid-free paper that meets the uncoated
paper ANSI/NISO specifications for permanence as revised in 1992.

Text design by Christopher Kuntze

Library of Congress Cataloging-in-Publication Data

Zuckoff, Mitchell.
    Choosing Naia : a family's journey / Mitchell Zuckoff.
    p. ; cm.
Includes bibliographical references.
    ISBN 0-8070-2816-9 (cloth)
    ISBN 0-8070-2817-7 (pbk.)
    1. Down syndrome—Popular Works. 2. Fetus—Abnormalities—Popular
Works. 3. Pregnancy—Complications—Popular Works. 4. Genetic disorders in
pregnancy—Popular Works. 5. Congenital heart disease in children—Popular
Works.
    [DNLM: 1. Child, Exceptional—Popular works. 2. Down syndrome—
psychology—Popular works. 3. Parents—psychology—Popular works. 4.
Prenatal Diagnosis—Popular works. WS 107.5.R5 Z94c 2002]
    I. Title.
    RG629.D68 Z83 2002
    362.3—dc21

                                                        2002006201

FOR
Isabel & Eve

# CONTENTS

PART III

# PROLOGUE

In November 1935, a child was born in the rural New Hampshire town of Twin Mountain. He was healthy and strong, with ten fingers and ten toes, but he wasn't what most people call perfect. Half his face was severely deformed.

Back then, less-than-perfect births were always a surprise. There was no way to predict whether a newborn would be greeted by smiles or tears.

The baby with the deformed face grew up under the protective watch of an older brother. As a boy, he suffered for his deformity, but he worked hard and made friends. As a man, he hiked and loved music and earned the respect of those who knew him. He never married or had children, and he never moved far from Twin Mountain. His older brother did, though, and when his brother's wife bore her third child, a girl, the man with the deformed face became godfather to his niece. When she was small, he got down on the floor and played with her. When she was older, he had a way of making her feel good about herself. He cherished that role.

The goddaughter grew into a lovely woman. She fell in love, married, and became pregnant. By then, less-than-perfect births weren't always surprises anymore. During the six decades between the godfather's birth and the goddaughter's pregnancy, a scientific revolution took place. Pictures made from sound waves could reveal a fetus's misshapen face, missing limbs, deformed spine, damaged heart. Other tests could peer inside a fetus's cells to detect Down syndrome, cystic fibrosis, dwarfism, muscular dystrophy, sickle-cell anemia, Tay-Sachs disease, and more. Tests on eggs fertilized in a petri dish could allow parents to choose which to implant and which to discard, based on predictions of good health or even whether they wanted a baby in pink or blue.

But all that knowledge came with a catch. There were no cures for most problems spotted during pregnancy, so a prenatal diagnosis of disease or disorder was usually followed by a life-altering choice: continue the pregnancy or abort the "imperfect" fetus. In the midst of grieving the loss of the healthy child they wouldn't be having, expectant parents had to face questions of laws and ethics, duty and discrimination, financial burden and emotional cost, freedom and faith, suffering and grace.

This is a story about those questions, and how they were answered by the goddaughter and her husband.

It is also a story about how the echoes of scientific discoveries travel far from the sterile laboratories where they're made, reverberating in the lives of ordinary people. And it is a story about how deformities can be worn on the face or hidden in the heart.

Most of all, it is a story about an overlooked truth, one that will forever escape detection by even the most advanced prenatal tests: Family legacies, good and bad, are handed down from one generation to the next as much by deeds as by genes.

# Part I

# CHAPTER 1 "DON'T WORRY, MOM. EVERYTHING WILL BE FINE"

"Mom, did you have a baby shower?"

"No, Tierney. But there was a reason."

Tierney Temple-Fairchild and her mother, Joan Temple, were passing time in Tierney's car, driving northeast on Interstate 84 outside Hartford. It was a late afternoon in early May. The sun was bright, the spring air was warm, and new leaves graced the trees lining the highway. Forsythia bushes were ablaze with yellow blossoms.

Mother and daughter had been talking about work, weather, and nothing terribly important. Then Tierney casually asked about the shower. The question brought to her mother's mind a memory, long buried in the place that stores unsent letters, unpaid debts, and unmade apologies. Joan could see no reason not to share it with her youngest child.

It was forty years ago, Joan began. She was a young married woman, around Tierney's age, pregnant with the first of her three children, Tierney's brother, George. As she neared the end of her pregnancy, one of her closest friends delivered a stillborn child. It came as a devastating shock; the friend had already painted the nursery, assembled a layette, and dreamed the dreams of all happy first-time mothers.

After her friend's loss, Joan told Tierney, she wouldn't allow anyone to throw her a baby shower. She didn't want to celebrate in the wake of her friend's tragedy, and she didn't want to tempt fate by acting immune to such pain. Lightning had struck someone standing next to her, Joan figured, and she wasn't about to wave an umbrella in the air. No one could persuade her otherwise, and Joan had dug in her heels right up to the moment her water broke. She had so refused to prepare for a baby that Tierney's father had missed the birth of his namesake son. He was out buying a crib.

Tierney listened quietly. Normally she loved hearing family stories. But as Joan spoke, Tierney gripped the steering wheel and kept her eyes trained on the road ahead. When Joan finished, Tierney quickly changed the subject.

Tierney had a secret she was keeping from her mother, and the last thing she wanted to talk about was a stillborn child. That could lead to thoughts about bad omens and a mother's intuition, and no good could come of that. The conversation moved on, and Joan let the memory drop.

What Joan couldn't possibly have known was that next to her on the front seat, tucked safely in Tierney's purse, were the first recorded images of her first grandchild.

One night several weeks earlier, Tierney had been at home with her husband, Greg Fairchild, in the book-filled one-bedroom apartment they shared in a convenient but unlovely part of downtown Hartford. They had just come home from dinner at a nearby restaurant, and they were alone except for their excitable black poodle, Onyx.

Almost on a whim, Tierney decided to break out the last in-home pregnancy test in her medicine cabinet. She had already gone through nearly a dozen, each one a disappointment. Tierney's urine had never revealed a pastel stripe, a red cross, or any other indication that parenthood was in their future. Tierney had equally low expectations for the plastic wand she held in her hand. She suspected that she had ovulated when she was out of town for several days on a business trip, costing them yet another month.

Tierney and Greg had known each other for almost nine years. They had been in love for eight, married for nearly four. A graduate student, Greg was thirty-four. A corporate manager, Tierney was thirty-one. They'd trash-canned their birth control almost a year earlier, feeling ready to start working on their imagined ideal family: three children, two biological and one adopted.

When Tierney hadn't become pregnant during the first few months of trying, both of them had grown anxious but neither felt panicked. Tierney had been on the Pill, and they knew it might take six months or so for her body to readjust its cycles and begin ovulating normally again.

When those six months passed and nothing happened, Tierney sought answers from her obstetrician/gynecologist, Dr. Michael Bourque, whom she had known since she was nineteen. A battery of tests showed that she still wasn't ovulating, so Bourque had started her on a relatively low dose of a fertility medicine called Clomid, a synthetic compound in a class of drugs called antiestrogens. Clomid is a first-line offense against infertility, designed to trigger a woman's body to produce an egg ready for fertilization.

Bourque had told Tierney not to worry, but it wasn't easy as more months came and went. She and Greg began wondering if they'd ever be able to conceive. They started thinking about costly and invasive fertility procedures. They discussed whether a sperm or egg donor might be necessary, or whether they might have to adjust their family plans altogether and go straight to adoption.

By spring, Tierney had reached what Bourque said was the highest dosage he would prescribe of Clomid before sending her to a fertility specialist. He knew that among patients treated with Clomid, 95 percent who become pregnant do so within the first six months of taking the drug.

As part of her treatment, Tierney was monitoring her body temperature every day, charting the peaks and valleys that indicate ovulation—the magic formula is a sudden dip, followed by a three-day rise of at least two-tenths of a degree over the highest temperature recorded during the previous six days. One sign that ovulation has been answered by conception is the woman's temperature doesn't drop back down after the three-day rise. Tierney doubted it meant anything, but that's what seemed to be happening the April night she took out her last e.p.t.-brand home pregnancy test.

Tierney went into the bathroom and shut the door. Watching her from the wall was a black-and-white photo of jazz trumpeter Dizzy Gillespie, his eyes closed and his cheeks pregnant with air. She followed the instructions—allowing the wand's absorbent tip to sop up some of her urine. She left the test kit on the counter for the two-minute lifetime it would take to show positive or join its predecessors in the garbage.

Though she had been through this drill too many times before, Tierney was nervous about returning to the bathroom. She paced around the apartment while Greg stayed in the living room, keeping his hopes and his head down. He sat quietly, reading in a high-backed burgundy wing chair. On a nearby glass-front china cabinet sat Greg's bronzed baby shoes, alongside a sepia-toned photo of him as an adorable, smiling baby. When she was certain enough time had elapsed, Tierney waited a little longer. She steeled herself and returned to the bathroom.

And there it was, staring up at her from the tiny round indicator window: a bold pink stripe. She had never seen one before, except in the picture on the package. "Oh my God, that's what it looks like when you're pregnant," she said, bounding from the bathroom. She ran to Greg and jumped on his lap, her cheeks flushed with joy. The moment had finally arrived: a first pregnancy for both.

They basked in the news. They kissed, they smiled, they touched each other's faces. Still, they remained cautious about the possibility of a false-positive reading from the over-the-counter test. It would be awful to announce that they were pregnant only to withdraw the news afterward. They agreed not to tell anyone until Tierney could make an appointment with Bourque for confirmation.

That visit took place April 15. A blood test, an ultrasound, and a physical examination confirmed the in-home test results. Tierney was indeed pregnant. Even Bourque was excited, circling the positive results on Tierney's patient record and adding two huge exclamation points. And he added a bonus: the due date was December 7, Greg's birthday. The ob/gyn also gave Greg and Tierney tangible proof of impending parenthood: black-and-white ultrasound images the size of baseball cards.

To the untrained eye, the pictures had all the clarity of Rorschach's inkblots. Was that a leg? A lung? Tierney's placenta? Bourque assured them he could see a healthy-looking, eight-week embryo taking the developmental leap to becoming a fetus.

It was about an inch-and-a-half long. Fingers and toes were becoming clearly defined. Organs were starting to work. Spontaneous movements were beginning. Taste buds were starting to form. Tierney and Greg studied the images and tried to convince themselves they could see what Bourque did, but for the most part they had to take the doctor's word for it.

Thrilled as he was to have the pictures, Greg maintained a certain detachment. "It's like looking through an aquarium glass. You can't touch fish, even though they really are there," he said later. "You can't pick them up and you can't hold them and you can't play with them. You can't do all these things with babies when they're in utero. It's still a photo on an electric screen. When there's someone there who's crying, moving around, with needs, I think that creates a much different response."

Still, the grainy images were confirmation enough for Greg to phone his parents, Bob and Mary Fairchild, at their home in a small central Virginia town called Rustburg. Long eager to become grandparents, but unaware that Greg and Tierney had been trying to fulfill that dream, the news caught Bob and Mary by surprise. Bob expressed quiet congratulations. Mary let out an ear-piercing scream. They hung up after promising not to tell anyone. That was a treat Tierney and Greg wanted for themselves.

Tierney specifically hoped to contain word of her pregnancy for another few weeks, until mid-May, so she could tell Joan on Mother's Day.

But then came the car trip.


Tierney and Joan were in Tierney's midnight blue Honda Accord, en route to Marlborough, Massachusetts, a gritty little city halfway between Boston and Worcester. Their destination was Marlborough High School, to attend a symphony concert featuring Joan's older daughter, Tara.

Tara was thirty-two, a year older than Tierney. She was single, living in Worcester, a veterinarian by profession and a violinist by avocation. If they tried, the two sisters could pass for twins, a fact that pleased them both. Growing up, they were both good girls, "A" students, pretty, well-mannered, and polite. As children, they shared a love for koalas, and they had even invented their own imaginary koala language. Their bond had held strong over the years. In their teens, they had clung to each other through their parents' divorce; they had remained close as adults by regularly making the hour-long trip between their homes and by talking frequently on the phone. Tara was the only person to whom Tierney had confided her difficulties trying to conceive.

When Tierney saw Tara before the concert, she knew she couldn't wait any longer.

"I have something to tell you. It's a secret," Tierney blurted out. They hurried off together to a bathroom. Tierney pulled out the ultrasound pictures.

"I'm pregnant!" she said.

The sisters hugged and cried and struggled to pull themselves together. Tierney didn't want to spoil her Mother's Day present to Joan. They composed themselves and left the high school bathroom like teenagers who had just snuck a cigarette, though they never would have dared such defiance as girls. They emerged straight-faced and bright-eyed. Their stealth worked, but it didn't last.

After the concert, they drove to Tara's apartment. Standing in the street, getting ready to say goodbye, Tierney decided she could wait no more—she wanted Tara to share their mother's joy. Impulsively, she pulled out the ultrasound photos. But night had fallen and it was too dark to see. So Tierney, Tara, and Joan moved into the glare of the Honda's headlights. They huddled together, their heads just inches apart.

"That's my baby!" Tierney said. Joan cried for joy. Mother and daughters hugged.

On their drive back to Hartford, Tierney told Joan about the months of fertility problems, the in-home tests, everything that happened on the long road to pregnancy. Joan listened quietly, feeling guilty the whole time. She told Tierney she wished she hadn't chosen that very afternoon to tell the story about her friend's stillbirth.

"I'm so sorry," Joan said.

"Don't worry, Mom," Tierney said. "Everything will be fine."

In the weeks that followed, everything had indeed gone well. As she approached the halfway mark to nine months, Tierney had no complaints beyond her inability to fit into her favorite clothes: a bulge was developing nicely on her normally flat stomach. She suffered through only one day of morning sickness, and that was only because she was so busy with work that she had forgotten to eat.

Although Connecticut was sweltering through one of the hottest springs on record, Tierney continued jogging to stay in something vaguely resembling her usual shape. She ran a route that took her from their apartment building on Imlay Street through their Asylum Hill neighborhood, past the Taco Bell, the halfway houses, and the little ethnic markets located hard against Interstate 84. She also maintained a rigorous weight-training program at her gym, and it looked as though she would be the first person to stick with the regimen long enough to be used in the data the gym trainer was collecting for a Ph.D. dissertation.

All the medical indicators had been equally good. In June, as a routine follow-up to the April ultrasound test, Tierney underwent a prenatal examination called a triple screen. The test, usually performed between the fifteenth and eighteenth weeks of pregnancy, is used to check the likelihood of several kinds of major birth defects, including neural tube and ventral wall defects, in which a fetus has an abnormal opening of the spine or abdominal wall. It's also used to screen for Down syndrome, the most common of all chromosomal abnormalities, a condition marked by mental retardation and signature facial features and often accompanied by various health problems.

Introduced in 1988, the triple screen checks a sample of a pregnant woman's blood for the levels of three substances: alpha-fetoprotein (AFP), estriol, and human chorionic gonadotropin (hCG). AFP is a protein produced in the yolk sac of a pregnant woman and also by the liver of her fetus. Estriol and hCG are hormones produced by the placenta. The e.p.t. pregnancy test that Tierney had used was designed to detect hCG in urine—its presence at certain levels is a sure sign of pregnancy. In fact, hCG was the substance used in the old "rabbit tests." Doctors in the 1920s discovered that rabbits injected with urine rich in hCG—the urine of pregnant women, that is—would undergo distinct changes to their ovaries. Doctors would kill the rabbits to see if those changes had taken place. Although the rabbit died regardless of whether a woman was pregnant, the phrase "The rabbit died!" became mistakenly synonymous with a positive result.

The triple screen, then, is a sophisticated rabbit test. Scientists discovered that elevated or lowered levels of the three substances at specific points in a pregnancy can suggest a host of potential problems. Proper levels suggest the absence of those problems—in other words, a healthy child. For instance, a high level of AFP at certain times suggests a greater likelihood of a neural tube defect such as spina bifida, a physical deformity that results from the failure of the spine to close properly during the first month of pregnancy. Lower-than-expected levels of AFP and estriol, combined with higher-than-expected levels of hCG, can mean Down syndrome.

There's little dispute about the value of the triple screen, but it's far from perfect. By their very nature, so-called screening tests such as the triple screen and ultrasound provide good indications of what's happening inside a womb, but no definitive answers. It's as though they hear thunder and automatically predict rain: the two usually go together, but not always. Screening tests are known for false negatives, where bad news masquerades as good. For instance, the triple screen only picks up about 60 percent to 70 percent of instances of Down syndrome.

Despite the test's less-than-perfect record, Bourque saw no reason for concern. Using a formula that combines the levels of AFP, estriol, and hCG with mathematical values for Tierney's age, weight, race, and family history, he concluded with great confidence that the odds of Tierney having a child with Down syndrome or a neural tube defect were extremely low.

The chance of Down syndrome was particularly small. Stamped across the bottom of the one-page report tucked into Tierney's medical file were two words: SCREEN NEGATIVE. It was only below that, in tiny print, that a disclaimer read: "It should be noted that normal test results can never guarantee the birth of a normal baby, and that 2 to 3 percent of newborns have some type of physical and mental defect, many of which are undetectable through any known prenatal diagnostic technique." Tierney didn't see the disclaimer, but she wouldn't have worried about it, anyway.

Instead, she and Greg focused on the big picture: SCREEN NEGATIVE. That result, combined with the first ultrasound performed on Tierney in April, meant Bourque had no reason to order more costly, complicated—and more definitive—diagnostic tests. A "Prenatal Diagnosis Screening" form Tierney had filled out also bolstered Bourque's confidence. Of twenty-two questions about her and Greg's personal and family medical histories—everything from hereditary chromosomal abnormalities and hemophilia to muscular dystrophy and sexually transmitted diseases—Tierney had answered "no" to every question but one. She wrote that she had an uncle with a birth defect, but she didn't elaborate. It didn't seem necessary, and Bourque didn't consider it significant enough to ask about it.

Tierney was a smart young woman with an impressive resume, on course for a successful future. She had an undergraduate degree from the University of Pennsylvania, a master's in business administration from the Darden Graduate School of Business Administration at the University of Virginia, and a Ph.D. in education from UVA as well. In 1994, she had been hired to manage education programs for United Technologies Corporation, a huge Hartford-based aerospace and industrial company.

Tierney was five-foot-six, slim and pretty, with large brown eyes, silky, shoulder-length brown hair, and a scrubbed peach complexion. She had her mother's voice, a teacher's voice, sweet in the lower registers and prone to cracking when she got excited and it soared by an octave. She was a hard worker—an overachiever since early childhood, her mother had always said—focused and organized, with a storehouse of energy that allowed her to work or play for long hours with little sleep. She had ready access to her emotions but usually displayed a professional exterior, steely at times. She had a wary side, and she would furrow her brow and narrow her eyes as she worked to understand a point and gain insight into the person making it. When she felt comfortable, she shared an effervescent laugh and a mischievous sense of fun. She had a gleaming white smile, and she was proud of it.

On a Wednesday night in late July when Greg was in Manhattan, Tierney sat alone on their uncomfortable living room couch. It was a fancy, Duncan Fife–style sofa that Greg's mother had reupholstered in green-and-gold brocade. Above Tierney on a high shelf was a photo from their wedding. It showed a handsome black groom in black tie, dancing with a beautiful white bride wearing her mother's white dress. The apartment windows were open, but it was little help. The temperature had topped ninety degrees during the day, and the night air was thick with humidity, a combination that was no friend to a pregnant woman. Trying to get comfortable, Tierney kicked off her shoes and put her feet up on the sofa.

All around her were applications from educators hoping to win grants from United Technologies. Part of Tierney's job was to make grant recommendations, and she was eager to finish reviewing the applications so she could start going over her department's budget for the next fiscal year. She always drove herself at work, but she felt even more pressed than usual. In two days, she and Greg were scheduled to head off on a weeklong vacation at a rented cottage on Martha's Vineyard. It would be their last vacation before the baby came, and she didn't want anything hanging over her head.

Feeling stressed by the work before her, Tierney began chewing absently on a paper clip. She bit down, hard, and felt the sickening crack of enamel: she had dented her smile.

Maybe it was the special care she took of her teeth, maybe it was the hormones of pregnancy, or maybe it was the anxiety of wanting to clear her plate before vacation. Maybe it was a combination of all those things. Whatever it was, the chipped tooth reduced her to tears. It seemed the worst possible thing that could happen, at the worst possible time. She called Greg.

"I really don't need this now," she told him. "I have to go away on vacation, I have to finish all this stuff, and this is the last thing I need." She made the same call to her mother. Joan and Greg echoed each other's assurances. Tierney, they said, it's no big deal. Your dentist will make your tooth as good as new.

Indeed, he would. But it would be a while before Tierney would need her smile again.

## CHAPTER 2 "IF YOU ARE GOING TO CRY, YOU CRY LATER. IT BLINDS YOUR EYES"

It was Friday, July 24, two days after the chipped tooth. The day dawned with a cloudless pastel sky. Two weeks of oppressive humidity had finally eased, and the forecasters promised a perfect summer day. Tierney and Greg rolled out of bed early to get ready for their long-awaited getaway to Martha's Vineyard.

Greg had arrived home the night before after several days in Manhattan, where he was teaching graduate students and completing his doctoral degree in business at Columbia University. He had an undergraduate degree from Virginia Commonwealth University in Richmond, and, like Tierney, he'd received an MBA from the University of Virginia's Darden School. His last major task before receiving his Ph.D. was to research and write his dissertation, a book-length treatise on finding ways to tear down barriers to new business development in the inner city.

Greg was average height but model-handsome, with thick, powerful shoulders, a strong chin, and rich chocolate skin. He was warm and funny, but retained a hint of the outsider. It was a remnant of his youth as an army officer's kid who had moved from base to base, and it reflected his journey as a black man climbing educational, social, and professional ladders. Still, his affable nature made people yearn to befriend him. Students wanted to learn from him, elders wanted to mentor him. Children rushed at him like porch-light moths; he played games with the little ones and asked probing questions of older ones. His voice was a distinctive, syrupy tenor that hinted of the South. When challenged, he would stand his ground. When stressed, his first defense was a nap followed by a long talk. He had a fencer's intellect —thrust and parry, advance and retreat—that allowed him to cut through illogic and hypocrisy with deadly finesse. He had a sudden, happy laugh, and a generous hug.

Greg dressed Vineyard casual that morning, while Tierney pulled on a loose-fitting, black-and-white striped dress that Greg had bought her a few days earlier. It was a practical gift: the elastic waistbands on her pants had been cutting into her expanding middle, and her closet was short on flowing dresses. A silver pendant that looked like a stylized star dangled on a necklace over her heart. It was an African symbol for "hope" that Greg had brought home from a trip to Ghana. He had given an identical one to Tierney's sister, Tara. Both wore them often.

Tierney spent the morning at work, while Greg straightened up the apartment. He packed a suitcase with shorts, sandals, and other vacation clothes, then went to a nearby Stop & Shop supermarket. He bought a hundred dollars' worth of meat, seafood, and other groceries, to avoid inflated Vineyard prices. He mixed up a batch of his tangy homemade marinade for barbecuing and packed the provisions into a cooler.

Greg loaded their luggage and the cooler into the Honda, then picked up Tierney at work. It was 1:15 P.M.

"Hey, I'm on time!" she laughed upon seeing him.

Only one obligation stood between them and their vacation: a scheduled visit to Saint Francis Hospital, located less than a mile from their apartment. A sprawling, century-old hospital with 617 beds, Saint Francis was New England's largest Catholic hospital. It also was one half of the nation's first Catholic-Jewish hospital merger, joining forces in 1990 with New York's famed Mount Sinai.

The hospital visit was part of Tierney's normal prenatal care, a routine second ultrasound to confirm the due date through a series of measurements as well as to make sure the fetus was healthy and growing. Tierney expected it to be no more complicated than her trip to the dentist a day earlier to fix her broken tooth.


Most expectant mothers consider ultrasound as common as weight gain and swollen feet. But few know its roots. The use of sound waves to "see" a fetus can be traced to the development of sonar for underwater detection in the early 1800s. Nearly a century later, visionary doctors realized the same principle could be adapted to detect tumors and other internal disorders without the pain and mess of "exploratory" surgery. It also had an enormous advantage over X rays: no known side effects.

By the 1970s, ultrasound had become a key tool in obstetrics. It could safely be used to detect major defects including spina bifida and anencephaly, a fatal condition in which a fetus's brain fails to develop. By the early 1980s, ultrasound tests were being used to diagnose fetal heart malformations, and in 1985, a Harvard Medical School researcher described how ultrasound could be used to screen for Down syndrome by measuring the folds of skin at the back of a fetus's neck. Thick folds are a common symptom of the disorder, and they usually show up well on ultrasounds. If the neck folds on a fetus in its twelfth week are more than three millimeters thick, a child is three times more likely to have Down syndrome. If the folds are six millimeters thick, Down syndrome is thirty-six times more likely. It's hardly a perfect indicator, but like other screening tests, it's a useful gauge. With booming demand for prenatal information—whether divined from neck folds, chemical levels in the blood, or any other method—tremendous efforts are being devoted to finding ways to improve speed and clarity, meaning earlier and more precise results. From the standpoint of maternal health, both physical and emotional, sooner and more certain are always better.

The sooner reliable information is available, the sooner prospective parents can know whether to relax or cry. And the sooner they know that, the sooner they can start considering whether to continue or abort.

Greg parked the Honda in the hospital garage and they walked cheerfully to the main entrance. Tierney mused that their next visit would be for the delivery. Her life was coming full circle: she had been born at Saint Francis, too.

Greg and Tierney took the elevator to the fourth floor, and Tierney peered excitedly down the hall to the maternity ward.

"Look!" she told Greg. "That's where we'll go next time."

But there was no time for a tour. Ultrasound works best when the woman has a full bladder, so that morning Tierney drank what felt like a gallon of water. She was eager to finish the test, use the bathroom, and then drive directly to Cape Cod for an 8:30 P.M. Vineyard ferry.

They went to the hospital's prenatal testing unit and met the ultrasound technician, Maryann Kolano, a petite, pretty woman with frosted hair. She greeted them sweetly but efficiently and led them to Room 1. It was small and well lit, with a tile floor, mauve walls, and homey touches. A flowery, impressionistic print hung on one wall, and the room's one window had polka-dotted curtains. Room 1 smelled hospital-clean, with a piney, vaguely antiseptic fragrance.

An Ultramark 9 ultrasound machine dominated the room. It was an impressive piece of equipment, a modern obstetrical marvel, though not quite top-of-the-line. It was all anyone expected Tierney would need for a sound-wave look at the progress being made by the fetus inside her.

Tierney pulled up her new dress and lay back on the padded examination table. Kolano took a special jelly from a warmer and spread it gently over Tierney's exposed stomach. Greg sat beside the table in a hard plastic chair reserved for husbands and birth coaches. Tierney could barely see the nine-inch ultrasound monitor from her supine position, but Greg had the best seat in the house.

Kolano moved the ultrasound wand over Tierney's jelly-covered skin like a pizza maker using a ladle to spread sauce on a mound of dough. With each movement of the wand, Kolano created a picture of the tiny creature inside. Greg studied the monitor, fascinated by the details emerging from what looked like a half-developed Polaroid. An arm here, a leg there, a tiny face in profile. Then the internal organs: brain, liver, kidneys. All looked to be in working order, Kolano said. Greg was impressed. The machine was far more sophisticated than the one Bourque had used for the first ultrasound, three months earlier in his office.

With each movement of the wand, Kolano spoke into a microphone to record what she saw: head circumference, 16.6 centimeters; foot, 3.4 centimeters; femur, 3.2 centimeters; and so on. Using a mathematical formula, the measurements would confirm or revise the due date and determine whether the baby was developing properly. Several times, Kolano told Tierney and Greg the measurements were all in the normal range and everything looked good. The ultrasound wand also acted as a microphone, capturing the sound of a beating heart. Kolano checked the beat count—153 per minute—much too fast for an adult, but just right for a fetus in the twentieth week of pregnancy.

Kolano made more notes. There was plenty of amniotic fluid bathing the fetus in the womb. The placenta looked healthy enough to provide all the nourishment needed for the nine-month journey. The umbilical cord was properly connected. Kolano spotted the gender but said nothing. Tierney and Greg had told her they wanted to be surprised.

A half-hour into the session, only one sour note was struck, but it was minor: the baby was in a breech position—head up instead of down toward the exit. But there was plenty of time to turn, Kolano said. Nothing to worry about.

As the minutes passed, they started to chat. Kolano told Greg and Tierney that she understood what they were going through: she was a new mother, too. Throughout their conversation, she referred to the fetus Tierney carried as a baby, just as Greg and Tierney had being doing for weeks. She mentioned several times how active the baby was, kicking and grabbing, moving to its own groove inside Tierney. It was great to see, Kolano said, but all that motion was making one part of her job more difficult.

"I'm having a hard time seeing the heart. Maybe the baby's turned," Kolano said calmly. Then it appeared, pumping in a confident rhythm. She stopped the moving image, capturing a vivid cross section, and Greg remembered his high school biology.

All mammals have four chambers in the heart, Greg thought to himself. He could see only three, one large and two small. He dismissed it at first, telling himself it was pretty incredible that ultrasound could see inside the heart at all. Greg also reassured himself by recalling that Kolano had said the heartbeat count was normal.

"You know," Kolano said tactfully, "I'm not as good at this as some other people. Maybe somebody else should take a look." She masked her alarm as she left the room.

Tierney and Greg waited patiently, though not without concern. Tierney was worried they might hit traffic on the long Friday night drive to Cape Cod, and it would be a huge hassle and a terrible disappointment if they missed the ferry. None of her anxiety was the result of Kolano's sudden exit.

A few minutes later, Kolano returned to Room 1 with her boss: Dr. James F. X. Egan, director of maternal/fetal medicine at Saint Francis. He was an avuncular vision of authority, with silver hair, red cheeks, and blue eyes behind tortoiseshell bifocals. Even before finishing with the introductions, Egan was looking at the screen on the Ultramark 9.

"We're only locating three chambers," he said, confirming what Greg had thought. Egan made the remark in a voice that revealed only information, not emotion. But then he added, "I think we have a problem here."

Tierney began to cry. Greg took her hand. "Stay calm. It's going to be OK," he said. "There's nothing to worry about yet."

"I've worried you," Egan said sympathetically. "I'm sorry." Maybe it's the machine, he added. They should move two doors down the hall, to Room 3, where he could use a more advanced ultrasound, the Ultramark 5000.

When they entered Room 3, Tierney and Greg saw a machine that looked like a cartoon robot made real, with a squat body and a video monitor for a head. On the market for less than two years, the Ultramark 5000 was a state-of-the-art obstetrical supercomputer. It could produce remarkably detailed, three-dimensional, real-time images of what was happening inside the womb, and it could even show color images of blood flowing through the vessels. With the Ultramark 5000, parents could start arguing early over whose nose or chin their baby had inherited. But the Ultramark 5000 wasn't used so casually. Its specialty was high-risk pregnancies, and it was being used on Tierney.

Still in tears, Tierney hoisted herself onto the table. This time Egan used the wand while Kolano stood by, watching and hoping for the best. But almost instantly, the Ultramark 5000 confirmed the initial diagnosis in bold color. Greg had been correct. There were three chambers where there should have been four. It was a defect, a serious one, caused by interior heart walls that had failed to form properly.

There was a hole in the heart. Tierney and Greg's baby had a diagnosis before he or she had a name. A hole in the heart. In their baby's, and suddenly, in their own.

Egan plowed ahead. He told them the medical term for the flaw was an endocardial cushion defect, sometimes called an atrioventricular canal defect. It was a malformation well known to doctors, a defect that deprives the body of the oxygenated blood that every cell needs to survive. Egan also noticed that the fetus's heart was situated at a slightly off-kilter angle. Their baby would be fine in the womb, he explained, because Tierney was providing all the oxygen it needed. But Egan told them that a child born with this condition would require major heart surgery before its first birthday.

Thoughts and emotions flooded Tierney. Was it something I did? Was it my fault? Did I hurt my baby? Rationally, she knew she wasn't to blame. But she wasn't feeling very rational at the moment.

"I'm sorry," Tierney whispered to Greg between rising sobs. "I'm really sorry."

"You don't have anything to apologize about," he answered gently.

But "sorry" was more than an apology. Tierney wanted to tell Greg she felt sorry for him, sorry for herself, sorry they wouldn't be having the healthy child they had tried so hard to conceive. There would be time and opportunity to say all that, but as she lay on the examination table, all Tierney could muster were tears and "sorry."

Again, Greg told her not to apologize, not to worry. He was shutting down his emotions, raising his academic antennae and trying to grasp the clinical issues. Greg remembered a television show about successful heart operations on babies, sometimes while they were in the womb. He asked Egan if the defect would hinder prenatal development, and Egan assured him it would not.

"Great," Greg said, regaining his equilibrium. We can handle this, he thought.

But Egan was only getting started. He knew that a flawed heart might be a sign of a condition that can't be fixed with surgery. He took a deep breath and plunged in.

A significant percentage of endocardial cushion defects—something like 60 percent—are found in children with chromosomal disorders such as Down syndrome, he began. It's not an automatic link by any means, Egan tried to assure Tierney and Greg. But . . .

Tierney and Greg didn't hear him finish the sentence. They were stunned, speechless, spinning. What was he talking about? Heart defect? Hole? Surgery? Chromosomes? Sixty percent? Down syndrome? Their baby?

To find out if that was the case, Egan first checked Tierney's triple-screen results. He was buoyed to see they showed no signs of trouble. A woman Tierney's age normally has about a 1 in 600 chance of giving birth to a child with Down syndrome. Based on her triple-screen levels, Tierney's odds were calculated to be far lower than normal: 1 in 2,146. An excellent sign, Egan thought. Also, in the ultrasound images, the fetus didn't appear to have notably thick folds at the back of the neck. Also good news. And, other than the heart defect, the ultrasound didn't find other physical markers of Down syndrome, such as certain kinds of bowel obstructions, short thigh bones, abdominal flaws, or kidney problems. Maybe it was only a heart defect—serious, to be sure, but fixable.

If they wanted to know for certain, Egan continued, they needed to make the leap from screening tests—ultrasound and the triple screen—to a tool on the next level of medical know-how: a diagnostic test. Tierney should undergo amniocentesis.

"When?" Greg asked.

"Right now," Egan answered. Tierney began to cry even harder.

*　　　*　　　*

Though it followed the discovery of the rabbit test by fewer than thirty years, amniocentesis made killing bunnies seem horribly primitive. To perform amniocentesis, usually called simply "amnio," a doctor inserts a long, fine needle into the uterus through the mother's abdomen and then withdraws an ounce or so of amniotic fluid. The fluid contains cells from the fetus, and those cells can be analyzed with near certainty for Down syndrome and other disorders. Results take ten days to two weeks.

The test was introduced in the 1950s as a way to determine whether dangerous blood incompatibilities existed between mothers and their fetuses. By 1978, it was the standard of care for pregnant women age thirty-five and older, who by virtue of their age were automatically considered at high risk for a child with Down syndrome.

By the late 1990s, medical researchers, including a group of doctors headed by Egan, began challenging routine amnios for women over thirty-five as unnecessary in terms of risk and expense. Instead, they argued, amnio should be reserved for situations where screening tests have already revealed indicators of problems—such as heart defects that show up on ultrasounds. Nevertheless, amnio remained a foundation of care for older pregnant women.

Amnio is considered safe in the hands of an experienced practitioner like Egan, working in a high-tech setting like Saint Francis. Yet its invasive nature makes it far riskier than ultrasound. On average, miscarriage occurs about once in every 250 amnio procedures.

Tierney was never the biology student that Greg was, and the combination of unwanted information and emotion left her feeling vulnerable. Keeping her dress pulled up just below her breasts certainly wasn't helping. She couldn't stop crying. She loved and trusted Greg, and she considered him as smart and capable as anyone she had ever known. Still, Tierney wanted to call her mother.

At sixty-two, Joan Temple was a substitute teacher with even less understanding of modern medicine than Tierney. But Tierney was terrified, and she wanted Joan's support and prayers. Maybe, for a minute, she wanted to feel like a child again, kept safe by her mother from the scary things in life's dark closet.

But Greg discouraged Tierney from making the call. It would only upset them both, he said, and they didn't know what they were dealing with. Calling Joan would be admitting there was a major problem, one they couldn't handle on their own. Greg wasn't ready for that.

Kolano remained in Room 3 throughout Egan's examination, standing to the side and trying to be helpful. "I feel so bad for you guys," she said. "This is so tough, but it's better that you find out now."

Greg and Tierney wondered what she meant and why she seemed so flustered. They didn't know how rare it was for even these obstetrical experts to have such a surprise, with no warning signs from earlier screening tests, maternal sickness, or advanced age. Later, Egan would estimate that of the two thousand or so ultrasounds performed every year at Saint Francis, only perhaps two yielded completely unexpected, heartbreaking news for prospective parents. This was shaping up to be one of those cases.

After allowing Tierney to finally empty her bursting bladder, Egan offered his sympathies again. He described how he would perform the amnio, then asked Tierney to sign a release form acknowledging the risk of miscarriage.

Tierney felt rushed and confused. Wasn't everything wonderful just an hour ago? Wasn't this supposed to be a quick stop before a glorious beach vacation? But through her tears she signed the form.


Her body shook as Egan inserted the needle, the pinprick familiar to anyone who has ever donated blood. She cried not in pain but in fear that the sharp point would jab her baby. She remembered how Kolano had joked about how active the baby was during the ultrasound, and Tierney worried that a sudden kick or turn might mean impalement. But the Ultramark 5000 was still turned on, and Tierney watched the needle pass harmlessly into the uterus and then back out. Greg helped her off the table.

Afterward, Greg overheard Kolano ask Egan if he was going to order something called the FISH test. It would come back in half the time of the amnio, she said. No, Egan answered, it's not accurate enough.

Tierney didn't catch the remark but Greg did, and it bothered him. You can't cure Down syndrome, he thought, so Egan must have meant just one thing: the doctor was telling the technician that this FISH test, whatever it was, wasn't accurate enough for use in deciding whether to get an abortion. The brief exchange between Egan and Kolano was the first hard proof that a clock had begun ticking.

Tierney was a little more than halfway through the normal forty-week course of fetal development from the mother's last period to delivery. The fetus she carried was about nine inches long and weighed nearly a pound. A coat of fine hair covered the body. Its senses were awakening. It had a regular cycle of sleeping, sucking, and kicking. It couldn't survive outside the womb.

Connecticut law allows elective abortions through the twenty-fourth week, the point at which a fetus is considered "viable" and abortion is illegal except to protect the mother's life or health. That meant Tierney and Greg had about three weeks to decide whether to continue or abort, and half that time would be eaten up waiting for amnio results. After that, they would have only a matter of days to make a decision that would affect them and their families for the rest of their lives.

Tierney grew up in Avon, Connecticut, a comfortable Hartford suburb, in a stone house on a large lot surrounded by old oak trees. She was raised a Catholic and as a girl was a regular at Sunday Mass. Her faith in God was a constant in her life. Yet she was socially liberal and departed from church doctrine when it came to reproductive rights: she believed strongly in a woman's right to choose. Like many Americans, she wrestled with questions about when life begins—conception? viability? birth?—but until that day at Saint Francis, she never imagined the debate would affect her personally.

Greg shared Tierney's mix of strong faith and socially liberal politics. When Greg was in his teens, his father had retired from the army as a colonel and the family had settled on eight forested acres in Virginia. They were Baptists in the heart of the Bible Belt, and the Good Book was alive in their house. Yet Greg didn't allow church teachings to dictate his thinking.

"I am not one of those people who believes on a religious basis or a moral basis that under any conditions this would be a wrong thing to do," he said once. "I understand why there are many reasons why people choose abortion, and I am not in the business of judging why someone might." That was at least partly because he knew that he could imagine himself among them.

Greg and Tierney's support for abortion rights put them among the 82 percent of Americans who say they feel that way in some or all circumstances.

After the amnio, Tierney signed the appropriate insurance forms and accepted caring words from the Saint Francis staff. Egan gave them the names of a pediatric cardiologist and a genetic counselor who could answer the questions he knew would torment them in the days ahead.

Shortly before Greg and Tierney left, there was a moment when Egan and Kolano mused out loud about having them drive the amnio samples across town to the University of Connecticut laboratory. It was getting late on a Friday afternoon, Egan said, and the courier might not make it before the lab closed for the weekend. The sooner the testing began, the sooner the results would come back.

The conversation struck Tierney as odd. Through her haze, she thought about an episode of the television show *Ally McBeal,* in which the title character, a scattered young female lawyer, gets pulled over by a cop while racing to drive a semen sample to a fertility clinic.

Egan sensed their discomfort and decided to stick with the courier.

Kolano showed them the back way out of the obstetrics suite, so they could avoid the waiting room. Tierney understood the reasoning, but it made her feel even more conspicuous. She looked at herself and her husband: a tear-drenched pregnant woman and a shell-shocked man. Walking zombies. They were the last vision any nervous patient wanted to see in an obstetrics waiting room. "If we went that way, people would look at us and think, 'Wow, they just got some really bad news about their baby,' " she said later.

The entire visit took two hours. It was the same spectacular summer day when they stepped back outside. But everything else had changed.

They drove home in a fog, silent except for Tierney's sobs. Greg left their luggage in the trunk but carried the food-filled cooler into the apartment. They wouldn't be leaving that night for Martha's Vineyard.

Tierney lay down on the sofa. Still crying, she apologized again to Greg. "What does this all mean?" she asked him. Greg had no answers, only comfort and the illusion of strength. He fell back into a chair and found himself spouting hospital drama clichés: There's nothing to worry about. We still don't know for sure. Everything will be OK. We'll play whatever cards we're dealt.

Greg called his parents. Bob Fairchild was sixty-five. He was quiet and kind, with none of the stereotypical bluster of an ex-military man who had commanded thousands of troops on bases in the United States and Germany. In more than two decades in the military, he had never fired a weapon during combat, and that pleased him. Mary Fairchild, ten years younger than her husband, was bright and warm, a talented seamstress who ran her own upholstery business. She had been a special education major in college. Greg and Mary were especially close, and he liked to tease her, calling his mother "the queen." She was independent, talkative, and—like Tierney's mother—deeply religious.

"We're really sorry for you both," Mary told Greg, the elder of her two children. Greg could hear disappointment in her voice. Bob listened silently on the line. Mary spoke of faith and prayer, holding back the tears she wanted to shed for the grandchild she already loved. "If you are going to cry, you cry later," she explained. "It blinds your eyes."

Mary knew that Greg's instincts would tell him to build a cocoon around himself and Tierney. If he could, Greg would close off the world and remain locked in their apartment at least until the amnio results came back. But Mary also knew that Tierney would go stir-crazy if Greg kept them there. Mary encouraged him to abandon his usual ways and take Tierney to the Vineyard, where she could walk the beach, take in the sun, relax. Greg was skeptical, but he promised to consider it.

Greg also called Tierney's sister, Tara. She was already out on the Vineyard and was expecting them to arrive later that night. Greg told Tara they were delayed at the doctor's office and that Tierney still had work to do and errands to run. They wouldn't be coming to the Vineyard that weekend.

Tara knew Greg well. She heard something in his voice. "Is everything OK?" she asked.

"Yeah, everything's fine," Greg lied.

Tara didn't believe him, but she didn't press.

Tierney called her mother, who was at home with a friend. They were reading an inspirational book, *The Cup of Our Life: A Guide for Spiritual Growth*. Tierney wished that Joan were alone, so she could talk more openly. Joan took the call in another room and listened as her baby talked about her baby.

"Tierney, you just have to believe and have faith," Joan said. "This is not something that is set in stone, and you don't have any information yet. There's nothing you can do right now, and you need to relax and not think the worst. Remember," Joan added before they hung up. "It's God's plan, not ours."

The only parent they didn't call was Tierney's father, George "Ernie" Temple III. Relations with Ernie were complicated, and he wouldn't be told for another eleven days.

The last call they made together was to Alicia Craffey, the genetic counselor on the list Egan had given them.

"I'm really sorry this happened to you guys," Craffey began. But unlike Egan and Kolano, Craffey didn't stop with sympathy. She asked questions—trying to find out what they had been told, what they understood, what they needed, what they were thinking, how they were feeling. She promised to assemble a package of information about the heart defect and Down syndrome.

"There are people who have faced similar situations, whose experiences might be helpful to you," she said. Some of those experiences were collected in a book, *A Time to Decide, a Time to Heal*. She'd include it in the package.

After they hung up, Craffey jotted down a half-page of notes about her new patients. Most of it was clinical, describing the situation, but one line stands out. Craffey noted how "shocked and very upset" both Tierney and Greg had sounded.

The calls made, Tierney forced herself to eat, for the baby. They listlessly watched TV. They talked for hours about everything and nothing. They fell into a fitful sleep. Overnight, the ice in the cooler melted. The food left abandoned inside turned rancid.

## CHAPTER 3 "I'M JUST SO SICK OF HAVING TO DEAL WITH DISCRIMINATION"

Greg woke the next morning in a foul mood. His calm, "let's wait and see" attitude of the day before had been replaced by anger and a search for escape. It was the first of several back-and-forth flips he and Tierney would make in the days ahead.

Not wanting to unload on Tierney, Greg called his parents. He unleashed a torrent of thoughts on being black, on imagining himself the parent of a mentally retarded child, and on discrimination based on race and disability. He had known from the day that he and Tierney had crossed the color line to marry that there would be challenges for any child of theirs. But he thought they'd be limited to skin color. He could handle that. But the thought of racial issues compounded by Down syndrome and a heart defect seemed too much to bear.

"I'm just so sick of having to deal with discrimination," he told Bob and Mary. "Why couldn't this have been visited on someone who believes discrimination is not a part of life? Why couldn't this have happened to someone who has lived the most privileged life of all? Then they would have some way of understanding that, yes, people do discriminate against people, and it does hurt and it does have impact."

He had dreamed, expected even, that his children would face less discrimination than his generation had, and that their children would face even less, until someday it no longer existed. "You know, you do your work so it's easier for the ones who follow."

Mary reminded him that there certainly were people of privilege in his situation. She recalled that conservative columnist George Will had written movingly about raising a son with Down syndrome, and about how it had affected him and his perspective. But that didn't help. If anything, it reinforced Greg's point about wanting that kind of news to arrive on the doorstep of people who otherwise wouldn't experience discrimination. Greg knew plenty about it already, and he didn't need his awareness raised.

Greg remembered a Bible passage he had learned as a boy. "Even Christ, when he knows that the next day he is going to be crucified, he himself was upset," Greg told his parents. "And he said, 'Lord, oh that this cup could pass from me.' Even Christ had this moment where he was saying, 'If I could just avoid this, it would be OK with me.' I confess," Greg said. "That's how I feel. I would like not to have to deal with this."

Mary tried to calm him. "You're jumping the gun. You don't know that it's going to be Down syndrome. You're really just going too far."

In the turmoil of the moment, neither remembered the next line of the Bible passage that Greg had quoted. On his knees in the olive groves of Gethsemane, Jesus did indeed seek to be excused from the pain of the cross. But then Jesus accepted the fate that awaited him: "Nevertheless, not as I will, but as Thou wilt," he told God. Much later, Mary Fairchild would say that was the message she had wanted her son to hear.

Greg wasn't finished. He described to his parents his limited experiences with Down syndrome. As a teenager, he had volunteered to help at a Special Olympics track meet, one of the worldwide athletic competitions for people with mental retardation founded in 1968 by Eunice Kennedy Shriver. Greg was part of a crew of people who were supposed to hug runners as they crossed the finish line, no matter if they placed first or last.

"I remember my own visceral reaction when you see a child with what I would call extreme Down syndrome—very large glasses, bulging eyes, tongue sticking out of the mouth. I didn't pull away, but you don't feel as comfortable reaching over and hugging. Clearly, after you do it, after you hug the first five, you find out, hey, there's nothing wrong." Remembering his initial response made him wince. It pained him to think that people would feel that way about his child.

"Look," he told his parents. "I know how people behave. I remember when I was a kid and we lived in Germany, there was this girl. I don't know if she had Down syndrome or not, but I remember that she was retarded. And little boys would go and ask her to pull down her pants. And her brother would come out and find them and get real upset." Greg envisioned himself in that role; it angered and exhausted him to even think about it.

His mind racing, he thought about the effects on his professional life. "When I have people over to my house and we have dinner parties, what will happen the moment when the child comes out and the people won't know what to say and do?"

Greg listened as his parents tried to calm him, but he hung up feeling even worse than when he had dialed the phone. Afterward, Bob and Mary would share the news with Greg's younger sister, Marla, a chef. The two weren't especially close; Marla would send a card offering support, but they wouldn't discuss the situation. After talking with his parents, Greg painted a bleak picture for Tierney. He told her that if they continued the pregnancy, they faced a frustrating future. They could never stop being vigilant, educating the ignorant, battling the cruel.

"If we have this baby, just get ready for the onslaught of stupid, maybe well-meaning, but stupid comments. We're going to have to deal with them for the rest of our lives," he said. "Tierney, we're going to have to go into our child's school, fighting with administrators, changing this and that. I'm going to have to make sure people aren't abusing my child, putting him in the back of the room or locking him in the closet. This is what we're going to have to do. But I'm mad about it."

"You know," he added, "it's not that I wasn't going to be an involved parent. But I don't want to be Greg Fairchild, the problem dad, here he comes. That's the deal now." To himself, Greg thought: Why shouldn't we exercise the privilege of avoiding this? Why shouldn't I get out of this? Why shouldn't we have an abortion?

None of Greg's feelings surprised Tierney. Not the ones he shared with her, and not the ones she suspected he was keeping to himself. They talked openly and often about race, class, and privilege. It was really one long conversation that had begun almost the moment they met.

The year they met, they were recent college graduates, working in Manhattan at Saks Fifth Avenue. Both were executive trainees, recruited to the posh department store through campus interviews. Neither had any great interest or experience in high-priced fashion retailing; it was something to do, a decent job, a chance to live in New York.

In college, Greg had thought about a job in banking—his father, after retiring from the military, had become a bank senior vice president. Greg had never even heard of Saks when a company recruiter named Kyle Rudy began talking to him at a college job fair.

Tierney was equally blasé about a retail job. She had thought about a career in advertising or publishing, or maybe teaching at a private school. But she had a heavy load of college loans. Those other fields would have been thrilled to have her, but at a salary of only $10,000 a year. The money was at Saks. Kyle Rudy recruited her, too, a year after he netted Greg.

Tierney and Greg worked on the seventh floor of the massive midtown store, across the street from Rockefeller Center, with views out the window of Saint Patrick's Cathedral. Greg was a manager in the dress department, and Tierney was an assistant manager in women's coats and suits. When Tierney arrived, Greg immediately pegged her as part of a clique of Ivy Leaguers with names like Troy and Scotty, privileged types who considered themselves too smart for retailing. As Tierney sarcastically put it years later, "To Greg, I was this snob and I had my friends from Harvard and Brown and Duke."

Greg was an army brat/country kid from Virginia who had come to New York wearing a plaid suit that he quickly realized made him look like a bumpkin. He called his father to ask permission to buy a new one, and then just about yelled "gee whiz" when he was told that it could be tailored overnight.

One day at Saks, Greg noticed Tierney and what he called her "all-male entourage." They were in a minor panic: for all their high-priced education, no one in Tierney's Ivy League posse could figure out how to void a sale. On her way to summon help from the customer service department on the eighth floor, Tierney ran into Greg and Kyle, who had evolved from recruiter to friend. They began to talk, and Greg realized that he had misjudged Tierney. Tierney realized that Greg wasn't just handsome, he was kind. Kyle stood by watching as something clicked.

Saks rules forbade managers and assistant managers in the same department from leaving the store together for lunch. So Greg would lunch with Tierney while his assistant lunched with Tierney's manager. Their lunches quickly evolved into wide-ranging discussions of retailing and values, with an emphasis on the latter. They talked about the women who shopped at their store. They wondered, as Greg put it, "Isn't there more to life than making sure that people own six thousand dresses?"

In time, they crossed the threshold of race. Greg attacked the Reagan administration policy of "constructive engagement"—doing business with the white minority that ruled South Africa as a way to encourage change. On any other continent, Greg argued, one that wasn't populated almost entirely by blacks, the United States would fly warplanes over there and solve the problem. "We're the country that puts down communist insurrections in support of democracy all over the world," he told his new friend. "So why won't we do it in a country where a small portion of the population rules by force and denies the majority the right to vote?"

Tierney had had black friends—she and her mother had been the only white voices in a gospel choir—but she'd never come close to interracial romance. Greg was the first black man she had dated, the first one with whom she had spoken so openly about race.

Although she tended to agree with him—though not always at first—she enjoyed playing devil's advocate, challenging his logic. She liked to prod and probe the mind of the passionate man sitting across the table with a deli sandwich in his hand. Things got heated sometimes, and their lunch hours ended tensely. Occasionally, when he was alone in his apartment at night, Greg feared they wouldn't even speak to each other the next day at work. But Tierney always came back, smiling, learning from him, teaching him, falling in love with him, and knowing that he had fallen in love with her.


Like Greg, Tierney awoke the Saturday morning after the amnio with a changed view. Unlike Greg, she felt at peace. For the moment, her confusion and sadness had passed with the night. "We both consider ourselves to be pretty strong people," she told Greg. "If this is going to be a worst-case scenario, then maybe we're the right parents to take this on."

She also reminded Greg, and herself, that they didn't have a final diagnosis—Tierney was holding on to hope that the amnio would be negative for Down syndrome and the heart defect wouldn't be all that bad. She had a cousin whose child had been born with a heart defect—but not Down syndrome—and it had been corrected without incident. Maybe, just maybe, this was a family pattern repeating itself.

While Greg stewed, Tierney sought to escape the apartment. The humidity had returned, and the temperature began rising toward the eighties. Tierney drove eight miles to the University of Connecticut Health Center genetics office to collect the package of materials that Alicia Craffey, the genetic counselor, had assembled for them. She brought home the thick manila envelope, and she and Greg settled onto their couch to begin the unwanted task of learning about Down syndrome and heart defects.

\*     \*     \*

John Langdon Down was a British doctor born in 1828, brilliant by all accounts, on track to win election to the staff of the prestigious London Hospital. But at age thirty, he veered onto a much different path, wrangling an appointment as medical superintendent of the Earlswood Asylum for Idiots in Surrey. It was a bold move, and, to many, a foolish one. He chose what his peers considered a second-rate career over an exalted profession. And not just any second-rate career. He was devoting himself to the generally reviled field of "idiocy."

In Down's day in Britain, there existed a three-tier classification system for mental deficiency: idiots on the bottom, imbeciles on the next higher rung, and the feeble-minded on what passed for a top rung. It was pretty much the same in the United States, though the term "moron" was substituted for feeble-minded. Down was a reformer, and he set about trying to improve the conditions of his asylum and the care of its residents. He also thought the existing classification system was overly simplistic and failed to take into account clear differences among the mentally retarded people whose lives he oversaw.

In 1866, he published the paper that guaranteed him a place in medical history. On first reading, outside the context of nineteenth-century Victorian England, Down's paper would make a white supremacist blush. Titled "Observations on an Ethnic Classification of Idiots," in a scant three pages the paper attempted to categorize mental deficiencies based on racial categories. He thought he had found evidence that some mentally retarded white Anglo-Saxon Protestant children ended up in what he considered their pitiable state of idiocy because their development had somehow been arrested in the womb, leaving them on the level of one of the so-called lower races. Of course, a corollary of such a conclusion would be that a mentally deficient WASP would be considered of "normal" intelligence among those "lower" races. As one would expect from such a system, the more severe the mental deficiency, the "lower" the race it was equated with.

Down must have believed he was working out his own version of Darwinian theory. At the time of Down's work, Darwin was all the rage for his writings on the evolutionary progression of species—sometimes represented in simplified versions as a ladder or a pyramid with humans (white humans, that is) at the very top. Down's paper reflected Darwin's ideas by suggesting that certain mentally deficient WASPs failed to make the usual progression in the womb and fell off at a lower rung of the evolutionary ladder. By that way of thinking, mentally deficient WASPs were evolutionary throwbacks.

Down wrote that many of the idiots and imbeciles in his care "can fairly be referred to one of the great divisions of the human family other than the class from which they have sprung." Down found British idiots who he thought had stopped developing around the "Ethiopian variety," and cited as evidence "the prominent eyes, the puffy lips, and retreating chin." He noticed that some had "the wooly hair." Down next offered up "the Malay variety" of idiots, with "shortened foreheads, prominent cheeks, deep-set eyes, and slightly apish nose." He was just warming up.

Down wrote that the real purpose of his paper was to call attention to the "Mongolian type of idiocy." He then wrote what is generally believed to be the first clinical description of physical characteristics common to people with the condition now known as Down syndrome. Although Down blew the big picture, he did a respectable job on the descriptive end. He based his work on a boy he knew: "The face is flat and broad, and destitute of prominence. . . . The tongue is long, thick and is much roughened. The nose is small. The skin has a slight dirty-yellowish tinge, and is deficient in elasticity, giving the appearance of being too large for the body."

As the evolutionary biologist Stephen Jay Gould has pointed out, for all Down's racist classifications, he was actually something of a liberal for his time. His paper argued that, as Gould put it, "all people had descended from the same stock and could be united into a single family, with gradation by status to be sure." This contrasted with the view of retrograde Victorians who believed that different races represented separate acts of creation, and that the "lower" races could never "improve" toward WASP-hood.

Down's theory imploded over time, in part because scientists observed the same features in people with the syndrome across all ethnic and racial lines. That finding, among others, undermined Down's view of arrested development on some sort of race ladder. Still, "Mongolian idiot" and its semantic cousin "mongoloid idiot" took hold. They haven't been completely erased, despite their racist, fallacious underpinnings and the best efforts of advocates for people with Down syndrome. Some of those advocates even regret the negative implication of the word "Down," and only half-jokingly suggest the condition's name be changed to "Up syndrome."

As Down's racial theories lost ground, scientists began speculating in the 1930s that Down syndrome had something to do with abnormal chromosomes. But it wasn't until 1959—almost a century after Down's paper—that someone proved it.

The literature that Craffey provided Greg and Tierney spelled out the complex science in relatively straightforward detail: The human body is built from billions of microscopic cells, and each cell has a nucleus. In the nucleus of each cell are rod-shaped bodies called chromosomes. Those chromosomes contain tens of thousands of genes, and the arrangement of those genes is an instruction manual for human development. Usually, there are forty-six gene-laden chromosomes per cell, organized in twenty-three pairs. One member of each pair is inherited from the mother and the other comes from the father.

Sometimes, however, the mother's egg or the father's sperm contains not the usual complement of twenty-three chromosomes, but an extra one, making twenty-four. In a majority of conceptions resulting in Down syndrome, the mother's egg contributes the extra chromosome. When a twenty-four-chromosome egg and a twenty-three-chromosome sperm come together at the moment of conception, the total number of chromosomes in the fertilized egg is forty-seven, one more than usual. Each time that fertilized egg replicates itself to grow, the error repeats itself, and every later cell in the body also has forty-seven chromosomes. Usually, the error corrects itself through self-destruction: 90 percent of eggs with extra chromosomes fail to develop and those pregnancies end in miscarriage. But that leaves the other 10 percent.

If the extra chromosome happens to be a twenty-first chromosome, the smallest chromosome of all, fertilization and prenatal growth can continue pretty much as usual. Miscarriage and stillbirth are far more likely than in typical pregnancies, but many such pregnancies survive. And every cell that develops from that original, forty-seven-chromosome fertilized egg looks just like the first: instead of the usual matched pair of twenty-first chromosomes, there are three. In most occurrences of Down syndrome, the extra chromosome floats around on its own in the nucleus. Occasionally, however, it attaches itself to another chromosome. Either way, the result is Down syndrome.

The third twenty-first chromosome gives Down syndrome its scientific name: trisomy 21. There are other trisomies, resulting from three copies of other chromosomes, but trisomy 21 is easily the most common.

Despite extensive study, scientists haven't quite figured out why the extra chromosome causes problems—it's not as though an ingredient is missing from the genetic recipe. People with Down syndrome have all the usual genetic material, plus a little more—too much salt in an otherwise perfect soup. What is known with certainty is that the added chromosome alters and interrupts the typical course of human development, causing a genetic stew of mental and physical impairments.

Tierney and Greg learned from their reading that children with Down syndrome are as varied as other children, though they have certain consistent features. All are mentally retarded, or in the more current term, developmentally disabled. Most have IQs between forty and seventy on a scale that considers one hundred average. A small percentage, perhaps 10 percent, are in the higher IQ range, and a similar percentage are in the lower range. The rest are spread through the middle, in the classic bell-curve arrangement. There's no way to predict in advance where a child with Down syndrome will fall on the IQ scale, just as there's no telling how smart any other child might be while in the womb.

Greg and Tierney learned that people with Down syndrome are often stereotyped as relentlessly happy and preternaturally sweet— "Angels on Earth" some people call them. Some observers even claim they have faint halos that, if the light hits just right, can be captured in photographs. In reality, people with Down syndrome do often tend toward friendliness and sociability. But they have the same range of behaviors and emotions as other people. They get angry. They can be stubborn. They get impatient. They can be disobedient. Hurt their feelings and they cry.

Among the most common physical infirmities—and the most life-threatening—are heart defects, affecting about 40 percent. Nearly all have loose joints and low muscle tone, which makes them seem more "floppy" than other babies. Thyroid disorders and seriously malformed digestive tracts occur far more often than in typical children. People with Down syndrome are fifteen to thirty times more likely to get leukemia, and 25 percent of adults with the condition develop Alzheimer-like symptoms of dementia after age fifty. They tend to be short, and obesity is a concern. Hearing and vision problems are common. Most have relatively small mouths, which, when combined with low muscle tone, often results in a protruding tongue. That characteristic contributes to the ugly and false stereotype of mentally retarded people as drooling, slack-jawed "idiots" with their tongues hanging out.

As recently as 1968, the average life span for a person with Down syndrome was just two years, mainly because of the large number of people with the disorder who died in infancy from uncorrected heart defects, blocked digestive tracts, and other ailments. Over the next three decades, however, new surgical techniques and changes in attitudes toward treatment of the mentally retarded led to a dramatic rise. By 1997, the average life span had reached fifty years.

But that was only for white people with Down syndrome. In 1968, blacks with the disorder on average died before their first birthdays. By 1997, their average life span had increased, but only to twenty-five years, or half that of whites. When the racial disparity was first reported in 2001 by the federal Centers for Disease Control and Prevention, an accompanying editorial concluded that because Down syndrome and its life-threatening physical disorders appear at equal rates among all races, shorter life spans for blacks were more likely the result of differences in "socioeconomic status, education, community support, (and) medical or surgical treatment of serious complications." In other words, blacks with Down syndrome had the same life-shortening disadvantages as blacks without Down syndrome.

Reading the information from Craffey, Tierney and Greg learned that although inherited factors play a role in a small percentage of cases, no one knows exactly why the extra chromosome appears in a given egg or sperm, or how to prevent it. It occurs in all races and in all countries, and births are equally divided between boys and girls. By some accounts, Down syndrome has been around as long as the human race, and there are estimated to be two hundred fifty thousand Americans with the condition. It appears once in almost every eight hundred live births. The only clue to its likely occurrence is the mother's age: women over thirty-five are significantly more likely to be mothers of babies with Down syndrome.

But Tierney became pregnant shortly before her thirty-first birthday. That knowledge led her and Greg to a surprising discovery: of the five thousand or so babies with Down syndrome born each year in the United States, 75 percent are born to women under thirty-five. The main reason is that, overall, most babies are born to younger mothers. The proportionately larger number of babies that younger women bear offsets their relatively low odds of having a baby with Down syndrome.

That helps to explain why the number of children born each year with the disorder has remained stable for decades, despite a high abortion rate among women who know in advance. Because younger mothers undergo fewer prenatal tests, most only learn that they have a child with Down syndrome after birth. Also, the number of older women who become pregnant has risen steadily in recent years. Even if many abort after prenatal testing, more older mothers mean an increased overall incidence of Down syndrome conceptions.

That was the scientific side. The emotional side was harder to digest. Greg read aloud to Tierney from a book that contained statements from parents of children with Down syndrome. He didn't sugarcoat it. In his newly dark mood, Greg tended to skip over the more positive comments and focus on the negatives. He read to Tierney about a woman who was never invited back to a new parent group when she mentioned that her child had Down syndrome. He told her about a woman who cried for a year. He described parents who received condolences instead of baby gifts. Among his selections, Greg read aloud the comment of one downhearted woman: "I wanted people to say congratulations, and they didn't. It was like my baby had died."

He added another twist, specific to them. "You know," Greg said, "people are really ignorant on genetics. Maybe this will never be said to our faces, but don't think there isn't somebody somewhere that's going to say, 'Well, gee, that probably happened because they were an interracial couple.' Don't be fooled. That will be thought of, talked about when you're not in earshot, mentioned to other family members why they shouldn't marry outside their race. All that."

Complicating matters further, Down syndrome wasn't all that Greg and Tierney had to worry about. They started learning about the hole in the heart from an article Craffey photocopied from a tome of parental nightmares called the *Birth Defects Encyclopedia*. They read that the defect spotted on the ultrasound could be corrected by surgery, but success was not guaranteed. Some babies are doomed from birth.

Using data in the materials supplied by Craffey, Greg tried to make rough calculations about the likelihood that a baby with Down syndrome would survive the necessary open-heart surgery. He figured it was about two out of three—encouraging but not worth celebrating. He also knew he needed to check his math with an expert.

No matter what she read or what Greg told her, Tierney wouldn't let herself spiral down to depression. While Greg was describing the racial issue as a negative, Tierney was thinking about all they already knew about challenges from being an interracial couple. "This might be our new calling," she said. "Maybe because of what we've been through, we're now able to handle this." Her main concern for the moment was the heart. If their baby's heart couldn't sustain life, if there was little hope for the future, that alone might be reason to end the pregnancy.

They called Craffey for clarification on some parts of their readings. They talked and read and talked some more. They cried.

Hours passed and the summer sun set. A sliver of a crescent moon rose in the sky. They went into their bedroom and said an impromptu prayer. They asked for doctors who would make good judgments. They prayed for accurate information and sound advice. They sought strength in making their own decisions and help in making them together.

Then Greg and Tierney crawled into bed.

# CHAPTER 4 "THE MIRACLE YOU PRAY FOR MIGHT NOT BE THE MIRACLE YOU RECEIVE"

When they awoke the next day, it was Sunday and both Greg and Tierney felt drawn to church. With no parish of their own, they drove to the Church of Saint Timothy in West Hartford, where Tierney's mother sometimes worshipped. It was a fine brick building surrounded by tall, strong trees.

Tierney chose Saint Timothy's because it was home to her favorite priest, the Reverend Henry Cody, whom she had known since she was small. Her father had even played basketball with the priest when they were young men. Tierney wanted his guidance. But Father Cody wasn't there. Some other priest was filling in, one she didn't know. Her disappointment gave way to serenity when she heard him speak.

Sitting in a pew, bathed in sunlight passing through stained-glass windows, Tierney and Greg heard the priest give a moving sermon about the role of prayer and the mysteries of miracles. He talked about the six million Jews killed in the Holocaust. He tried to imagine what they were praying as they were herded into boxcars on their way to Nazi death camps. He contrasted those prayers with the prayers of people who seek God's help to find lost keys or missing earrings.

The more the priest spoke, the more deeply the message resonated for Tierney and Greg. He talked of having faith through trials large and small, and he spoke of prayers being answered in unexpected ways. "The miracle you pray for," the priest concluded, "might not be the miracle you receive."

They never caught the priest's name, but from that moment, his words became a mantra for Tierney. She said it repeatedly, sometimes to Greg but often just to herself: "The miracle you pray for might not be the miracle you receive."

With those words ringing in her ears, Tierney decided there would be no more prayers for the baby not to have Down syndrome. What's done is done. She reasoned that if her baby had the condition, that might somehow be a miracle in itself, in ways they couldn't yet imagine. In her most private thoughts, she continued to hope the amnio would come back negative, even if she wouldn't officially pray for that. Instead of focusing their prayers on the genetic recipe written at conception, Tierney and Greg would pray that the heart defect was routine and could be fixed by surgery.

After church, they drove to Joan's house for an uneventful lunch, then went home to resume their reading about Down syndrome and heart defects. Midway through the day, they called Alicia Craffey. It was one of several conversations during that first weekend of their new lives. After each call, Greg and Tierney hung up the phone feeling better, even if only a little. In one of the calls, Tierney asked questions about the triple-screen results. The report had clearly been stamped SCREEN NEGATIVE.

Craffey offered some encouragement. She told them that despite the heart defect, Tierney's triple-screen odds of having a baby with Down syndrome—1 in 2,146—meant there remained a good chance their baby didn't have it. "The FISH test will be a good indicator," Craffey said.

There it was again, this FISH test. Greg and Tierney told Craffey they didn't think Egan had ordered one. And, they wanted to know, what was it, anyway?


Craffey had grown up in Connecticut, the oldest of six children. She went to Trinity College in Hartford and received a master's degree from Sarah Lawrence College in Bronxville, New York, home of the nation's oldest and largest training program for genetic counselors. Half of all the genetic counselors in the United States were schooled at Sarah Lawrence, and the deans of many other genetics training centers traced their professional roots there. The school boasts that several countries in South and Central America, Europe, and the South Pacific each have only one genetic counselor, and that one was trained at Sarah Lawrence.

Craffey's office had plants on the windowsills, two Monet prints on the walls, and a bookcase with titles such as *Giving Sorrow Words, Maternal Serum Screen for Birth Defects,* and *The Anatomy Coloring Book.* Notably absent were pictures of babies; some of the people she counseled didn't take one home.

When she began working with Tierney and Greg, Craffey had been a genetic counselor for a dozen years. She had recently celebrated her fortieth birthday. She had shoulder-length brown hair and glasses, with a loud but pleasant voice, a big laugh, and a therapist's gift for making an immediate connection.

Though charming and intelligent, she had never married. More than a decade earlier, Craffey's true love had taken up with one of her coworkers at a Rhode Island school for severely mentally retarded and autistic children. Heartbroken, Craffey couldn't stand seeing them together, so she quit the school. She had loved that job, loved being needed, loved helping children whom others thought were beyond help. She fondly remembered an autistic girl named Jeanine who spent much of her childhood engaged in obsessive, self-abusive behaviors—pinching herself, tearing out her hair. By the time Craffey had left the institute, Jeanine's behavior was significantly improved. Her unblemished skin and the unbroken landscape of her thick, brown hair were proof.

Craffey was a single mother, having adopted a one-year-old girl from China just eight months before meeting Tierney and Greg. There was a certain synchronicity to the adoption: as a genetic counselor, Craffey knew better than anyone that her daughter, Maya, might never have been born if her biological parents had known in advance they would be having a girl. China's population control policy of one child per couple led families to favor boys, who are considered more likely to provide for aged parents.

Whenever she worked with new clients, Craffey began by acknowledging that they were going through an awful time. She offered sympathetic words. But she never stopped at "sorry." She asked about their marriage, about their families, about the extent of their understanding of the prenatal diagnosis they feared or had already received. All the while, she would prepare them for whatever the fates of the womb had in store. She challenged false, preconceived notions. Most of all, she offered information and a ready ear.

Craffey had scores of happy patients to her credit, but she often told a story of failure to illustrate how she envisioned her role as a genetic counselor. A couple had tried desperately for years to conceive a child, but their efforts had been fruitless. Eventually they turned to a sperm donor, and the wife became pregnant. They were overjoyed, but they were adamant that no one know that the husband wasn't the baby's biological father.

As it happened, the couple both had blue eyes. The sperm donor had hazel eyes. When they chose the donor, the couple shared the common but mistaken belief that hazel eyes resulted from a genetic combination of blue and green eyes. So, they thought, no one would wonder about paternity if their child was born with blue or hazel eyes. If the child's eyes were blue, it would look just like them and no explanation would be needed. If the child had hazel eyes, they could simply say one of their parents or grandparents had green eyes, and the genetic combination with their blue eyes had made hazel.

But to their horror, they learned during the pregnancy that in fact hazel eyes result from a blend of genes for green and brown eyes. No blue in the mix. And because genes for brown eyes tend to dominate over genes for lighter-colored eyes, there was a good chance that the fetus the woman was carrying would become a child with brown eyes. The couple was devastated. They were certain that brown eyes on a child with blue-eyed parents would be a dead giveaway that they had used a sperm donor. They wanted to abort.

Craffey tried to tell them that a famed geneticist had proved that brown-eyed children could indeed come from blue-eyed parents. By itself, eye color is not always a sign of paternity. She reminded them: You've been through so much and worked so hard to conceive a child. Now you've done it, and you want to end this pregnancy over eye color?

As hard as she tried, Craffey couldn't dissuade them. The woman aborted.

The way Craffey saw it, the failure wasn't the abortion—she strongly supports a woman's right to choose. She failed, she thought, because she was unable to help the couple understand the genetics and come to terms with their emotions. She strived to help people do both. "What's hard is feeling like I let someone down, that I wasn't skilled enough, I wasn't *there* enough for them," she said years later.

On the other hand, Craffey consoled herself by saying maybe there was no way to get through to some people. And if she couldn't make them understand that eye color was meaningless, maybe they had made the right choice by aborting. "If the child had brown eyes, and every time they looked at their child they thought about it not being theirs, what kind of life is that for that kid?"

More often than not, though, Craffey believed she succeeded. "The best part of my job is feeling like I make a difference. Here are these people in crisis, and some of the things I do or say will help them get through it. And, if I wasn't there, they'd still get through it, but maybe they wouldn't feel as good on the other side."

Her philosophy remained consistent regardless of whether she was helping people deal with cases of unwanted eye color or spina bifida, anencephaly or Down syndrome: parents' feelings were paramount. "If they decide they are going to terminate a pregnancy with Down syndrome, even if I think they would be great parents to a child with Down syndrome, I just have to feel like they made the best choice for them, with all the best information I can provide. They know themselves a hell of a lot better than I do."

At the same time, Craffey sometimes found herself frustrated by the very tests that made her work so necessary. "It's unfair that when you have a prenatal diagnosis of Down syndrome, that's the only thing people know about their baby." When birth precedes the discovery of Down syndrome—or any other unwanted diagnosis—parents are able to see that as just one aspect of their newborn child. "We'll know that he or she has Down syndrome, but it will take its rightful place. It won't be the only thing we know."

Craffey tried to stay in touch with patients long after their crises passed. She led monthly counseling sessions for parents who, in her words, "terminated" or "interrupted" their pregnancies, and she held an annual, candle-lighting memorial service for them as well. Some patients who aborted moved on with their lives with little evident effect, but sometimes patients who made that choice needed more support than the ones who continued their pregnancies. Craffey gave out her home telephone number whenever she thought new patients needed it. Tierney and Greg needed it.

"How are you doing?" Craffey asked during the Sunday phone call.

"Not doing very well," Tierney answered through tears. Greg was on the line, listening. Part of the problem, Tierney said, was the anxiety of not knowing and the difficulty of having to wait so long for the amnio results.

But what about the FISH test? Craffey asked.

"There's that FISH test again. What is it?" Tierney said.


FISH stands for fluorescent in situ hybridization, a scientific mouthful that describes a process familiar to any 1970s teenager who owned velvet black-light posters. When used to screen for Down syndrome, the FISH test treats cells from the fetus with tiny, fluorescent molecules that bind themselves to the twenty-first chromosomes. Examined by microscope under an ultraviolet light, FISH-treated twenty-first chromosomes give off a distinctive glow. If the nucleus of a treated cell displays two glowing twenty-first chromosomes, the test is negative for Down syndrome. If three chromosomes glow in the dark, the test is positive.

While Greg and Tierney were learning about FISH, a team of Virginia scientists was preparing to announce that they had used a nearly identical method to enable couples to preselect their child's gender. The researchers stained DNA of sperm cells with a fluorescent dye, then shined lasers on them to make the dye glow. The amount of fluorescent light produced depended on how much DNA the cell contained. Sperm cells with the Y chromosome—which produce boys—contain slightly less genetic material and therefore glow less. The researchers separated the sperm cells by how much they glowed, and then performed in vitro fertilization using sperm that fit parents' desires for a boy or a girl. The number of happy customers was multiplying rapidly.

While the sex selection method was in its infancy, FISH had been widely in use since the mid-1990s for prenatal testing for Down syndrome and other chromosomal disorders. Its biggest advantage was speed—results were usually available to patients within three days, sometimes as little as one. The main drawback was that FISH wasn't quite as accurate as amnio. Craffey told Greg and Tierney its accuracy rate was 97 percent, though in fact it was slightly higher. A complete amnio analysis remained the gold standard for prenatal testing, approaching 100 percent accuracy.

Both tests were considerably better than the triple screen's accuracy rate of 60 percent to 70 percent. Yet the small difference in accuracy rates between FISH and amnio was significant. It was the reason Egan had said FISH wasn't accurate enough. Ninety-seven percent accuracy meant it was wrong, on average, in three cases out of a hundred. If the three cases were false positives for Down syndrome, those women might abort during the days before the amnio results showed they were in fact carrying healthy fetuses. That kind of mistake was Egan's concern.

After Craffey explained it to them, Greg and Tierney agreed to hold off any final decision on abortion until the amnio came back. In the meantime, they wanted FISH. Craffey faxed a consent form to Greg and Tierney's home fax machine and promised to call the lab early the next morning to see if part of Tierney's amnio sample could be used for a FISH test. She was unsure how they would get Tierney's insurance to pay the $210 cost, since it wasn't ordered initially. Tierney didn't care.

"Even if we have to pay, this is a kind of agony here. We really want to know," Tierney said. Craffey said she would handle it. When they hung up, Greg and Tierney had the same thought about Craffey: This woman is amazing.

Craffey was equally struck by Greg and Tierney. Usually one half of a couple acts as spokesperson for both, but not with these two. They were on the phone together nearly every time they spoke. Both were engaged in the discussion and deeply familiar with the reading material she had given them. They both asked smart questions and pressed for answers. They followed up each other's thoughts and fears in an intellectual and emotional two-part harmony. She found herself admiring them.

But Craffey had one other impression as well. Greg and Tierney seemed to be focusing exclusively on the negatives. They kept asking about the problems they and their baby would have. It was a sign Craffey had seen before, and it usually meant a couple was planning to abort, whether they had admitted it to themselves or not.


As Sunday wore on, Tierney began to feel claustrophobic. She tried to pass the time by reading a book Craffey had left in the package for them, *Babies with Down Syndrome: A New Parents' Guide*. But she quickly felt overwhelmed by early chapters that offered scientific discussions of the disorder and a catalog of medical problems associated with the condition. She called her mother.

"You know, I'm upsetting myself," Tierney said. "Should I even be reading this if this isn't the case? We don't know yet."

"I don't think you should be reading things you don't necessarily have to read," Joan answered. Tierney closed the book and tried to figure out what to do next. Even with the FISH test, it would be days before they would get results. Tierney was supposed to be on vacation, but it didn't feel that way. It was summer in the city, and a hot one at that. She was shopping in her same supermarket, driving the same streets, living the same life they lived all year, week in and week out. She wanted to go to Martha's Vineyard.

"I'm picturing a calm beach, soothing waves, and maybe I'm a little fearful of it just being us here, by ourselves, dealing with all this stuff," she told Greg. "I'm thinking it would be better, for me, to be somewhere I could just walk and think and pray and do all the things that I want to do to get myself in good health. Good mental health." They hadn't even unpacked their suitcases, she reminded him.

Greg would just as soon have stayed home, preferably in bed. But he remembered what his mother had said, and he knew she was right. Tierney needed this trip. Reluctantly, he brought the suitcases back out to the Honda. He came back inside and began refilling the cooler. He grabbed some food for Onyx the poodle, who'd be joining them on vacation. He stuffed the books and articles from Craffey back into their envelope, then tossed the envelope into the trunk.

# CHAPTER 5 "I'M REALLY SORRY TO HAVE TO TELL YOU THIS"

When Bill Clinton was looking for a summer beach getaway, presidential pal Vernon Jordan thought he knew just the place. There were beautiful beaches, beautiful sunsets, beautiful people. There were Kennedys. There was Carly Simon. There were restaurants that served exquisite meals and ice-cream shops with triple scoops. There were bookstores, boutiques, and Black Dog bakery treats. There were bike paths and nature trails and golf courses and nightspots. There was Chappaquiddick, but that could be avoided.

Martha's Vineyard was all that, and more, and Jordan knew it. The island eight miles off the Massachusetts coast was the ideal vacation spot for a man who said he considered himself America's "first black president." As Clinton was quick to learn, beyond the surf and celebrities, beyond the literary luminaries and gray-shingled mansions, beyond the bicycle-renting day-trippers and sunburned cell-phone millionaires, Martha's Vineyard had a history largely unknown to white America: it was the preeminent resort for the nation's black elite.

*Ebony* magazine had made it official back in 1947, declaring, "The most exclusive Negro summer colony in the country is at quaint historical Oak Bluffs on Martha's Vineyard." The boosterish piece swooned, "Negro and white swim together on the public beaches, rub shoulders at public affairs." It wasn't quite that idyllic; some longtime Vineyarders recall blacks not being allowed on certain beaches in the 1940s and 1950s. Yet when one prominent black doctor questioned why a favorite beach was made private, he was quickly invited to join. Social status, not skin color, was the primary concern of Vineyard beach owners.

As the *Ebony* writer understood, the center of the black social whirl was Oak Bluffs, one of six towns on the triangle-shaped island. The roots of Oak Bluffs's popularity among the black elite were laid down in the nineteenth century, when free blacks boarded ferries from the Massachusetts mainland and flocked to the town's religious revival meetings. Soon they began inquiring about buying property. When no one tried to stop them, they built the foundations of a black resort community. Some married members of the Wampanoag tribe, native Vineyarders who had lived on the island and fished its waters for thousands of years. The blacks congregated around the Baptist Tabernacle in the town's Highlands section, known for its brightly painted gingerbread cottages. They built homes large enough for themselves and then their extended families, and then they opened some of the first black-owned guest cottages in the nation, led by the still-open Shearer Cottage, established in 1912.

For more than a century, black and white children enjoyed an equal chance of grabbing the brass ring on the Flying Horses Carousel in Oak Bluffs, the nation's oldest operating merry-go-round. They and their parents and grandparents took in the noonday sun on The Inkwell, a stretch of beach the length of a football field that had felt the footsteps of many of the twentieth century's most notable black public figures. The tawny sand and blue waters of Nantucket Sound had attracted Martin Luther King Jr., Congressman Adam Clayton Powell Jr., Sen. Edward W. Brooke, actor-singer Paul Robeson, and Madam C. J. Walker, whose hair and beauty products made her America's first self-made, African-American millionaire. They were followed by Oprah Winfrey, Spike Lee, legal scholar Charles J. Ogletree Jr., journalist Charlayne Hunter-Gault, and lawyer/presidential golf buddy Vernon Jordan, who had summered on the island for a quarter-century.

Most tourists lined up to buy clothing featuring The Black Dog, the island's unofficial mascot. But the hip crowd at Oak Bluffs wore T-shirts bearing The Black Dawg, an attitudinal Labrador complete with dreadlocks.

Just as it had drawn Clinton, the island's history of racial tolerance and diversity had been an important attraction for Tierney and Greg. They set out early Monday, July 27, for the 150-mile drive from Hartford to the ferry dock at Woods Hole, Massachusetts, at the base of Cape Cod. They were subdued in the car, thinking more than speaking, but Tierney was happy to be out of the house. Greg was wishing he were in bed, but he tried to make the best of things.

Tierney drove the Honda onto the lumbering 233-foot ferry. Most Vineyard visitors consider the forty-five-minute ride across Vineyard Sound an essential part of their vacation, a physical reminder to leave their worries on the mainland. They lean against the rail, buy hot dogs and Cokes, and toss bits of bread to the screaming seagulls that hover around the boat.

But Greg was in no mood for any of that. He was too tired, too depressed. He spent the ferry ride napping in the car, below deck, in the dark belly of the boat. Tierney took Onyx topside, but the ride was no fun for her, either. She was struck by a feeling she had first experienced a day earlier in church. Wherever she looked there were children, healthy, happy children, none of them mentally retarded or infirm. They seemed perfect and carefree, and so did their parents. It made her sad.

The ferry eased its way into the Vineyard dock, and Tierney carried Onyx down the boat's metal stairways to rejoin Greg in the Honda. When the ferry was tucked tight against its slip, they drove off and headed directly to their rental cottage on the far western end of the island.

It was an area known to Wampanoags as Aquinnah, an Algonquin word for "high land." Most non-Vineyarders called it Gay Head. The cottage was weathered and cozy, with flower boxes below the windows and a fence adorned with colorful lobster trap floats that had washed onto nearby beaches. The cottage was owned by a local Wampanoag woman who had given it a traditional name: Medicine Man's Lodge.

Tierney's sister Tara had rented the place with a friend for the summer, and Tierney and Greg were subletting it for a week. The original plan was for Tara and her friend to crowd in with Tierney and Greg for a fun weekend, then return to the mainland and leave the couple to themselves during the week. But by delaying their trip until Monday, Greg and Tierney arrived to find the cottage empty. They were glad of it.

The pattern that began on the ferry continued on the island. Greg stayed holed up in the cottage, reading some but generally not doing much. He had planned to work on his dissertation, but that was before the new reality. Now he lacked the energy and concentration for it. Tierney and Onyx spent part of each day at nearby Philbin Beach, a favorite of locals, known for its tranquility and the occasional nudists who swung by.

To get there, Tierney drove a half-mile from the cottage to a tiny roadside parking lot. She grabbed her beach gear and led Onyx along a path of soft sand through tall beach grass. That led them over a dune and onto the rocky beach. To the west, Tierney could see the Gay Head

Light, whose alternating red and white flashes had warned sailors away from the beautiful but dangerous Gay Head cliffs since 1844. To the east was more of the endless beach that circled the island. With Onyx nestled on her lap or playing at her feet, Tierney read and reflected under blue skies and a healing sun.

Tierney and Greg spent part of each day on the phone with Greg's parents and Tierney's mother. There were nightly calls from Alicia Craffey. Tierney called Tara and confessed that Greg had lied about why they had missed the ferry the previous Friday. Tara had suspected something was wrong, but she was shocked by the news. She heard the pain in her sister's voice and offered solace and support. She fought to comprehend what she was being told. Tierney said they weren't sure about anything, bad or good, or about what to do if they heard the worst. She promised Tara they'd talk again soon.

Tara hung up and her sister's words swirled in her mind. There was "abnormality" and "heart defect" and "high correlation to Down syndrome." As a veterinarian, Tara's expertise lay with animals, but her medical training and her deep connection to her sister told her this was serious bad news.

As the days passed, Tierney and Greg felt their moods roll in and out, cresting and crashing, high then low, low then high. They alternated roles. One was hopeful, the other resigned. Then one was depressed, the other upbeat. One worried that the heart defect was irreparable, while the other stewed about Down syndrome. They switched positions then met in the middle, then switched again, like insomniacs trapped together in a narrow bed.

Their minds were bursting with new, unwanted information, swimming with words like "false negative" and "maternal age," and with numbers like 1 in 2,146, the triple-screen odds. Another number in their thoughts was twenty-four. It was the number of chromosomes they feared one of them had contributed at conception. Twenty-four was also the date of the fateful ultrasound. And, coincidentally, twenty-four was the number of weeks of pregnancy until viability.

Yet, as intense and frightening as it was during those first few days, there were times when the situation didn't seem quite real. With one phone call, one sheepish doctor or genetic counselor could admit that it had all been an awful mistake. "Really sorry to have scared you like that . . ." Everything could go back to normal. They could have their lives and their happiness back. Maybe someday they could even laugh about it while holding hands and walking barefoot on Philbin Beach, their healthy child dancing in the nearby waves.

On Thursday night, as the fading light marked the end of their fourth day on the island, Greg answered the ringing phone. It was Tierney's obstetrician, Michael Bourque. He had news about the FISH test, and he asked Greg if Tierney could pick up on another extension. They braced themselves.

"I'm really sorry to have to tell you this . . ." Bourque said, bringing down the curtain on their hopes. "It came back positive."

Three twenty-first chromosomes had glowed brightly under the microscope. One of the three was on its own and the other two were stuck together. It was a rare configuration; in 95 percent of cases of Down syndrome, all three twenty-first chromosomes are separate individuals inside the nucleus. Regardless, it meant there was extra genetic material in every cell of their growing fetus. If born, their baby would have Down syndrome.

Chances for a different result were slim, Bourque said, but the diagnosis wouldn't be official until the amnio results arrived the following week. He told them about a doctor in his practice who had a two-year-old with Down syndrome, and he offered to introduce them to her. He told Tierney and Greg he wanted to see them in his office when they returned from the Vineyard, and he promised to clear his calendar to fit their schedule. They choked out "thank yous" and hung up.

Greg took it hard, but he had seen it coming. Something about the conversation the night before with Craffey had made him think the tests would be positive for Down syndrome. Craffey had told them there were no FISH results and, in fact, she had been telling the truth. Maybe he had only imagined it, but Greg had convinced himself that Craffey was holding back. That night, when Greg told Tierney what he was thinking, she had refused to believe it. "I'm not going to give up my hope that this isn't going to happen to us," she responded.

After Bourque's call, Tierney alternated between numbness and pain. As the results sank in, Tierney knew she needed to stop hoping it wouldn't be Down syndrome. It wouldn't be easy. All her positive vibes drained away. "I was dealing with it and trying to stay strong, and appealing to my better half that I could handle it," she told Greg. "I was going to be there with you." If anybody could cope with such a challenge, Tierney had told herself, she and Greg could. But that was to keep her spirits up, before she knew for sure.

"Now, all of a sudden, it *is* going to be us," she said.

Craffey called an hour later. She said she was surprised, given the low odds on the triple-screen results. But it was time to look ahead, she said, and she promised to provide all the information and support they needed, no matter what they decided.

They called Greg's parents. "Well, you'll deal with it if that's the situation," said Mary. Greg was too spent to ask exactly what she meant. Bob was quiet.

They called Tierney's mother. Joan had been praying as hard as anyone. She had confided the situation in several friends of similarly strong faith, and they all had been taking to God overtime, asking for a miracle. Tierney explained to Joan about the genetic testing and about how unlikely it was that the FISH test would be wrong. "I need you to tell people who think that there's going to be some miracle that there's just not going to be one," Tierney said. Sadly, Joan agreed.

During their first few days on the Vineyard, the fat envelope from Craffey had remained undisturbed in the Honda's trunk. Call it wishful thinking. Call it denial. Before the news from Bourque, it was possible to hope it wouldn't be necessary to read any more about chromosomes. Maybe the envelope could be handed off to some other couple. Maybe Greg could drive to the Gay Head Post Office and mail it right back to Craffey. That would be the end of that.

But with Bourque's call, those thoughts had faded away. Greg went to the car, opened the trunk, and fished out the envelope. He brought it inside the cottage and tore it open.


The next day, Friday, July 31, Tierney called her brother, George, to let him know what was going on. George was thirty-six, an architect and former Air Force captain. He was a newlywed; his wife, Allison, was a doctor, an anesthesiologist. They were living in Boston's historic Charlestown neighborhood, best known for the Battle of Bunker Hill and, more recently, for the "code of silence" that prevailed when murder was committed by one Townie against another. But George and

Allison weren't part of that insular world. They were among the young professionals who had flocked to Charlestown in search of relatively affordable homes, views of Boston Harbor, and five-minute commutes to downtown.

While not as close to Tierney as Tara, George saw himself as very much her big brother. By nature, he was the type of guy who wanted to fix things, to come through in tough spots, to save the day where family was concerned. "What can we do?" George asked when Tierney called. "I really want to be with you. I'd like to come out there immediately."

Tierney and Greg were grateful, but they decided they should talk about it and call George again later in the day. After he hung up, George paged Allison at work. They began calling around to doctors she knew to collect information, advice, and referrals.

When Greg and Tierney called George back, Tara was at George and Allison's house as well. She was en route to the Vineyard to join Tierney and Greg for the weekend, and had dropped by before heading to Cape Cod to catch the ferry. By the time Greg and Tierney called, George, Allison, and Tara had already spent several hours on the porch talking about what they knew about Down syndrome, heart defects, and the combination of the two.

Based on the medical information gathered on the fly by George and Allison, the three had reached a consensus: this was a misbegotten pregnancy, one that would lead to grief. Tierney and Greg were young and should try again. They should abort.

No one said so, at least not directly, during the phone call that night with Greg and Tierney. Allison gave them names of a pediatric cardiologist and a geneticist. Then she tried to gently broach the larger subject. You guys are going to have a really hard time with this decision you're facing, she said. You guys are going to have a lot to focus on and a lot to decide.

Greg and Tierney hadn't raised the issue of "deciding" with George or Allison, and both were taken aback by her comment. Though Allison's words troubled them, neither Greg nor Tierney rose to the bait. Before hanging up, they all agreed that Tara and George would come to the Vineyard the next day; Allison had to work, so she couldn't join them. Tara would take an early ferry, accompanied by her golden retriever, Winnie. George would follow later that night.

\*       \*       \*

The next morning, Greg hibernated in the cottage while Tierney went to pick up her sister at the ferry dock. When Tara and her dog climbed into the car, Tierney was already crying. She had driven around in circles, growing more frustrated as the ferry emptied, the minutes passed, and she couldn't locate her sister. Her emotions were already frayed, and she didn't need this. When they were finally together, Tara asked almost immediately how Tierney was feeling about the conversations with George and Allison.

"They were helpful," Tierney said. But there was more to it than that. Tierney was open with Tara, and her emotions began tumbling out. "Frankly, they made me a little bit fearful. I was surprised by that. And then this whole issue of a decision was coming before me, and I was thinking about that. I got the sense that if this was them, they would make a decision to terminate. They never said that, but that was the sense I got from the gloom-and-doom information they were giving me. And they had all this medically based information, and I had nothing else to go on, no way to answer them."

Tara tried to calm Tierney, saying she thought George and Allison didn't know how best to communicate what they knew and what they felt. "They clearly were upset for you and Greg," Tara said. But yes, she confirmed, based on the information they had gathered about the heart defect and what they knew about Down syndrome, George and Allison believed the pregnancy shouldn't continue. It was clear Tara didn't disagree.

The conversation fueled Tierney's worst fears. She loved the baby kicking inside her. But if the heart defect was irreparable, and if Down syndrome added to an impossible burden, maybe abortion would be the right choice, for the sake of the baby and themselves. Still, hearing it from Tara was devastating.

Greg was outside on the porch of Medicine Man's Lodge when Tierney, Tara, and Winnie drove up. When they got out of the car, he could see the sisters' reddened eyes were turned from each other. When Tara went inside to unpack, Tierney began crying again.

"They think this is a big tragedy. And they scared me," she told Greg.

"You know what?" he said, his voice growing hard. "I believe that people talk to a few people who know a little something about the things they're talking about. Then they take that and try to make decisions for you based on their own experiences and their own fears."

Just then, Tara walked back outside. Greg and Tara were close, not just as in-laws but as friends. They often sparred verbally about everything from race to how much money a pet owner should reasonably spend on veterinary care to save a sick animal. Those talks were sometimes heated, but the stakes had never been so high.

"Here's my opinion," he told her. "I understand that you're all thinking that this is going to be a terrible thing and we should probably consider termination."

"Yes," she answered. "That's what we discussed. And our concern was that because of your faith, you might not consider that option."

Greg told Tara that they were, in fact, actively considering abortion, regardless of religious beliefs. But he also told Tara that, based on his reading, he believed that she, George, and Allison were overstating their supposedly objective medical knowledge of the heart defect and its interaction with Down syndrome. He suspected their goal was to justify abortion, as a way to spare Tierney and Greg—and perhaps, even themselves—from a difficult future.

"People don't want to give up the shield they have from discrimination," Greg said. "And people know that a child with Down syndrome will feel discrimination. And because they don't want to deal with that, people will tend to seek out information that confirms their belief that this is something you shouldn't do."

"You know," he added sharply, "when this is all said and done, if it turns out more positively than everyone expects, some people will see us as having been pioneers."

Tara shot back: "And if it doesn't turn out as positively as you expect, some of them will see you as having been stupid."

Tierney tried to cool them both. "You know, we haven't even talked with the specialists yet," she said. "We're not at the point of having this conversation yet. We should wait and see."

They moved on as best they could, talking about Tara's job and trying to avoid more conflict. As the night wore on, Tierney and Greg nested in front of the television. Tara went out late to pick up George at the ferry dock. When they returned, there were quick hugs and greetings, and soon everyone was asleep.

\*　　　\*　　　\*

The next morning, Tara and Tierney sat together in the cottage's sun-drenched upstairs bedroom.

"I'm sorry," Tara began. She regretted having grilled Tierney as soon as she got off the ferry, and she wished she had taken a different approach with Greg. Tara said she recognized that she had been thinking about herself as much as them.

"I was wondering how I'm going to feel in public with this child at age two or five or ten," she said later. "I knew I was going to be called on in some way to support this child, and I was thinking, 'Can I do this?' They were selfish feelings, about how this was going to affect me."

Tierney accepted the apology and the two fell into conversation. Tierney wistfully mentioned how the children on Martha's Vineyard all seemed so perfect.

Not true, Tara said. On the ferry, a pretty four-year-old girl came over and asked to pet Winnie.

"She was so cute and so sweet," Tara said. "I don't know why I didn't get off the boat and tell you this: she had Down syndrome."

"Oh, Tara!" Tierney cried. "I don't know why, either. That's what God wanted you to tell me all along. That's what I needed to hear."

Tara felt terrible, but something awakened inside her. She realized Tierney would need as much support to continue the pregnancy as she would to end it. The two sisters remained upstairs for more than an hour, talking and crying. It was a return to the closeness of three months earlier, when Tierney had dragged Tara into the high school bathroom before the concert to show her the ultrasound images.

Tierney told Greg afterward: "For the first time since all this happened, Tara said she had a real joy inside her about this baby. She's feeling joyful, and she hopes I can feel that way, too." Greg was pleased, but he was on edge.

After lunch, Greg, Tierney, Tara, and George decided they could use a respite on Philbin Beach. While waiting for a spot in the tiny parking lot, the lingering tensions between Tara and Greg found a misdirected outlet. They flared into a dispute over whether the car could squeeze into a tight space. The argument escalated far out of proportion with the issue, and Tara decided she no longer wanted to go with them to the beach. She left them there and drove back to the cottage, alone.

Tierney, Greg, and George found a sandy place among the rocks and watched the rolling waves. Tierney sat between her brother and her husband, and Greg and George talked about the weather, about George's plans to leave Boston, and about this and that and not much of anything at all.

"Why aren't we talking about this?!" Tierney demanded suddenly.

"Tierney," George said. "I'm here, I'm going to be here. We're going to support you."

But then, gently, George began pressing the case for abortion. He said the doctors with whom he and Allison had spoken warned that the heart defect could mask other deformities and could even be devastating all by itself. It might well be irreparable, dooming the baby to a brief and horrible life. If you add mental retardation to the equation, why should you put yourselves and this child through such an ordeal?

"George," Greg said, "that may be true. But I can tell you I remember distinctly that, during the ultrasound, up until the heart everything was 'normal, normal, normal.'" Greg said he knew that George thought he was being objective, but they wanted to hear for themselves how the experts assessed the problems, the risks, and the chances.

Tierney didn't say much, but she was wavering. On the one hand, she didn't see herself aborting because of Down syndrome—but she wasn't certain about that. On the other hand, she feared that the heart might be something else entirely—maybe a big enough problem to follow George's suggestion and abort. She wanted, needed, more answers.

There was nothing more to say and no time to say it. They needed to get back to the cottage to change for a cocktail party at the summer home of one of Greg's professors. Just before they left the beach, Tierney pulled out a camera. They took pictures of each other, partial family portraits on a rocky beach. The pictures show various combinations of two men and a woman, all young, healthy, and attractive, but with wan smiles and wary eyes.

# CHAPTER 6 "WHAT DO PEOPLE USUALLY DO?"

G reg and Tierney sat like defendants awaiting a verdict. Or, more accurately, a reversal of judgment on appeal. Their backs were stiff, their jaws clenched. Holding hands in their obstetrician's office, they braced for the results of the final test that would reveal whether their unborn child had Down syndrome.

Michael Bourque leaned across his desk. He tried to meet their eyes with his. Softly he began: "I'm really sorry . . ."

They were prepared for bad news, but tears washed Tierney's face. Greg felt the air rush from his lungs. The amnio had confirmed the FISH findings: if they continued Tierney's pregnancy, their child would be mentally retarded and marked by the distinctive features and ailments of Down syndrome. Some doctors referred to the visible effects as the "stigmata" of the condition. On top of that, the child would have a life-threatening heart defect and who knows what other problems the tests couldn't see.

"I know this is really tough," Bourque said. A long pause followed.

Greg caught his breath. "What do people usually do?" he asked Bourque. "I mean, in terms of keeping the baby."

Bourque leaned back in his chair and considered the question.


It was Tuesday, August 4, eleven days since Greg and Tierney had received the first hint of trouble. They had returned home the night before from Martha's Vineyard.

The cocktail party at Greg's professor's house had gone smoothly after Tierney overcame her anxiety about what would happen if someone asked about her pregnancy. She had feared her distress would show itself as clearly as her rounded middle.

"Tierney, you don't have to tell anyone anything," Greg had told her on the way to the party. "Just be yourself and don't worry. No one is going to ask you really in-depth questions."

He had been right. Their hostess had asked how she was feeling, and Tierney had answered, "I'm feeling good." And that had been that. Afterward, Tierney thought: "I'm telling the truth. I'm doing fine. My baby's not fine. But I'm fine. I'm not lying, and I really don't need to go into it any more."

Once back home in Hartford, Tierney and Greg knew they weren't ready to resume their normal routines. Before their appointment with Bourque, Tierney had called her boss at United Technologies, Jacqueline Strayer, to say she needed more time off. Trying to contain her sobs, Tierney had explained only that there were "complications" in her pregnancy.

"Don't even worry about work, Tierney," Strayer had said. "Whenever you want to, check back with us and let us know."

Greg had made the same call to his colleagues at Columbia University, and he had received the same response.

Before leaving home for Bourque's office, Tierney couldn't stop herself from checking her office voice mail. She regretted it immediately. There was a message from a man she knew professionally, but not well. He had spoken with her in the past about his wife and children, and he had just heard she was pregnant.

"Congratulations! I'm so excited for you," he bubbled on the message. "I can't wait to tell you about all the wonderful things you're in for! I'll give you tips on parenting." He went on and on, innocently clawing at her emotions. They should get together soon, he said. Tierney burst into tears listening to the message. She never returned the call.


The appointment with Bourque was their first return to Saint Francis Hospital since the ultrasound had discovered the hole in the heart. Their moods reflected the changed circumstances. When they heard Bourque say the amnio had confirmed the FISH test, they felt as though their last hope for a reprieve had been denied. There would be no last-minute pardon. That only happened in the movies. So they pressed on, seeking Bourque's guidance.

"People do all sorts of things in this situation," answered Bourque, dark-haired and youthful-looking at forty-eight, an ob/gyn since 1981 who had trained at the University of Connecticut School of Medicine.

The more he spoke, the more Greg and Tierney thought they detected discomfort in his voice and body language. Through a welter of emotion, they heard him ramble through a noncommittal answer. He cautioned them that he was a general obstetrics practitioner, not a specialist in Down syndrome or pediatric heart defects. He said some people don't abort under any circumstances, and others abort if the child isn't a boy. He also let them know an abortion would have to be done elsewhere; Saint Francis is a Catholic hospital.

"It's really your decision. It's up to you," Bourque concluded. More than once, he said, "I'm sorry." And each time he said it, without elaborating or enlightening them about what lay ahead, it seemed to confirm for Tierney that they were facing a catastrophic event. The "sorrys" made Greg angry.

They walked out of Bourque's office and Tierney was still crying. Just as when they left after the amnio, Tierney imagined how she must have looked to those around her. "I probably scared all the other pregnant women in the office," she told Greg.

The farther they got from Bourque's office, the more irritated Greg became. He felt they had gained little useful information about Down syndrome or the faulty heart. They didn't even get good advice about ways to approach their decision. He wondered why Bourque didn't seem to know more. "OK, this is the number-one birth defect involving chromosomes, and among children with Down syndrome, this particular heart defect is very common. He should know this," Greg said. He thought they might want to consider finding a new doctor.

But that wouldn't be easy for Tierney; Bourque was her first ob/gyn. She had seen others when she lived elsewhere, but when she returned to Connecticut after grad school, she had gone right back to him. She liked and trusted Bourque, but she suspected he knew more than he was saying. She thought to herself: Is he worried about being sued for giving out information that's incomplete or misleading? Does working in a Catholic hospital limit what he can say about abortion? Is he going overboard trying not to influence us?

The way Bourque saw it, he was walking a thin line between informing and influencing a patient he knew well, one he liked and admired. "We have to be very careful that we try not to color things one way or the other," he said later. "It's wrong for someone to make a choice that really isn't in their best interest only because it arises from where the doctor is coming from."

And yet, Bourque acknowledged there were certain limitations to working at Saint Francis—where, like Tierney, he had been born. "I do practice at a Catholic hospital, and we hold to the principles that religion and the hospital espouses," he said. "My practice does not encourage, or carry out, or perform abortion choices, but it's our duty to make people aware of them. If they ultimately choose those paths, then it's our job to ensure they seek providers who will handle their care successfully."

Even as he was offering his sympathies, Bourque knew they wouldn't do Tierney and Greg much good. To some extent, Bourque admitted later, he was helping himself. "We're not just doctors. We're parents, we're fathers. We have our own problems with our own families. You're trying to connect to your patients as a human being," Bourque said. "Saying, 'I'm sorry,' probably helps the caregiver to continue to function. It helps to resolve his feelings of inadequacy over what happened and his powerlessness to make it right."

Greg and Tierney pulled out of the Saint Francis parking lot and drove across town to Connecticut Children's Medical Center. Opened in 1996, the 123-bed teaching hospital offered state-of-the-art pediatric care with the slogan "Kids are great. We just make 'em better!" They had an appointment with their first specialist, pediatric cardiologist Dr. Harris "Hank" Leopold.

There, for the first time, they got an upbeat assessment from a medical professional. It came from Leopold's nurse, Karen Mazzarella. "Everything will be fine," she told them. "Your biggest worry is going to be whether your child wants to ride a motorcycle or get a tattoo."

They knew she was exaggerating, but it felt good to hear. It couldn't have come at a better time—they were still reeling from Bourque's news about the amnio. There were no "sorrys" from Mazzarella, a sprightly woman with short-cropped hair. In the hallway outside her office were bulletin boards covered with hundreds of photos of children who had undergone successful heart surgery. They were babies, little kids, and teenagers, in a rainbow of colors. Some had Down syndrome.

As they waited, Greg and Tierney saw a tall, unassuming man walk through the office. Mazzarella sprang into action: "Dr. Ellison, these are the Fairchilds." They exchanged greetings while Mazzarella explained that Lee Ellison was a pediatric surgeon who routinely and expertly repaired defects like the hole in their baby's heart. When Ellison left, Mazzarella told Greg and Tierney in a stage whisper that he was one of the best pediatric heart surgeons anywhere. Greg and Tierney took her word for it.

She led them into Leopold's office, and he was just as encouraging

as his nurse, even in his body language. Rather than separating himself with a desk, he cozied up close to Tierney and Greg, pulling his chair forward so their knees almost touched. He was a soft-spoken man with glasses, a receding hairline, and a Harvard pedigree. With detailed charts he illustrated the heart defect, described its effects, and showed how it would be fixed. Over the next half-hour, Leopold explained that the phrase "hole in the heart" was more than a metaphor when used to describe an endocardial cushion defect.

In a normal heart, there are four chambers, two upper and two lower, two on the right side and two on the left. Blood enters on the right side, and from there it's pumped to the lungs to be enriched with oxygen. From the lungs, it goes back to the heart, entering on the left side. The left side then pumps the blood to the rest of the body. After dropping off its oxygen and nutrients to hungry cells from head to toe, the blood returns to the right side of the heart, depleted. It's sent back to the lungs for more oxygen, and the cycle continues, endlessly until death. By the time a child reaches kindergarten, the heart will have pumped about 150 million times; an average lifetime requires more than two billion beats.

Normally, walls of muscle inside the heart separate oxygen-rich blood from oxygen-depleted blood. Small, perfectly designed valves built into the walls open and close to allow the blood to move from one chamber to the next. In the hearts of people with an endocardial cushion defect, parts or entire sections of those walls are missing, and the two valves that are supposed to separate the upper and lower chambers are malformed as a single, large, ineffective valve. Oxygen-rich blood sloshes from one chamber to another, mixing with oxygen-depleted blood. As a result, less of the rich, oxygenated blood gets pumped to the body, which can't thrive without a full supply of oxygen reaching all its cells.

In an attempt to compensate, the heart pumps more blood than normal, furiously trying to keep pace with oxygen demand. That extra pumping can enlarge and damage the heart muscle. Even with all the heart's best efforts, the defect makes it impossible to keep up with the body's needs. Making matters worse, all that extra pumping builds up pressure in the blood vessels of the lungs, putting them at risk of serious damage.

Leopold explained all this to Tierney and Greg with diagrams that illustrated the problems and showed how surgery would correct them. Leopold also mentioned that before the defect could be fixed, there was a risk of "blue baby syndrome," named for the bluish hue in the skin of children whose bodies aren't getting enough oxygen. It was yet another syndrome for Greg and Tierney to deal with, as if Down wasn't enough.

Also, Leopold said, babies with this defect tend to pant as they try to take in added oxygen to nourish their bodies. And because their baby would spend its first months of life in a New England winter, Greg and Tierney would have to be vigilant about colds. Sniffles that turned into a respiratory infection could be fatal.

Despite all their reading, it was a lot for Tierney and Greg to digest. But Leopold knew exactly what he was doing. He piled on the bad news first, saving the best for last: "The success rate for this surgery is better than 90 percent." And there actually appeared to be a slight benefit when the defect accompanied Down syndrome. Doctors weren't certain, but it appeared that for reasons involving the shape and development of the heart valves, the prognosis was best among children with three twenty-first chromosomes.

Leopold told Greg and Tierney that based on the ultrasound, it looked as though the fetus Tierney carried would not be in any immediate danger after birth. No cardiologist would need to be present for the delivery. "Your baby will be on some medication, but other than that, your baby is not going to be connected to a machine or anything like that," he said. "Your baby is going to go home with you."

Greg felt vindicated. His reading about the heart defect had led him to believe the odds were good, and now an expert was confirming it. Even better, the two-thirds survival odds that Greg had calculated at his kitchen table now seemed too pessimistic in light of Leopold's claim of a 90 percent success rate. Greg had more support than ever for rejecting George's bleak scenario of a baby suffering a brief and painful life.

But Tierney was oddly unsettled. On Philbin Beach, she had told her brother she would only abort if she learned that the heart defect meant certain death. Now, despite Leopold's encouraging assessment, she was gripped by new doubts. She wondered if he was downplaying the effects of a damaged heart on a child with Down syndrome. They

had heard ominous warnings about the heart defect, and Tierney was having trouble shaking them.

She probed Leopold for a darker outlook relating to Down syndrome: "Will there be some kind of interaction between the two, so having the heart defect will stunt development and make it even harder for this child?" She asked the question several times, in several ways. Each time, Leopold gave essentially the same answer.

"We're in the business of doing this," he said. "This is what we do. We work on these hearts. I'm very aware of what we can do and what we can't do. I'm not here to tell you there is no risk and there aren't going to be problems. But it is no way near as dire as it could be. The real issue is how you'd handle Down syndrome after the operation."

When they left Leopold's office, Mazzarella reinforced the message by taking them page by page through a booklet called "To Mend a Broken Heart: Pediatric Heart Surgery." It starred a bright-red, diaper-clad, cartoon heart, complete with blood vessels sprouting from its head. In easy-to-understand terms, the booklet gave a clear description of the surgery their baby would face. When Mazzarella finished, she moved to put the booklet away, but Tierney asked for a copy. Mazzarella smiled and handed it to her; it was a sign that Tierney hadn't given up hope.

Mazzarella brought them on a tour of the intensive care unit, where their baby would be cared for after surgery. She showed them the dormlike rooms where parents could stay while their children were in intensive care, and the common kitchen where they could prepare meals. It struck Tierney as funny to imagine Greg cooking for them there. Tierney also noticed how the halls were brightly colored and filled with children's playthings: Big Wheel riding toys, Tonka trucks, crayons and coloring paper, blocks and wooden beads. More like a daycare center than a hospital.

Before they left, Tierney noticed a tiny baby in an ICU bassinet. She had Down syndrome. Mazzarella read Tierney's mind. "This baby has many more complications than they saw on your ultrasound," she said. "She's two months old and she's never been home. She just had the surgery, and she's doing fine."

Greg mentioned how young the baby's parents seemed. Mazzarella reminded them that most babies with Down syndrome are born to younger mothers. Mothers like Tierney.

*     *     *

On their way home, Greg was fuming. Leopold and Mazzarella had given them a much-needed dose of good news. But the questions Tierney had repeatedly asked Leopold, and the way she had asked them, seemed to Greg to reveal her true feelings, feelings she had kept hidden from him.

"Do you really want this child?" he demanded. "What's wrong here? You've got doctors telling you that everything is going to be OK. Why don't you believe them?"

"I don't know," Tierney said, the hope that sustained her ebbing away. "Maybe it's their job. Maybe they only tell you the good parts because this is what they do. I'm not sure they're giving us the right information, or maybe he doesn't really know about Down syndrome. I just don't know."

She thought back to a videotape Alicia Craffey had given them. The twenty-five-minute video, produced by the Connecticut Down Syndrome Congress, told rosy stories of families whose children had Down syndrome. An infant was rolling over. A three-year-old was baking in a preschool class. An eight-year-old was playing soccer. A twelve-year-old was taking karate. And a delightful teenager named Ashley Wolfe was talking about graduating high school and getting a job. The video showed her typing on a computer. With patented teenage nonchalance, she told an interviewer, "All you're doing is inputting data."

The mother of the three-year-old with Down syndrome looked into the camera and said: "For new parents, I would say to you, it's going to be OK."

The video closed with the happiest note of all. Chris Burke, an actor with Down syndrome who played "Corky" on the television series *Life Goes On,* a performance worthy of MTV. He sang a song with the lyric "Love—let it shine, and let it grow, in all of us, together." While he sang, he smiled, danced, and clowned around with the guitar player accompanying him.

Yet Tierney knew from her reading that a small percentage of children with Down syndrome were profoundly retarded, unable to speak, much less sing. They needed basic care their entire lives. And she knew it would be impossible to know in advance whether their child would be like that or like Ashley Wolfe and Chris Burke.

Inundated with conflicting information and intense emotions, Tierney told Greg she was growing skeptical of almost everything she heard and everyone who was saying it.

"You have the cardiologists who do the work with children, and if children didn't have heart defects, we wouldn't have pediatric cardiologists. So of course they're fine about this," she said. "And then you have the Down Syndrome Congress, which is basically dealing with families whose children have this condition, so they want other families to feel good and comfortable, and that's what they're trying to put out in the video—a positive message.

"I guess I'm thinking, everybody is doing this because they have their own interest, maybe even their own agenda. I don't know what to do about it."

Though discouraged, she wasn't ready to give up. Before making any decisions, she wanted to see Dr. Robert Greenstein, a geneticist who was an authority on Down syndrome. He worked closely with Craffey and even appeared on the Connecticut Down Syndrome Congress video, as the voice of expertise. Balding, bearded, and professorial, Greenstein faced the camera and explained how Down syndrome occurs and how it's not the end of the world when it does. Their appointment was scheduled for two days later.

First, though, there was unfinished family business.

# CHAPTER 7 "THIS CHILD WILL CAUSE TRAUMA AND TRAGEDY FROM THE FIRST BREATH"

Greg and Tierney knew they couldn't wait any longer to share the news with Tierney's father. He was the only member of their immediate families who hadn't been told. It wasn't exactly an oversight.

George "Ernie" Temple III was three weeks from his sixty-seventh birthday, an engineer by training and temperament, a man as solid—and at times, as unmoving—as the granite of his home state of New Hampshire. Tierney was in the eighth grade when her parents split up, and in some ways the rift had never healed.

She was always close to her mother, and the history between father and daughter was at times tempestuous. She stood up to him, and he didn't always like it, but they generally got along during their semiregular phone calls and the few times a year they were together. Tierney tended to downplay the conflicts, though she believed that her brother George was Ernie's No. 1 child in every respect, and that Tara seemed to have an easier time with their father than she.

Tara was more blunt about the family dynamic. The way she saw it, in their father's eyes Tierney was the odd child out, "on the bottom of the totem pole." Like Tierney, Tara thought their brother held an exalted place as Ernie's firstborn, a son in his own image.

Tara had her own special niche as Ernie's first daughter. When he moved away from Connecticut after the divorce, Ernie had enlisted Tara's help; she spent her sixteenth birthday carrying boxes for him. Tara thought Tierney was supported less by Ernie, prized less, given fewer opportunities. Only Tara was sent to private school, though both girls were "A" students and Tierney was eventually chosen salutatorian of her high school class. Tierney also played piano and excelled in student drama productions—she played the title role in *Oliver* in junior high. Although Ernie at times expressed pride in her, Tierney never seemed to shine as brightly in her father's eyes. "It was never easy for Tierney with him," as Tara put it.

After the hospital visits to Michael Bourque and Hank Leopold, Tierney and Greg went home, made dinner, and settled in for Tierney's call to Ernie. He was in Maryland, visiting a lady friend. When the small talk was finished, Tierney got to the point.

"We've had some bad news about the baby," she said. After explaining the medical issues, Tierney laid out the situation: "We only have a little bit of time. But we're trying to find out information and we want to make the best choice for us."

"Well, Tierney," Ernie said, as Tierney recalled afterward, "that's really too bad. But you know, the way medical services have improved, with technology, there's a lot that can be done."

Tierney felt oddly soothed by the comment. They hung up with a mutual promise to talk again soon. But almost as soon as she put down the phone, Tierney thought she caught Ernie's real meaning. He didn't mean medical services and technology to help a disabled child. He meant medical services and technology to end a pregnancy. She called him back.

Tierney asked flat out if he was talking about abortion. Ernie said yes, and Tierney asked him to explain his reasoning.

"Do you understand what having a child with these disabilities is going to bring to your life, to both of you?" Ernie said. "You've got career goals. You're both professionals."

"Yes, I recognize that, but who better than us?" Tierney said. "Who better than us?"

Ernie knew it was a rhetorical question. Tierney tried to probe deeper, to find the source of his discomfort. "Is it the mental retardation that's concerning you?" she asked.

Ernie didn't answer directly, but he told Tierney a story. When he was a boy, his family rented out rooms in their oversized New Hampshire farmhouse, a place they always called "Home Sweet Home." Tierney knew it well. She had visited the family spread often as a girl, and a framed, turn-of-the-century photo of the house sat that very moment on a shelf in her and Greg's apartment. Ernie told her that one of the people who lived and worked with them was a young, mentally retarded woman. She might have had Down syndrome—he wasn't sure—but he did know she wasn't capable of much beyond menial tasks.

"Did she have any education?" Tierney asked.

"I don't know. Maybe a couple of years," he said.

"Well, Dad, you know, that could be a contributing factor to the fact that she wasn't able to do very much," Tierney said.

Ernie shifted gears. "Do you understand the baby is going to be in pain? Do you want to put the baby through that? This child will cause trauma and tragedy from the first breath."

Tierney was stunned, but she pulled herself together and tried again. She told Ernie that she and Greg were gathering information about what kind of challenges they and the baby would face. She said they hadn't decided which course to take. But, she added, if they did continue the pregnancy, there were services available to help them. Tierney mentioned state-funded early intervention programs that Alicia Craffey had told them about. She described how the programs were designed to promote physical and mental development. Tierney hoped her explanation would help Ernie to see how much had changed since the days of the young woman at his family farmhouse.

But Ernie heard it differently. He heard it with the ears of a man steeped in the "Live Free or Die" ethos of antitax New Hampshire.

"Tierney, I probably shouldn't say this."

"Go ahead. Say what you think," she said.

"Do you really think it's fair to keep the baby?" Ernie asked.

"What do you mean, 'fair'?"

"Knowing what you do about this child, is it fair for you to take state money, resources?" Ernie said. "It's fine for people who don't have that decision. They have to have the baby, and they have to take state money. But is it fair for you to do it?"

Tierney let the comment pass; she had no response. Later she would think: That is the harshest thing my father has ever said to me.

There was little else for either of them to say. Tierney promised to consider Ernie's points. She asked, "Will I have your support if we decide to keep the baby?"

"How much support did you think I was going to give you?" he answered. "Did you expect I'd be around more once you had a baby?" He said it without rancor—he meant it as a question, a genuine inquiry to learn what she expected. But it came out wrong. He tried to soften the blow by quickly saying he would support whatever decision she and Greg made.

"If you need to talk further," Ernie said before hanging up, "you can call anytime. Three in the morning. Whenever."

Afterward, Tierney felt exhausted. She hadn't realized that her father still had the power to hurt her that way. She told herself that she had invited him to say what he thought, so she shouldn't be surprised that he did so with his trademark bluntness. As for the part about being around and involved, maybe he meant to contrast himself with her mother, Joan, who lived close by. Ernie was often on the road for work, and he frequently traveled between his home in New Hampshire and his girlfriend's place in Maryland. It wasn't as though he was going to be changing diapers or babysitting for them on a regular basis, even if their baby didn't have special needs.

Then again, Tierney couldn't help thinking that Ernie's reaction would have been different if George were the one making him a first-time grandfather. Also, she realized, on some level what she wanted wasn't her father's advice, opinions, or even his presence. She wanted his approval. And yet, despite that yearning, she wouldn't bend to his wishes just to please him. "I've kind of been the one in my family who has taken on my dad," she once told Greg. "It's like, 'I'd love to have your support, would love you to understand, would love to keep our relationship. But I'm not going to do it at the expense of something I feel personally strong about.'"

When Tierney told her sister about the conversation, Tara vowed privately to speak with their father, to make sure he didn't upset Tierney again. Tara knew how they tended to lock horns, and that wasn't what Tierney needed.

When Tierney recounted the conversation to Greg, he went into a slow boil. He wasn't shocked that Ernie was repelled by the thought of a grandchild with Down syndrome. That was Ernie. But, now of all times, he shouldn't have taken such a headstrong approach with Tierney. And maybe, Greg thought, Ernie was less concerned about mental retardation than he was about something else entirely. Greg's thoughts rushed back nearly a decade, to Ernie's reaction when he first heard the two were dating.

Several months after their Saks lunch hours had turned to romance, Tierney brought Greg to a family gathering at George's house. Greg was on guard. Tierney had prepared him for her family, and he wondered whether he'd be received as Tierney's latest run-of-the-mill boyfriend or as Tierney's black, hopefully soon-to-be-ex-boyfriend.

Ernie had recently returned from a business trip to Germany, Greg's home for several years as a boy during his father's army career. Ernie and Greg quickly fell into conversation about their impressions and experiences there, and Greg was pleasantly surprised by how well they were getting along. During the same visit, Greg noticed that Ernie seemed to be ignoring George's live-in girlfriend, a blue-eyed blond who preceded Allison in George's life.

It struck Greg as odd that Ernie would act that way toward her when he was a guest in her house. But on the other hand, maybe there was some bad blood between she and Ernie. And, Greg thought, if Ernie was rude to her and nice to me, it doesn't seem like this guy makes judgments based on race.

Greg had had a lifetime of experience gauging the attitudes of white people around him, and he thought he possessed sensitive racial radar. As a military kid, he and his family had moved every eighteen months until he was thirteen years old. He was born in Texas, and in addition to Germany, the Fairchilds had lived on or around army bases in Kansas, Virginia, and Alabama, where Greg's younger sister, Marla, was born. Each move had made him the new kid, and that had left him ever alert to social signals.

While growing up in a military environment, Greg never felt second class; he was the son of a ranking officer in an organization that prided itself on the ideal that there was no black or white, just army green. He had playmates of all races and several friends whose parents had interracial marriages. But through his own sensitivities, and with guidance from his parents, Greg became keenly aware of the racial tensions in the troops his father commanded. He knew there were times his father had to roam the base to keep those tensions from exploding into intramural hand-to-hand combat.

Greg also came to understand that some foreign-born officers' wives felt they were treated like second-class citizens by some of the white, American-born officers' wives. The foreign-born wives confided their frustrations in Greg's mother. Although Mary Fairchild was one of the American-born officers' wives, she was also a black woman from the South. The foreign wives knew she would understand the prejudices at play.

Greg got more firsthand experience with racial distinctions when his father retired from the army and the family moved to Rustburg, not far from Lynchburg, in the fertile foothills of the Blue Ridge Mountains. Mary had grown up there, and she had family in town. Greg's cousins took it upon themselves to enlighten him about small-town Southern life in the 1970s. They figured he needed the training, and fast. Although his childhood on army bases meant he didn't talk like them or think like them, he looked like them. And that, his cousins believed, was enough to guarantee he'd be treated like them.

"My cousins said, 'Blacks live on one side of town, whites on the other. When you go to school here, people are definitely going to discriminate against you. They're going to make it really hard for you,'" Greg recalled. "The whole attitude was that the system is designed to keep you down. This is not a place where there are a whole lot of people saying, 'Hey, let's all get together,' like it was when I was in Germany. There's no interracial anything here."

Greg took his cousins' warnings seriously but skeptically. When he went to school, he learned they were at least partly correct. In a racially mixed high school, he was one of only two black students placed on the academically accelerated track. He soon discovered there were no blacks on the track or basketball teams. It wasn't that they didn't run or play ball, but they were certain the white coaches wouldn't want them. It was a two-way street, blocked at both ends: they didn't go out for the teams, and the coaches didn't come looking for them.

Greg decided not to conform to expectations—this was something of a character trait for him—and as a result, he learned a lesson that would stay with him: warnings about worst-case scenarios, even if well intentioned, aren't necessarily true. Rather, they're often based on the fears and misconceptions of the person delivering them. Despite his cousins' predictions, Greg excelled in his advanced classes. He went out for the track team and became its first black member. He got ambitious and ran for student body president. And won.

And yet, for all the acceptance he found, for all his achievements, some things never changed. "I'll never forget this as long as I live," he said once. "There was this guy, and we were friends, we were on the track team together. And one night I was spending the night at his house. And this guy, Randy, makes a point to me. He says, 'Fairchild, you are like a brother to me. You are the closest person I know. But you could never date my sister.' I mean, it was out of the clear blue sky. There had never been a conversation about me dating his sister. He just wanted me to know that."

During college, Greg worked summers in a steel mill outside Lynchburg. He watched as men who sweated side by side for twelve hours a day went to separate company shower rooms at the end of their shifts—one for black workers and one for whites. It wasn't forbidden for white workers to shower with the blacks or vice versa. It just wasn't done. But if Greg and a white friend were in the middle of a conversation in the locker room, they would occasionally ignore the unwritten rule and enter the same shower area. It was a small act of defiance that earned them stares of disbelief and, from some, quiet contempt.

In that sense, Greg's world wasn't all that far removed from that of his father's father, Robert Fairchild Sr. When Greg's grandfather was growing up in Tulsa, Oklahoma, his friend Dick Rowland, a black shoeshine man, was accused of accosting a white elevator operator. Rowland was arrested and a *Tulsa Tribune* headline blared: "Nab Negro for Attacking Girl in Elevator." The newspaper ran a front-page editorial titled "To Lynch Negro Tonight" and, predictably, a lynch mob quickly gathered.

"The Negroes saw that article and said, 'Oh no, there ain't gonna be no lynching tonight,'" Robert Fairchild told an interviewer before his death in 1996 at age ninety-two. "'If there is, we gonna be in the middle of it.'"

"So there was a white man about sixty-five years of age, about five feet five inches, weighed about 135, 140 pounds, walked up to this six-feet-five-inch Negro and said, 'Nigger, what you doing with that gun?' He said, 'I'm gonna use it if I need to.' He said, 'No, you're not. You're gonna give it to me,' and he tried to take it. And that's what set the riot off."

The result was the Tulsa Race Riot of 1921. An estimated three hundred people were killed—far more blacks than whites. Fires in Tulsa's prosperous black neighborhood of Greenwood wiped out twenty-three churches, dozens of businesses, and a thousand homes. The "Negro Wall Street of America," as Greenwood had been known, was destroyed. Only later did police conclude that Rowland had told the truth when he claimed he had stumbled accidentally into the woman on the crowded elevator. The charges were dropped and Rowland was set free.

None of the racial issues Greg personally experienced had ever escalated to violence, but the same wasn't true for his cousins. A few years back, one stopped at a roadside market to get a sandwich. He was minding his own business when a white guy announced, "There ain't going to be any niggers in the store with me." Greg's cousin was the lone black person in the store. He got his sandwich and left, but the troublemaker followed. The white guy went to his van, where his mother was waiting. He reached in and got a knife, then told his mother to use the van to block Greg's cousin's car. She did so, and the son stalked over to Greg's cousin, brandishing the knife. Among countless other mistakes, the white guy didn't anticipate that Greg's cousin was an ex-Marine and a karate expert. They struggled, and the white guy fell to the pavement, dead.

"The police came," Greg said, "and everyone who was there agreed that my cousin was doing nothing, was harassed, and killed the guy in self-defense. So there were no charges. It ends up in the local paper as a story about a bully who was killed in the process of attacking someone. So, you could say the South has changed, because years ago, my cousin would have been in jail. On the other hand, the South hasn't changed, because you can still drive up somewhere to get a sandwich and a guy and his mother will try to kill you."

Years later, after marrying Greg, Tierney got a taste of it, too. In 1967, the U.S. Supreme Court issued a ruling in a Virginia case known as *Loving v. Virginia* that struck down all laws in the country that banned interracial marriages. "Marriage is one of the 'basic civil rights of man,'" Chief Justice Earl Warren wrote for the majority. "Under our Constitution, the freedom to marry, or not marry, a person of another race resides with the individual and cannot be infringed by the State."

In handing down that decision, the high court skewered the opinion of a Virginia trial judge who had upheld the antimiscegenation law by claiming to have special insight into the Good Lord's plan: "Almighty God created the races white, black, yellow, Malay and red, and He placed them on separate continents. And but for the interference with His arrangement there would be no cause for such marriages. The fact that He separated the races shows that He did not intend for the races to mix."

Three decades later, that judge's opinion still wasn't completely foreign in rural Virginia. At least it wasn't one morning when Tierney was driving with Greg and his father to the post office in Rustburg. She was in the back seat while Greg drove and Bob rode shotgun. "People were staring, like they couldn't believe a white woman was sitting in the back with two black men up front," she recalled, incredulous years later. "It was too much."

\*       \*       \*

As it turned out, Greg's positive first impression of Ernie turned out to be only half right. Greg was correct that Ernie didn't have a problem with black people. Generally speaking, that is. He did, however, have a problem with a black man dating his daughter.

At their first meeting at George's house, Ernie didn't realize that Greg was romancing Tierney. He was under the mistaken impression the two were work friends. If Greg were only a pal from Saks, Ernie wouldn't have had a problem with that. He prided himself on having sponsored the first black member of his fraternity at the University of New Hampshire, and he figured Tierney was following his example. Platonically.

When Tierney explained the real situation, everything changed. Ernie made clear his disapproval, a position that made him the only one of their parents who didn't embrace Greg and Tierney as a couple. Joan had quickly recognized the love between them, and Mary and Bob credited Tierney with strengthening their relationship with Greg. As Bob once said proudly: "You don't find many daughter-in-law relationships like the one we have with Tierney."

The next time they were together, Ernie gave Greg the silent treatment. As Greg put it, "I said hello and he literally is not talking." That continued on the few occasions they saw Ernie over the next year or so. But slowly, with time and the inevitability of their relationship, Ernie relented, at least outwardly. There was no dramatic confrontation, no big discussion of what had happened between them, no examination of what had changed. Ernie just seemed to warm up to Greg. When Greg donned a graduation gown to receive his MBA from the University of Virginia, Ernie drove down to Charlottesville to cheer him on. And when Greg and Tierney got married in the picturesque stone chapel on the university grounds, Ernie walked Tierney down the aisle. He danced at the reception and made sure the newlyweds' car was ready to whisk them away afterward.

By the time Tierney called Ernie to tell him the difficult news about her pregnancy, neither she nor Greg considered him racist. Greg had reached the point where he thought he was on good terms with his father-in-law, able to engage Ernie in conversation on current affairs and even race without tripping family land mines. Improbably, Ernie also grew close to Greg's parents, exchanging Christmas gifts and often visiting Bob and Mary at their home in Virginia, even when Greg and Tierney weren't around.

After Tierney's phone calls to inform Ernie about the problems with the pregnancy, Greg tried to make sense of Ernie's reaction. He looked inwardly, through the prism of his own experiences with race and his hard-earned understanding of his father-in-law's perspective. "I've come to believe his concern is about protecting his daughter, helping you avoid a life of discrimination," Greg told Tierney. "As your father, he would prefer you not have to deal with it. When we met, his attitude was like, you could just stop dating me. And now, he's saying technology can help us avoid the problem, the discrimination, that comes with Down syndrome."

Just when it seemed Greg and Tierney's life couldn't possibly get any more complicated, it got more complicated. The next day was Wednesday, August 5, the twelfth day of their new reality. Craffey called with the kind of news that begins, "I don't quite know how to tell you this, but . . ."

There was another piece of information gleaned from the FISH test and amniocentesis that they needed to discuss. The fetus had a relatively rare kind of Down syndrome, one that occurs in fewer than one in twenty cases. The problem, Craffey explained, was that this unusual kind of Down syndrome shows up most often when either the mother or the father is a carrier for the disorder. Their baby's Down syndrome might not be a completely random event after all.

There are three kinds of Down syndrome. The least common is called mosaicism, affecting just 1 percent of people with the disorder. In those cases, the sperm and the egg start off with the usual complement of twenty-three chromosomes each. When they join in conception, everything begins the way it's supposed to: a fertilized egg with forty-six chromosomes. The problem arises when that first cell begins to duplicate itself to divide and grow into more and more cells. In mosaicism, one of the first four or eight divisions leads to an uneven distribution of chromosomes. One of those early cells ends up with a third twenty-first chromosome, and one ends up with only one twenty-first chromosome. The cell with a single twenty-first chromosome dies off. But the cell with three twenty-first chromosomes lives on. And each time that cell replicates itself, the resulting cells also have extra chromosomes. The other early cells replicate themselves without incident, and they and their descendents have the usual number of chromosomes. As the embryo develops into a fetus and then enters the world as an infant, some—but not all—of its cells have the Down syndrome signature. As a result, people with mosaicism are likely to have fewer physical features and developmental delays than other people with Down syndrome. Laypeople sometimes call mosaicism a "mild" case of the disorder.

The second and by far the most common kind of Down syndrome is called nondisjunction trisomy 21. In those cases, every cell has an extra twenty-first chromosome, so unlike mosaicism, the Down syndrome is "complete." Nondisjunction results spontaneously and without explanation, and can be traced to one extra twenty-first chromosome tagging along when either the egg or the sperm was first formed. When a sperm with twenty-three chromosomes meets an egg with twenty-four, they combine to make forty-seven, a geneticist's dozen. Every replication and division after fertilization repeats the error, and it reveals itself as three separate twenty-first chromosomes floating around independently in the nucleus of every cell. Ninety-five percent of people with Down syndrome have nondisjunction trisomy 21.

Until Craffey's call, Greg and Tierney figured they were part of that crowd.

The third kind of Down syndrome, called translocation, occurs in the remaining 4 percent of cases. It's similar to nondisjunction because every cell of the body has three twenty-first chromosomes. The difference is that one of those three chromosomes isn't floating on its own in the nucleus. Instead, it's permanently affixed to another chromosome. The fetus Tierney carried had an extra twenty-first chromosome that was stuck to one of the two other twenty-first chromosomes, a rare formation. If the pregnancy continued, the baby would have a complete case of Down syndrome—this wasn't like mosaicism. But unlike mosaicism and nondisjunction—for which there was no known explanation beyond the risk factor of maternal age—most cases of translocation Down syndrome have a clearly established, genetically inherited link.

In fact, Craffey told Greg and Tierney, some 75 percent of cases of translocation Down syndrome occurred when either the mother or the father was genetically predisposed to passing on an extra chromosome. Carriers have the usual complement of forty-six chromosomes, so they show no signs of Down syndrome. But two of their chromosomes are stuck together. The result is a significantly higher chance that when their bodies create eggs or sperm, they will pass on an extra chromosome to their offspring, producing a baby with forty-seven chromosomes per cell. Craffey explained that Greg and Tierney's cells would have to be microscopically examined to determine if either of them was a carrier.

"If one of us is a carrier, that essentially means we can't have other children, right? Or we'd likely have another one with Down syndrome," Tierney said.

"Let's wait and see," Craffey said. "We don't know if either one of you is a carrier. You should both be tested, and then we'll know."

After they hung up, Greg and Tierney spent the night trying to stay calm. They discussed hypothetical worst-case scenarios for family building. If it turned out that Greg were a carrier, he didn't have a brother, so maybe they could ask Bob to donate sperm for a future pregnancy. Or if Tierney were a carrier, maybe they could ask Tara to donate an egg. Or, if neither of those options worked, maybe they'd use a more distant relative, or an unrelated egg surrogate, or an unrelated sperm donor. It was an ominous reprise of the "what if" conversations they had had months earlier, when they were having trouble conceiving.

When the genetic complications and family permutations started to overwhelm them—the idea of asking Bob to be the grandfather of his biological child was enough to give them both headaches—Greg and Tierney talked about simple adoption. As much as possible, they resolved, they wouldn't let this latest twist become the dominating factor in their decision whether to continue this pregnancy.

Before their lives had turned upside down, Greg routinely cooked them creative, healthy meals with an emphasis on fresh vegetables and well-chosen seasonings. He even liked to make his own ice cream—a current favorite was peach. But in the days since they first got the news, they had relied on nightly runs for pizza, Chinese, or take-out chicken. Craffey's latest call did nothing to improve the menu.

After yet another dinner-to-go, Greg and Tierney went to sleep, one day closer to the twenty-four-week deadline and no closer to a decision.

80

\*　　　\*　　　\*

They woke, still tired, and faced another day of temperatures in the mid-eighties with no promise of relief. It was Thursday, August 6. They drove to Connecticut Children's Medical Center to see Robert Greenstein, professor of pediatrics at the University of Connecticut and director of the hospital's Division of Human Genetics.

He was fifty-six, as warm and scholarly as he had appeared on the Connecticut Down Syndrome Congress video. Like Leopold, he sat close to them, looked them in the eyes, and asked what he could tell them.

"We're still not sure what to do," Tierney said.

Greenstein went through the full rundown of physical and mental effects of Down syndrome. The bottom line, he said, was that although all children with Down syndrome are developmentally delayed, extremely few are the helpless creatures of your worst fears.

"Almost everything you want to happen will happen. It's just going to happen at a different schedule," he said.

After that, Greg asked Greenstein one kind of question, and Tierney asked him another kind altogether. Greg's questions were about what they could do to help a newborn with Down syndrome develop physically and cognitively. What should they read? Whom should they speak with? Could they do exercises, Greg asked, to tone the baby's muscles? Would that decrease the "floppiness" seen among most newborns with Down syndrome?

Greenstein gave him a few recommendations then told him: "Don't get all wrapped up in the fact that your baby is floppy. You want to focus on eye contact, listening, attention span, and all the things that discourage behavioral problems and encourage cognitive and language development."

Tierney, meanwhile, asked about all the things that could go wrong. She questioned Greenstein about whether the baby might arrive prematurely and be even worse off. Greenstein told her that was a possibility, but not a significant one in her case. Tierney mentioned that she had read about a sharply increased chance of miscarriage or stillbirth with Down syndrome. Greenstein confirmed that was true. She expressed her fears about the heart operation and her worries that the physical problems could interact and compound the mental deficiencies. Tierney continued along that line of questioning until her eyes brimmed with tears. She knew her questions revealed that she was afraid, maybe too afraid to continue. Privately, she traced at least some of it to her conversations with her father and brother.

"Tierney," Greenstein said softly, "you seem to have some unfinished issues. Take a leadership position on this. You're going to have a lot of people saying things to you and you're going to have to be your own best advocate. Nine out of ten things people are going to tell you about Down syndrome are going to be wrong. So it's up to you. If you choose to have this baby, you have to be the expert. Take leadership. People are going to follow your lead. If you're really positive about it, other people will be positive about it."

He told them stories about children with Down syndrome whom he knew well. One had recently called to announce that she was trying to get her driver's license. Another was in her first year of college. Certainly, Greenstein added, those children are quite high-functioning. But they're not as much the exception as you might think.

After the hour-long meeting, Greenstein directed them to a hospital clinic. A technician would draw blood from both, to determine whether either was a carrier for the translocation type of Down syndrome. He wished them well and urged them to stay in touch.

That night, Greg and Tierney got an unexpected telephone call from Alicia Craffey, who worked closely with Greenstein. She told them that Greenstein was left with the impression that they had different attitudes about the situation, which if true could spell trouble down the road. Greenstein also had mentioned in passing to Craffey that Greg and Tierney were a mixed-race couple, and he wondered if that might be a factor in their apparently different outlooks.

The racial issue took Craffey by surprise—until Greenstein raised it, she hadn't known that Greg was black and Tierney was white. All their work together had been done by phone. Despite feeling as though she knew them intimately, Craffey had never laid eyes on them. She mentioned Greenstein's comment to Greg and Tierney, and it disturbed them.

"Tierney, we've got to get it together," Greg said afterward. In Greg's experience, whenever race entered the picture, the results were infinitely more complicated. Until that moment, race hadn't been seen as a wedge between them, and he was determined not to let it become one.

"We have to be on the same page," he told Tierney. "I'm not saying you have to be in the 'keep' group. But what more information do you need to know? We've talked to the cardiologist. You've now heard from the genetic specialist. What is it you're waiting to hear that will convince you one way or the other?"

"I want to talk to people who've been through this," she said. "I want to talk to people who have children with Down syndrome."

# CHAPTER 8 "SO, YOU'RE JUST GOING TO GO WITH THE ABORTIONIST?"

It was Friday, August 7, one day after the visit with geneticist Robert Greenstein, fourteen days since the ultrasound. Only seven days remained until the fetus would be considered viable, and Tierney and Greg were in flux. Adding to their confusion, they found themselves switching positions yet again on whether to continue the pregnancy.

Tierney's turnabout, a move toward keeping the baby, began with a call early in the day to Dr. Kenneth Warner. He was a pediatric cardiologist from Boston who had been recommended by George's wife, Allison. Warner reviewed a video copy of the ultrasound test that spotted the heart defect, and he endorsed the encouraging assessment from Hank Leopold, the cardiologist Tierney and Greg had seen two days earlier.

Warner told Tierney the defect would require a major operation during the baby's first few months. He then reviewed the extensive precautions necessary to keep the baby healthy until surgery. But, like Leopold, he said the success rate was better than 90 percent.

"Is this something we should consider termination for?" Tierney asked. She thought she knew what he would say, but she decided to ask anyway. That way she could relay the answer not just to Greg, but also to George and Allison. Warner wouldn't answer with a simple yes or no, but he said the prognosis was good. He recommended surgery. Tierney got the message, but she wasn't quite through.

She asked him about the heart defect's effect on a child's development. Warner echoed Leopold again, saying the surgery was safe, complications affecting the brain were rare, and children with Down syndrome tended to fare better than other children. As the questions mounted, Warner sensed that Tierney was waiting for something more.

"If you're leaning toward keeping, there's no reason not to," he said.

"Thank you," Tierney said, and hung up.

Leopold's nurse, Karen Mazzarella, helped Tierney to get in touch with a local woman named Jean Riccio, whose daughter with Down syndrome had successfully undergone the same heart surgery sixteen years earlier. The girl recovered completely and went on to attend regular classes in her neighborhood school. Riccio proudly described her daughter as a happy, healthy seventeen-year-old who competed on a swim team and liked to attend movies with friends. It was a brief call, but it helped.

Buoyed by all that she had heard, Tierney began moving past her fears about the heart and its effect on development. She called her brother. With practiced self-control, she reined in her desire to tell George how wrong he was and how much he had scared her. Instead, she told him how the cardiologist that Allison had recommended had given a thumbs-up. Tierney also repeated Warner's answer to her question about whether to abort.

George took the call in the spirit it was made. "Wow, Tierney, we didn't know," he said, as Tierney recalled afterward. "That sounds great. I'm really glad for you." Before hanging up, Tierney told George that she and Greg were still deciding, but she was leaning toward keeping the baby. He repeated his promise of support.

But Tierney didn't tell George everything. She didn't mention that the situation was complicated by Greg's sudden change of heart. Now he was edging toward abortion.


For days, Greg had been feeling confident about the heart surgery. He had accepted the idea that he would be the father of a mentally retarded child. Despite the relatively high odds that he or Tierney would be identified as a genetic carrier for translocation Down syndrome, he wasn't terribly worried about that—they were due for some good news, he figured, and maybe that would be it.

His new worries were subtler than any of those concerns. Greg began to focus on what this child would mean for the lives of their later children. He feared that he and Tierney might be placing an unreasonable burden on them. "What about the younger children being required to take care of their older sibling, possibly for the rest of their lives from a financial perspective?" he said. "Would keeping this child mean we aren't able to adopt a child later?"

He worried that there might be places they couldn't go, things they couldn't do as a family, promises they couldn't keep to themselves and the other children they might have. He thought they might have to forfeit the spontaneity that he and Tierney enjoyed and had hoped to pass on to their children.

"Being a good parent to me means having all your children feel like they got the best they could get from you," he told Tierney. "One day, you know, the second or third child might come to us and say, 'You had the option of not being in this situation, and you've brought all this weight down on us, and we're not happy about it.'"

"Oh boy," Tierney said. "Isn't this interesting? I'm finally comfortable and now you're having issues. You know, these are things I thought about and worked through a week ago, and you didn't pay much attention to them then."

Greg called his parents. Bob and Mary listened quietly and tried to calm him, just as they had during more than a dozen calls during the two preceding weeks. But as Greg went on, it was unmistakable that he was building a case against the pregnancy. Mary couldn't hold back any longer.

"So, you're just going to go with the abortionist?" she blurted out.

"Whoa," Greg said, taken aback. "I don't think the situation is as simple as that. I think these are valid things to bring up."

Bob, quiet by nature, decided it was time to express his thoughts. "Gregory," he said to his beloved only son, "this is not a tragedy. This is not the end of the world. All of us are born with defects. If you and Tierney give this child the love you have for each other, this child will be all right."

The call helped to soothe Greg. But he realized that, like Tierney, he wanted to hear from people who had lived through it. People who had had a child with Down syndrome and had gone on to have more children. Tierney was already hard at work making that happen. She had called Alicia Craffey and asked for phone numbers of families whose firstborn children had Down syndrome. Craffey talked to Greenstein, and he thought back nearly two decades to his experience with a family named the Mallins.

On the day she was born, Laura Mallin was perfect. Limbs and digits in proper number and working order. A doll's face, a tummy ripe and round as a grapefruit. Her mother, Ann, a fourth-grade teacher, and her father, John, a Harvard-trained lawyer, congratulated each other on their work and proudly took her home.

Five days later, Ann Mallin began to cry over her daughter. She cried every day. She didn't stop for six months.

Ann thought everything changed for the worse on that fifth day. Not just everything about her formerly perfect child, but everything about her formerly perfect life. She believed she'd never be happy again. She was convinced she'd be too embarrassed to ever take her baby out of the house. She imagined the other children she wanted to have, but she thought their lives would be ruined. Just like hers. By Laura.

"It was like a death," she said twenty years later. "I felt I had a normal child for three or four days and I was feeling euphoria. Then this happens. It changes your whole perception, and I felt like I was grieving. She wasn't the child I wanted to have."

No one had noticed any problems when Laura was born. The doctors and nurses at Saint Francis Hospital cared for her and Ann for a couple days then sent the new family home with good cheer and warm wishes. But during her first two days at home, Laura fed less and less. Worried, Ann and John brought her back to Saint Francis. The doctors diagnosed a blocked intestine. It was frightening news, but the Mallins were pleased to learn that it wasn't life-threatening if quickly treated. But the doctors suspected something else was afoot. They called in a bright young geneticist named Robert Greenstein.

Greenstein knew that such a blockage was sometimes a symptom of a chromosomal disorder. First he examined Laura for the classic physical tip-offs—upward slanting eyes, or maybe a single crease on the palm of each hand instead of the usual two. Laura showed none of those symptoms. So Greenstein looked deeper, into her cells, and there he found what he had suspected: an extra twenty-first chromosome in every cell. Ann and John Mallin's beloved newborn girl, their first child, had Down syndrome.

"I was devastated," Ann recalled.

John took the news better, though he, too, was pained. Maybe he saw it coming. He had had a premonition days before the birth that there would be "something wrong" with their baby. Also, John had personal experience with the condition. He had an older cousin with Down syndrome, a gentle man who lived his life peacefully at home. He was loved, cheerful, and able to take care of his basic needs. Though he never received formal education or training, he had taught himself to speak by watching television. To John, his cousin's life certainly wasn't enviable, but neither was it tragic.

While Ann continued her daily crying jag, Laura underwent surgery to open a pathway through her intestinal track. She spent nearly a month in intensive care, and then she came home a second time. Ann cared for Laura—changing diapers, washing bottles, bathing her, rocking her to sleep—but for months Ann's heart wasn't in it. She was twenty-nine, a bright, attractive blond with a good and successful husband, and she now lived every day with the belief that she was in store for a miserable life. Laura wasn't perfect anymore.

Then one day in June, when Laura was nearly six months old, she smiled up at her mother. Then she did it again. Then she laughed. As the days went on, the smiles and laughs chipped away at Ann's anguish. In countless small ways, Laura began showing she was her own tiny person, with her own identity. Ann stopped crying and started getting to know her daughter.

"I saw delays, but I started to love her for who she was. You love who you have," Ann recalled. It wasn't easy. Ann and Laura went to play groups where children Laura's age were starting to walk and talk, skills far beyond Laura's reach. Nevertheless, Ann held on to her improved outlook. "She was social and happy, and that compensated for the delays."

Almost as soon as she pulled out of her depression, Ann got pregnant again. It was a long nine months. Ann didn't want amnio; she couldn't imagine getting an abortion, and she knew by then she would make the best of whatever came along. Fifteen months after Laura was born, Ann gave birth to a son, John. He was healthy from the start, with the usual chromosomal complement of forty-six per cell.

Laura and young John became fast friends, playing in the family backyard, tumbling and laughing together, even creating a secret handshake. John progressed quickly past Laura intellectually, but he never moved past her emotionally. Two-and-a-half years after John's birth, they were joined by a third sibling, Sarah, who toddled along behind her big brother and sister.

Almost from the time she came home from intensive care, Laura was enrolled in Connecticut's Early Intervention Program, a system designed to provide developmentally delayed children with the extra help—physical and speech therapy, for instance—they need to reach their potential. When Laura was old enough for school, her parents saw to it that she was included in regular classrooms as much as possible, even if it only meant mornings for attendance and the pledge of allegiance, or lunch and gym, before moving over to a special-education classroom.

Concerned that Laura would be overlooked at school, the Mallins remained watchful. John Mallin remembers visiting his daughter's second-grade classroom several months into the school year. He opened her pint-sized desk to find two perfectly sharpened pencils, an unopened box of crayons, and a glue stick whose contents had long since spilled out and hardened. By then he was a founder of the Connecticut Down Syndrome Congress and had served as its first president. That experience, plus his legal training, made John Mallin a formidable advocate for his daughter. He approached the teacher, a woman he liked, and pointedly asked what Laura had been doing in the class.

"I don't know," the teacher replied. "She's in the back of the room with her aide all the time." The Mallins immediately found Laura a different class, with a teacher who better understood her needs and potential.

Some teachers saw Laura's delays as a learning opportunity and assigned other students to be her classroom "buddies." Ten years later, one of Laura's third-grade buddies turned into a girlfriend for her brother, John. Ann's experiences with Laura's schooling inspired her to shift her professional emphasis away from traditional classroom teaching. After spending ten years at home raising her children, Ann went back to work with a focus on special education. Eventually, she became a vocational coordinator, helping special-education students like Laura make the transition from school to work.

By the time she was a teenager, Laura was relatively self-sufficient in terms of her daily activities. She dressed, fed, and bathed herself. She had her own strong taste in music—Disney songs were high on her hit parade. She liked to watch videos, especially *Grease,* starring Olivia Newton-John and John Travolta. She followed instructions and obeyed her parents' safety warnings. She went to summer sleepaway camp for children like her, swam in the family's backyard pool, went skiing in Vermont with her dad, and vacationed with her whole family. Her favorite ride at Disney World was "Pirates of the Caribbean." She was trim, fit, and competed in Special Olympics. She won medals in softball throws, swimming meets, and running races, and she liked to wear them around the house.

She attended school proms, more than once with her boyfriend,

Tim, a handsome young man with Down syndrome. A picture from one shows Laura in an elegant, baby-blue satin dress. Her hair is swept up on her head, and a corsage from Tim covers her wrist. She is wearing a big smile. Tim stands next to her. Dashing in a tuxedo, he sports the canary-eating grin of a guy who knows his date is beautiful.

Laura held the photo as she sat one afternoon in the living room of the Mallins' gracious home in the Hartford suburb of Wethersfield. "We had supper at prom. We danced. We missed dessert. We were dancing," Laura explained in a delicate voice. The family's little black dog, Chloe, played at her feet. Laura was wearing fashionable nylon running pants and a stylish sport vest over a white T-shirt. Sitting nearby, her sister Sarah quietly urged Laura to untuck the T-shirt: It's cooler that way.

As part of her school program, Laura stuffed envelopes at a law office and worked low-level jobs at an Ames department store. But her favorite job was at a Red Lobster restaurant, where she liked to buy her own lunch. "I wash tables, roll silverware. I make garden and Caesar salads," she said. She used her first paycheck to buy the video *Matilda*, based on the book by Roald Dahl about a magical, optimistic girl who uses her mental powers to defeat an evil headmistress.

For all her accomplishments, Laura was not among the highest-functioning children with Down syndrome. Her words were often hard for those outside her family to understand. She read at a barely functional level. She couldn't drive. She didn't know that she was supposed to dial 911 in an emergency. Instead, she knew to run to a neighbor's house. "So she will call the cops," Laura explained. Time was an elusive concept for her. She knew what her watch said, but it had no meaning when someone told her work would be over in three hours. She couldn't make change from a twenty-dollar bill. She knew she was different but didn't know why. She said she liked having Down syndrome but the words lacked meaning. She couldn't explain them.

None of Laura's shortcomings diminished her family's devotion. "For most people, it really is a fear of the unknown," her father said. "It's a condition that has been around for all of mankind's history, but because it was kept in the closet very few people understood it. There's a lot worse out there. When you look at other conditions—autism, cerebral palsy—this is OK."

"Well," Ann jumped in, gently, "you wouldn't choose it. But it's all right."

That comment sent John Mallin into a reflective mood. He told a story about a man he knew whose son had a degenerative disease that would end his life by age twenty. Even when the young man's body was failing, his mind remained sharp. He was able to engage his father in rich conversation.

"I talked with his father about knowing all along he was only going to have his son for twenty years, and me having a daughter who will live until who knows how old, but never knowing who she would have been. We talked about which one you would choose. We didn't come up with an answer to that one." But then, he added, "Some of the things I've seen I know I couldn't handle. But having Laura, to me, seems relatively easy."

John and Ann planned to eventually move Laura from their house into a group home. Because of long waiting lists, they discussed developing their own group home with other families in similar positions. Laura understood the plan as well as she could, and she liked the sound of it. "I would live with friends," she said. It wasn't entirely clear if she knew that meant she wouldn't also be able to live with her family.

Her brother and sister said they were never embarrassed by Laura or considered her a burden. "I don't know any other way. That's just the way she was," said Sarah, a pretty teenager with long blond hair. On the other hand, Sarah admitted she sometimes wished she had an older sister with whom she could talk "about boys and stuff." Then again, there are advantages: when they visited Disney World, workers at the amusement park brought Laura to the front of long lines, and the rest of the family tagged along.

Her brother, John, a strapping six-footer with close-cropped blond hair, said the only problems he ever encountered weren't from Laura. They stemmed from his friends' choice of words. When teenage boys consider something unworthy, a common epithet is "That's retarded." More than once, John squared his shoulders and made clear that wasn't an expression he would tolerate. His friends caught on.

"Having Laura as a sister has allowed me to accept people who are different from me," he said. "It's about understanding the good of a person whoever they are. Laura's glass is always half full. She always asks my father, 'How was your work day?' She asks Sarah and me, 'How was school?' She's always interested in other people. I've used her as a role model in some ways. I look up to my sister."

\*   \*   \*

Greenstein passed along the Mallins' phone number, and Greg and Tierney reached them after dinner that Friday.

John Mallin answered the phone. "When would you like to talk?" he asked.

"Right now, if that's OK. It's kind of urgent," Tierney said.

In eighteen years as parents of a child with Down syndrome, John and Ann Mallin had never before received a call from someone in the midst of deciding whether to abort a pregnancy.

John Mallin told Greg and Tierney about Laura's challenges and her independence, her achievements and her deficits. He explained about early intervention and described the summer sleepaway camp she attended. John told them how he and Ann used Laura's two weeks at camp to devote extra time to their two younger children. On the other hand, he said, they sometimes took Laura on vacations and left the other kids behind. He told Greg and Tierney that Laura got along fine with her brother and sister, and that any problems were more the result of normal sibling rivalries than Down syndrome.

The Mallins had recently returned from a trip to Hawaii, and they told Greg and Tierney about a boy with Down syndrome who spotted Laura in the rental car line. The boy recognized a promising opportunity when he saw one. He grabbed a flowered lei and brought it to Laura, gently slipping it around her neck. The Mallins' pride in their daughter pulsed through the phone lines.

Greg questioned the Mallins about family dynamics and whether having a child with Down syndrome had robbed them of opportunities or spontaneity.

"She's actually more flexible than our other children," John Mallin laughed. The closest he came to a complaint was mentioning that it took Laura longer than usual to toilet train, so they had three little ones in diapers at the same time.

That amused Ann. "Oh, like he was the one changing them!" she said.

John Mallin told Greg and Tierney that although he and Ann didn't know Laura's condition ahead of time, now they couldn't imagine life without her. "You've been given advance warning, but remember, you haven't been dealt the worst card in life," John said.

Then Ann spoke directly to Tierney, veteran mother to young mother-to-be. "You shouldn't overthink things and seek out too much information. Once the baby's here, it'll be a lot easier. You could drive yourself crazy. Your worst fears are probably not going to be realized, so try to balance it. Try to enjoy the rest of your pregnancy."

## CHAPTER 9 "NO PROBLEM"

The call to the Mallins helped Greg. He identified with their outlook, and he hung up feeling as though their family life sounded like everything he and Tierney wanted. But the call had a mixed effect on Tierney. Now she was the one wavering.

At first, the Mallins had strengthened her growing resolve to continue the pregnancy. But by the next day, Saturday, August 8, Tierney found herself consumed by doubt. As a full moon rose, she and Greg flipped positions yet again.

"I'm really conflicted about this whole thing," Tierney told Greg. "I'm feeling good about all the information we've heard, from the Mallins, the doctors, pretty much everybody. But maybe we're just trying to do too much. I guess I'm feeling like maybe we should do the termination."

Her turnabout surprised Greg, but he could tell she wasn't speaking with conviction. It was almost as though she needed to work it through one more time, to test how the words sounded, before making a final decision.

Tierney watched the Down syndrome videotape again, then read from the books that Alicia Craffey had given them. She wept at the stories of people who kept their babies and also at those who aborted. She found herself in the strange position of envying parents who had learned during a pregnancy that their children would have even more devastating conditions than Down syndrome. One such case involved trisomy 18, also called Edwards syndrome, which is similar to Down syndrome but with more severe effects and a far worse prognosis. Babies with trisomy 18 rarely live to their first birthdays.

Tierney saw an advantage to that diagnosis: "That way it would be clear-cut"—she would abort, she told Greg. "For some people, I guess Down syndrome is clear-cut, too, but not for me. I'm sort of wishing, good or bad, why can't we have it clear-cut?"

In the articles and books from Craffey, Tierney read about several women's experiences going to abortion clinics. She started to think the "cure" sounded worse than the disorder. "One woman feels like everyone is looking at her, and her husband is with her, and everybody is shocked that her husband is there. You know, it's the whole scene, protesters outside. It sounded horrible."

Tierney was even more disturbed by a graphic account of how a woman who chose abortion near the twenty-fourth week essentially had to deliver the fetus, "and they put the baby on her and the baby dies. How could I do that?" she asked Greg, sobbing.

She read about another couple who decided to abort because they thought they couldn't handle it financially. Greg and Tierney had talked about financial strain, but unlike many prospective parents in their situation, that issue played little role for them. Both had already made career and educational choices that put personal goals ahead of monetary concerns—both could have parlayed their MBAs into hefty six-figure salaries, but Greg decided instead to get a Ph.D. so he could teach, and Tierney focused her career on the rewarding but less-lucrative field of businesses' role in education. Their only decision about money was that if they continued the pregnancy, they'd open an "independent living fund" instead of a college fund for their child. And they'd work and plan to make sure the financial burden didn't fall on younger siblings.

As the day went on, the more she read and the more she considered it, the less Tierney thought abortion was the answer for her. "Some people terminated because it was clear the baby wouldn't survive. I don't have that. Another couple terminated because of financial distress. We don't have that." She read about a woman who continued her pregnancy in part because she had recently lost her father. "She felt like this baby was a message and a gift. And I'm thinking, 'Hmm, I feel like I've heard that before.' Since we got back from the Vineyard, my sister has been saying she thinks this baby is a gift, that there was something important about this for our family."

There was one last set of worries Tierney and Greg shared, expressed to each other in the form of several questions: How severely mentally retarded might our baby be? What if he or she is in the minority of children with Down syndrome who are profoundly retarded? What if that's more than we can handle? Is there someplace we could turn? Could we put him or her up for adoption? Who would adopt such a child?

Using another telephone number supplied by Craffey, Greg called a woman in White Plains, New York. Her name was Janet Marchese, and few people on the planet were better equipped to answer those questions.

\*      \*      \*

Janet Marchese liked it when her appearance surprised people.

Before meeting her, most people expected a "fat old lady," in her words, with twinkling eyes, an apron, and a tray of fresh-baked cookies. That's the image they thought fitting for a woman devoted to finding adoptive homes for children with Down syndrome. Instead, they found a slim, hip, and attractive woman, with long dark hair, chunky silver jewelry, and a spicy vocabulary delivered with a thick New York accent.

When Marchese was a girl, she lived in fear of a mentally retarded man known around her neighborhood as "Crazy Raymond." That was the extent of her contact with Down syndrome. But then, in 1976, she and her husband, Louis, a police officer, decided to adopt two little girls from Korea. They already had two biological children, a boy and a girl, and they figured they had room in their lives for two more.

As they were finalizing those adoptions, a woman from the agency called and asked if they could take temporary, emergency custody of an abandoned three-week-old boy with Down syndrome. OK, they said, until you find him a home. When the adoption worker brought the boy to their house, Marchese thought someone had made a mistake. He was blond, blue-eyed, and beautiful. She immediately fell in love with Todd Jonathan, or T. J.

The placement was supposed to be temporary, but Janet and Louis realized they couldn't part with T. J. They adopted him. Word spread through the social service grapevine, and Janet started getting calls asking her to take more children with Down syndrome. She couldn't, but she also couldn't turn away. Those other kids were just like T. J., and they needed homes just as badly. She started playing matchmaker, helping to arrange one adoption, then another, then another, all involving babies and children with Down syndrome.

Marchese evolved into a one-woman clearinghouse for Down syndrome adoptions. By her estimate, she eventually played a role in more than three thousand such adoptions, a figure no one in the field disputes. Working from her kitchen table, it was common for her to make and receive one hundred calls a day to and from social service agencies, doctors, adoption professionals, birth parents looking to place their children, and couples and individuals considering adopting a child.

Then there were the "just thought you'd like to know" calls she received regularly from happy adoptive parents. She also frequently took calls from people facing difficult choices. People like the Fairchilds.

Over the years, Marchese had placed infants and toddlers, school-age kids, and even a seventeen-year-old girl who was profoundly retarded and functioned on the level of an eighteen-month-old. The girl's adoptive mother, Colleen Roth, told an interviewer: "People do not understand the pleasure that goes with this child. She has the most precious giggle."

Marchese swore that none of the adoptions she arranged was ever reversed, but she declined praise. "It's not a credit to me. It's a credit to the families."

"I'm driven. I cannot say no. I don't have control over it. I have no choice but to try to do something. Once I hear of a situation, I have to do at least something to help solve it," she once said. Marchese said she doesn't judge people who place children with Down syndrome, at least not in their presence. But she admitted to ill feelings toward "certain middle- and upper-middle-class couples who are not indigent, not poor, who are not single parents—people who have lots of advantages but simply cannot fit it into their lives to have a child with problems."

At the same time, she never soft-pedaled her explanations to people who asked what their lives would be like. "I tell them to cry. I tell them to go ahead and get really upset, that it's a terrible break," she said. "I tell them to go ahead and mourn the healthy child that they never had. And then I try to show them . . . that they can have wonderful lives if they keep their baby."

Her own family was proof. T. J. graduated from high school with help from special-education classes. He learned to read, write, and play harmonica. He earned a green belt in karate. "He skis and swims. He works on a computer better than me. He's had his own house key since he was twelve," she once said. "And he has normal friends who call on him. That's something I never dreamed would happen twenty years ago."

She never took money for her work with her organization, called A KIDS Exchange, an acronym for Adoption, Knowledge, and Information on Down Syndrome. "For us, it's our life," she explained simply. When her husband retired from the police force, he worked as a plumber to help support them. To raise more money, Marchese used her matchmaking gifts to become a leading dealer of collectible dolls.

She got some financial help from grants, including six years of support from the Joseph P. Kennedy Jr. Foundation, but the work nearly bankrupted them. Not just financially but physically.

By 2001, she had effectively shut down the exchange and left the work to others who stepped in to fill her shoes. "I just needed a break, at least for a while," she said. Marchese said she realized, however, that she might find herself drawn back into it. One motivation would be if she learned that agencies weren't finding enough homes for children with Down syndrome. Over the years, she had developed something of a love-hate relationship with adoption agencies, particularly ones that she believed treated children with Down syndrome as impossible to place or not worth the effort. In other words, the way she once viewed the mentally retarded man in her neighborhood.

"It's still those same people who are saying, 'Run for your life, it's Raymond!'"

Greg reached Marchese on Saturday afternoon, the day after the phone call with the Mallins. Marchese's adoption exchange was in full swing at the time, and as usual, she was inundated with calls. Greg thought she sounded rushed at first, but she slowed considerably when he got to the point.

"What if it's more than we can handle after the baby's born?" Greg asked.

"No problem," Marchese answered. "I have a long waiting list for these babies. You want to put the baby up for adoption, it's not a problem, not an issue." When she explained that she had a hundred people waiting for babies with Down syndrome, Greg was skeptical. That seems like a lot, Greg thought. Could she be exaggerating? Lying? Would she say that just to keep people like me from aborting children with Down syndrome? He gently asked her questions to get at those concerns.

Marchese never wavered. A lot of people on the waiting list had firsthand experience with mentally retarded children, she explained, so they knew just what they wanted. And what they wanted was a baby like the one Tierney was carrying. Marchese said others on the list were people who simply understood the value of these kids and knew how much they needed families.

Greg found himself believing her. "What if it takes three years or more to determine how severely mentally retarded the baby is?" he asked. "Could we put it up for adoption then?"

"No problem."

"OK then," Greg said, dropping what he thought was his biggest bomb. "How about finding a home for an interracial child, with Down syndrome, and a heart defect?"

Marchese didn't blink. "No problem."

Greg thought a minute. He had nothing more to ask. He thanked her and hung up.

Greg told Tierney about the call, and both knew there were no more questions. After all the twists and turns, all the changes of mind and heart, the only thing left was to decide.

They sat together in their apartment, at their dining table, on the sofa, in their bedroom. They talked about the encouraging medical outlook from the doctors they had spoken with. They recounted the upbeat family stories from Ann and John Mallin and Jean Riccio. They looked over the well-thumbed package that Craffey had given them, making sure there wasn't something they had missed. They discussed Marchese's promise of available adoptive parents if it proved too much for them. They reviewed the mechanics of abortion. They talked about their sense of themselves and each other. They talked about their families. They talked about love. They talked about God. They prayed.

There was nothing either one could say that would relieve the anxiety about the unknowable: unseen complications with the heart; the possibility of profound mental retardation; the long-term effects on their lives and future children. They also didn't know if one of them was a genetic carrier, but they held on to their resolve not to let that determine their decision.

Hours went by, and finally there was nothing more to say. The time had passed for talking and crying, listening and reading, praying and wondering. It was time to add it up in their minds.

They looked at each other and knew: The total didn't equal abortion.

Maybe it would have for most people—Tierney and Greg understood and empathized. At various points, each had been ready to abort, and both were grateful they had had that option. But that was a path they wouldn't take. It wasn't any more complicated than that. There were no fireworks, none of the excitement that accompanied the pink stripe on the home pregnancy test four months earlier. Just a quiet acknowledgment that their lives were about to change in ways they couldn't imagine and might ultimately regret.

Both had the same thought: We're having this baby. This high-risk, not-what-we-expected, not-what-we-wanted, much-loved baby. Our baby. They called it a leap of faith.

"If I had to terminate, I could bring myself to do it," Tierney said afterward. "But to terminate in a circumstance where I was afraid of taking on a challenge, I just don't think I could live with the repercussions it would have on my life. On our life together. Why wouldn't I allow God to take this pregnancy where it needs to go? And if my baby is going to die in heart surgery, my baby is going to die in heart surgery. My dad might say, 'Tierney, why do you have to go through that,' or, 'Why does your baby have to go through that pain?' But I have to trust."

For Greg, it came down to balancing risks versus rewards. "A lot of things have happened odds-wise that aren't in our favor—just the fact that the baby has Down syndrome when Tierney's triple screen said it was more than a one in two thousand chance. But we also know that the odds are in our favor that a child with Down syndrome won't have severe mental retardation. So, for me, to terminate on the offhand chance that situation presents itself is just not something I'm going for."

In the back of his mind, though, he was happy to have an escape hatch provided by Marchese: "The option, the adoption option let's call it, closes the deal."

"Yes," Tierney said later. "That sealed the deal."

They had made their decision with six days to spare. Exhausted, but at peace, they slept soundly through the night.


They woke the next morning, Sunday, August 9, and went to church with Tierney's mother. Father Cody, Tierney's childhood priest, was back on the pulpit. It was good to see him, but Tierney remained entranced by the other priest's words: "The miracle you pray for might not be the miracle you receive."

Afterward, Greg and Tierney took Joan to lunch at a Friendly's restaurant. Tierney began eyeing a sundae, a big one, with a cherry on top. Greg urged against it.

"I know," Tierney told him, reading his mind. "I'm still pregnant, and with everything that's been going on, I haven't been exercising. I'm going to get fat. Right?"

Greg smiled, Tierney ordered a salad, and they all laughed.

## CHAPTER 10 "THERE'S NOTHING TO BE SORRY ABOUT. I'M NOT SORRY"

O k, what if someone asks you the nature of the problem?" Greg asked Tierney.

"I say, 'There are some medical concerns with the baby, but I'm fine. I'm back to work, and I'm moving on,'" Tierney answered.

"OK, good," Greg said.

It was Sunday night, hours after their Friendly's lunch, and Tierney was growing increasingly anxious about returning to work the next day. She would never be the same person she was sixteen days earlier, when she dashed out of work for a quick doctor's visit before a Vineyard vacation. Too much had happened since.

Her colleagues had only the faintest idea of what she had been through. When asking for an extra week off, she had told her boss that there were "complications." Nothing more. The more Tierney thought about seeing her coworkers at United Technologies, the more she feared they would probe for information about the problems. She wondered if some might even question her about their decision.

Greg tried to comfort her. "Your worries are so far beyond what they would ever ask you. Nobody is going to pry like that," he said.

Tierney knew he was probably right, but she wanted to be ready, just in case. At the same time, she knew that he wouldn't face the same kind of inquiries. People didn't work as closely with each other at Columbia University, so Greg's two-week summertime absence wouldn't raise nearly as many eyebrows, if any. Also, Greg wouldn't be returning to New York until midweek, so it wasn't as urgent for him to think about the reaction. Most of all, though, there was simple biology to consider.

"I'm the one carrying the baby," she told Greg. "I'm the one who was out, and everyone knows it was because of something about the baby. What am I going to say?"

So Tierney asked Greg to role-play, to help her build a ready supply of polite but nonresponsive answers to intrusive questions. Even if she didn't need them, the exercise would be an important part of taking control of the situation, just as Robert Greenstein, Alicia Craffey, and other experts had recommended. Only when she was certain she had the answers down cold would she allow Greg to stop grilling her and go to sleep.

\*      \*      \*

Tierney was already perspiring when she arrived at work the next morning. It was partly the raging hormones of pregnancy and partly the heat—another midsummer day in the high eighties, with no rain in sight. But it was more than that.

She went to see her boss, Jacqueline Strayer, and both kept the conversation light. They focused on the Vineyard weather and generalities about how Tierney was feeling. Strayer didn't ask for details and Tierney didn't offer them.

The morning flew by, and the people she worked with asked only the most innocuous questions. When afternoon came, Tierney felt ready to share the news for the first time outside her family.

Tierney left her third-floor office in United Technologies' Hartford headquarters, a square-shouldered skyscraper known as the Gold Building. She took the elevator to Marie O'Brien's office on the twenty-second floor. O'Brien was forty-nine, dark-haired and attractive, a married mother of two teenage boys. Professionally, she was director of state government affairs for United Technologies and a mentor for Tierney. Personally, she was a friend. O'Brien knew that Tierney had extended her vacation by a week, but she hadn't been worried.

O'Brien was sitting at her desk when Tierney came in. It was a clear day, and Tierney could look out O'Brien's picture windows to see the golden dome of the state capitol and, beyond that, the lush, green Farmington Valley stretching out to the west.

"There's something I want to tell you," Tierney began. O'Brien sensed this wasn't going to be a discussion of corporate-sponsored education programs. She came around from behind her desk, closed the door, and took a seat next to Tierney.

Tierney used none of the evasive lines she and Greg had prepared. She told O'Brien flat out that the child she was carrying had Down syndrome and a heart defect. She talked about the need for surgery and the uncertainties of mental retardation. As she spoke, Tierney found herself feeling more relaxed. It pleased her to feel in control of the information, to share it without breaking down, to talk about her baby without regret. Tierney never mentioned that she and Greg had made a decision. But O'Brien knew.

"You guys are going to be great parents," O'Brien said. It was just what Tierney had hoped to hear.

O'Brien told her about Lowell Weicker, the maverick former Connecticut governor and U.S. senator, who was the father of a boy with Down syndrome. She talked about United Technologies' longtime commitment to Special Olympics. She mentioned the Kennedy family's involvement with mentally retarded children. "It's not like this is a rare and difficult disease or condition," O'Brien said. "This is something that's well known. You've got prominent public officials who have been actively advocating for the kind of understanding and support that people with Down syndrome need. Those people have been trailblazers, and that's how I see you and Greg. And I'm sure there are advances that have been made that you and Greg will learn about and take advantage of."

Two weeks later, O'Brien and her husband Tom would invite Tierney and Greg for a weekend at their beach home in Rhode Island. Greg would have a rollicking water fight with the O'Briens' sons. Tom would tell Greg that he and Tierney would be wonderful parents to a wonderful child. Tierney would let the seawater lift her body and her spirits. They would rise even higher at the sight of a girl with Down syndrome walking along the sand, just another happy beachgoer.

The conversation in O'Brien's office gave Tierney the courage to begin taking others into her confidence, at least in a general way. Another opportunity came soon after she returned to the third floor, when she ran into Heidi Sandling, a friend who worked in human resources.

"Hey, how're you doing?" Sandling asked as they walked down the hallway toward Tierney's office.

"I'm OK, but I'm in a high-risk pregnancy," Tierney said, reverting to her practiced, unrevealing speech.

"I can really understand that," Sandling said. "My sister and her husband are missionaries and they had a baby, their last child, who was born with Down syndrome and two holes in the heart. He's in third grade now." "Um," Tierney stammered, "funny you should mention that. That's pretty much exactly what I'm dealing with." So much for the script.

"Oh," Sandling said, surprised but calm. "Well, he's wonderful. His name is Daniel. He just got a part in the school play, and he's reading almost on grade level. One of the best things is to see the change in my father. He was transformed from being so concerned about what this would be like, how bad it would be, to really embracing and loving Daniel."

Tierney was near tears. Her voice deep with emotion, she whispered, "That's really amazing." She didn't elaborate about her own father's negative reaction, but after Sandling left, she called Greg to share what she thought was a good omen.

The conversations with O'Brien and Sandling were the first of what eventually would be scores of instances in which people told Tierney and Greg about their personal experiences with Down syndrome, mental retardation, and high-risk pregnancies. Nearly all the stories had happy endings.

Sandling mentioned Tierney's situation to her sister, Patti Long, who followed up with a heartfelt, eight-page letter that told her family's story. "I'm sure you have experienced some of the same shock, fear, and loss that we felt at first," the letter said. "However, let me assure you that although you are facing some difficult challenges, your little girl or boy is going to enrich and bring more joy into your lives than you ever imagined possible. Like most kids, Daniel can be stubborn, disobedient and gets into trouble at times, but mostly he is lovable, sensitive, determined, and 'one of the gang.'"

She ended the letter by offering nine pieces of advice, including: "Expect and let yourselves be sad and apprehensive about entering the world of persons with disabilities—don't feel guilty about being sad or mad. The unknown for all of us is scary." And, "Remember, your life as you know it isn't stopping or being totally overturned. You are just branching off into new adventures that will enrich you forever. We wouldn't trade having Daniel in our family for anything."

Tucked inside the envelope was a photo of Daniel and his oldest sister at the edge of the Grand Canyon, her arms wrapped lovingly around him. Both are smiling.


In the days that followed, Tierney told her boss, Strayer, select colleagues, and several other people she worked with inside and outside United Technologies. Each retelling took twenty to forty-five minutes, and each one exhausted her. And yet, with each retelling she felt less raw about the decision, less tentative. More in control.

Some people she told got teary, but none cried. Some hugged her. One invited her to pray with him, and she did. After, he reached over to a shelf behind his desk for some tiny Guatemalan worry dolls, colorful little people each just an inch high. He told her to pick some and place them in a box. Legend has it that Guatemalan children share a single worry with each doll before going to bed at night, and then place the dolls in a box or pouch under their pillows. By morning, the dolls have taken away their worries. A few weeks later, she got a call from the dolls' owner: mission accomplished. They've absorbed all your worries, he said.

Of the dozen or so people she told in and around her company, only one said, "I'm sorry." Tierney had expected the comment, and she was ready. "There's nothing to be sorry about," she responded, gathering herself up. "I'm not sorry."

He didn't mean any harm and she knew it, but it was important to let people know that she and Greg weren't feeling sorry for themselves or their baby. And they certainly didn't want pity. Later, the coworker told her sheepishly, "Well, I certainly won't say 'sorry' again."


While Tierney was back at work that first day, Greg got a call at home from Craffey. She had the results of the tests to determine whether either was a genetic carrier for Down syndrome. The laboratory at the University of Connecticut Health Center had examined their cells in essentially the same way the FISH test and amniocentesis had looked at the fetal cells, searching for errors among the chromosomes.

The results for Greg read: "Cytogenic analysis has been carried out on phytohemagglutinin-stimulated lymphocyte cultures from the above-named patient. This analysis has revealed an apparently normal male karyotype with no consistent chromosome abnormality or re-arrangement event." Identical language was used on Tierney's results, only with the word female substituted for male. It was a tongue-twisting way of saying they had finally beaten the odds. Neither was a carrier.

Although three out of four cases of translocation Down syndrome result from a parental carrier, the fetus Tierney carried was among the 25 percent of cases that occurred at random. If they had more children, they would face no greater chance of Down syndrome than any other healthy couple their age. They wouldn't need sperm donors, egg donors, or surrogate mothers, and their plans for adoption could wait.

"We were due," Greg said simply. Relieved, he called Tierney with the good news.

\*       \*       \*

The next night, Tierney knew it was time to share their decision with her father and brother, who were together at the family's home in New Hampshire. She and Greg had already told the rest of their immediate families—Joan and Tara, and Bob and Mary—and all had responded with pledges of support. Greg's sister, Marla, had learned through their parents and had sent good wishes through them.

The conversation with Ernie was brief, less than five minutes. Tierney wasn't seeking a confrontation, so she went right to the point: They were keeping the baby.

"I'll be there to support you," Ernie said.

In a conversation later that month with Ernie, during a family gathering in New Hampshire, Greg went a step further. "I know you said you're going to be supportive, but you also said some things that indicate maybe you're not going to be," Greg told him.

Ernie repeated his pledge of support, but didn't back down from his original stand.

"I'm supported in what I believe," he said, Greg recalled, referring to his comment that continuing the pregnancy would be a tragedy. "I've made my decisions based on good knowledge and information."

"Maybe you have, but we've been reading a lot, too," Greg said. "And for us, having looked at it all different ways, we decided that we are going to go ahead. Whether you agree or not with our decision, it's important that you be involved with Tierney. She needs you and wants that."

Greg tried to explain that sometimes there was a fine line between a child asking for a parent's opinion and a child seeking a parent's approval. "Even if they're grown up and married and professionals, you're still their dad. So I understand you were giving your candid assessment, but you need to know that carries a weight of approval or disapproval with it."

Ernie reflected on that a minute, then said he understood. The issue wasn't unfamiliar to him: he told Greg he had experienced similar conflicts with his own father. Before the conversation ended, Ernie struck a conciliatory note: "Well, nobody knows what the future is going to hold." Greg agreed, though he knew that he and his father-in-law both expected that, in the end, the other would be proved wrong.

*      *      *

After Tierney's brief conversation with Ernie, she asked him to put George on the phone. At first it was pleasant, with George wishing her well and saying he knew that she and Greg were doing what they thought was right. But Tierney wouldn't let it end there. Though unwilling to confront her father, she was ready to take on her brother. She told him the information he had provided was frightening, often wrong, and reflected his personal biases.

"In the future, when you're dealing with people who are going through a crisis like this, it might not be the best thing to go and give them information from secondhand sources who aren't experts in the field," she said. By contrast, his wife, Allison, had given them what they needed by providing them with names and numbers of experts like Warner, the cardiologist.

George grew defensive, saying he had only been trying to help. How could she question his motives? That was the information given to me, he said, and I gave it to you. I wasn't biased. It was objective information from doctors we had spoken with. How am I supposed to know what you can and can't handle?

They went back and forth a while, with neither giving much ground. Afterward, Tierney told Greg: "I've got to calm down. I've really got to cool out on these kinds of conversations. This is not healthy for me or the baby."

George sensed it, too. Tierney's words resonated with him, and he wanted to make amends. Several days later, Tierney and Greg's doorbell rang. Tierney figured it was the Jehovah's Witnesses again. Greg seemed to enjoy engaging them in conversation and spiritual debate, and they dropped by often. But this time it was a flower delivery man with a bouquet. Attached was a card from George and Allison: "We love you and look forward to meeting our new niece or nephew."


Greg returned to Columbia University the next day, Wednesday, August 12, and began methodically making the rounds of friends and colleagues. Unlike Tierney, Greg more than once found himself passing out tissues.

"I'm not crying because it's a bad thing. I just cry. That's my style," said Elizabeth Elam, administrative director of the doctoral program.

"Please don't be upset for us," Greg told her and other friends who took it hardest. "We're going to do what we have to do. It's serious, but it's not the end of the world."

Sometimes the responses surprised him. One of his professors, an outgoing, friendly man, was stunned into silence. He was supportive, but clearly uncomfortable, seemingly unable to look up from his computer screen. Greg left quickly, disappointed. Later the same day, Greg ran into another faculty member, one Greg had always viewed as reserved, distant, and buttoned-down, a study in blue blazers and khaki pants. "That's different from what you were expecting," the professor said. Unexpectedly, he added, "But that's great. You're going to have a great child."

A third faculty member, one with whom Greg had never felt quite comfortable, shocked Greg by coming around his desk and embracing him. "I almost cried," Greg said later. The spirit of prayer seized one friend, a fellow doctoral student named Matt Bothner. "God take Tierney and Greg and strengthen them to go forward. Do your will and bless this child," began Bothner, a lay minister in a Pentecostal church. The prayer went on uninterrupted for nearly ten minutes.

Two other doctoral students, separately, demonstrated why they were studying business and not biology. Both told Greg they were surprised to hear that Tierney was carrying a mentally retarded child. They thought that sort of thing happened most often when people who were genetically similar procreated. Like when cousins married. And since Greg was black and Tierney was white, the students figured, they couldn't be genetically similar.

Greg gave them a quick tutorial on Down syndrome, and resolved to redouble his efforts to enlighten people about genetics. A teacher by training and disposition, Greg gave several impromptu lessons about Down syndrome, chromosomes, and mental retardation, even getting as specific as to describe how translocation occurs. He also pointed out that many reputable scientists believed that genetic variations among humans of different races were medically insignificant.

In the first weeks after the decision, Greg grew obsessed with making sure people had correct information. He even called his mother and mother-in-law and quizzed them, making sure they understood exactly what had happened scientifically, so they could communicate it clearly to their friends. When they got something wrong, he explained it again. And again. At the peak of his ardor, he told his mother: "If you can't explain it, then I don't want you telling anybody anything at all!" Knowing her son's intensity, Mary went along with him, reviewing the material enough times to win a passing grade.

Tierney did the same kind of teaching with her mother, though with a softer touch. As Joan came to understand the science, she underwent her own conversion. No longer would she pray for miracles. Instead, she resolved to "celebrate this child," as she told Tierney.

As soon as Greg covered everyone in his immediate circle, he pretty much stopped talking about it and went on with his life. "It's not anything that I'm embarrassed about," he said. "I've just decided that I'm going to be matter-of-fact about it and let other people know after the birth. Then I'll say, 'I should let you know . . .' and that's it. And you know, there's a wall in the secretaries' office where all the people who have children on the floor put their baby pictures up. Of course I'm going to put a picture up, too."

The deadline for abortion came and went on Friday, August 14, another hot and sticky day in a summer filled with them. Greg and Tierney didn't talk about it. Greg was in New York, at Columbia, and he didn't remember the significance of the day until later. Tierney was at home, and she remembered. She felt a twinge of misgiving, but it came and went as quickly as the sudden kicks she was feeling in her uterus.

Her doubts had been replaced by something approaching relief. Before the deadline, she had moments when she felt she was back at school and there were days to go until a big exam. Whatever she was doing, the test was always in the back of her mind. Had she studied enough? Did she understand it all? What was she missing? Was she ready? But then, test day came and those thoughts wafted away. It was too late to worry anymore, and she couldn't spare the energy on what-might-have-beens. It was time to buckle down and do the best she could. That was how this felt.

She had reached the twenty-fourth week of pregnancy. The fetus she carried was about eleven inches long and weighed perhaps one-and-a-half pounds. Its footprints and fingerprints were forming the distinct swirls and patterns of individuality. Its eyes had all the components needed for sight. It had a startle reflex, and it could be bothered by loud noises. It could be soothed by a voice. If born that day its chances were only fair, a long shot at best, but then again it might survive outside the womb. It was legally viable.

There was no turning back.

# Part II

## CHAPTER 11 "I CAN'T REMEMBER THE LAST TIME THE BABY KICKED"

Two days after the deadline for abortion, Tierney and Greg remembered what Alicia Craffey had said about the biggest drawback of prenatal testing: When a defect is revealed after birth, new parents can confront the problem within the context of an adorable, needy little person sleeping in their arms, suckling at their breasts, or responding to the sight, sound, and smell of them. The defect is only one part of the picture. They could look into the bassinet at their "imperfect" baby and find joy. They could see a father's nose, a mother's eyes, a grandfather's chin. But when news of a defect or disorder comes during pregnancy, that's the sole, depressing focus because it's the only information expectant parents know with certainty about their unborn child.

When Tierney first became pregnant, she and Greg wanted to be surprised by the baby's gender. But now, knowing whether they'd be having a boy or a girl seemed just what they needed to move forward. They would know something else about their baby, something other than Down syndrome and a heart defect. Something that might help to restore the excitement of anticipation.

On Sunday, August 16, they called Craffey at home with a single question: Do you know the sex? The call made Craffey smile. She saw it as a clear sign that Tierney and Greg had fully embraced their decision.

"Yes," Craffey said. "It's a girl."

Greg and Tierney were thrilled. They were having a daughter. Not just an anonymous, amorphous baby with a bad heart, mental retardation, the physical markings of Down syndrome, and who knows what other problems. A daughter. Their daughter. Craffey noted the call in her records, with an exclamation mark. Her work with them was done.

Not long after, Craffey called Tierney to ask a favor: A Yale biochemist named Lawrence Cole was working on an alternative to the triple screen. As Tierney knew all too well, the triple screen caught only about 60 percent to 70 percent of Down syndrome cases—meaning a lot of false negatives, like hers. It also occasionally registered a false positive, which led to an unnecessary and potentially dangerous amnio.

Craffey explained that Cole was developing a urine test he thought might be 97 percent accurate, and to continue his work he urgently needed fresh urine from a pregnant woman known to be carrying a fetus with Down syndrome. Tierney was happy to oblige. She arranged for Cole's wife to pick up a urine sample the next day and rush it to her husband in New Haven. Suddenly, that *Ally McBeal* episode about driving wildly to get a sample to the lab didn't seem so farfetched, after all.

A few weeks later, Craffey was leafing through her mail when she saw "Fairchild" on a return address. She tore open the envelope and inside was a greeting card. On the front was a reproduction of Picasso's iconic 1959 drawing *Circle of Friendship*—colorful human figures, holding flowers, dancing under a bird in flight.

> Dear Alicia,
> There really aren't words to express our gratitude for your tremendous support through the difficult period of our pregnancy. While we know many challenges still lay ahead, we could not have reached the peaceful and joyful place we are now without your help. Your constant attention to our needs and professionalism throughout this time makes us thankful to know you. We look forward to our continued friendship.
>
> > Best Regards,
> > Tierney and Greg

Craffey tucked the card away for safekeeping.

In a financial footnote to their relationship, Craffey's employer, the University of Connecticut Health Center, was never paid for all the time Craffey had devoted to helping Tierney and Greg. All of their counseling sessions were done by phone—the situation was urgent, and that was the best way she could be available to them day or night, weekday or weekend.

Tierney and Greg's medical insurance only paid for office visits, so the health center's accountants couldn't file a claim seeking payment for Craffey's extraordinary services. And so, in a case study of insurance bureaucracy illogic, the main reason Craffey was so valuable to Greg and Tierney—her around-the-clock availability—turned out to be the very same reason her employer got stiffed.

In late September, Tierney and Greg took part in another ritual of modern maternity: the hospital tour. It was a warm fall night, and they were among eight expectant couples who converged on Saint Francis, all of them due in the coming months. The obviously pregnant women seemed excited and nervous. Their partners looked like boys dragged into the ladies' plus-size underwear department. Tierney wore the same black-and-white dress that she had on during the fateful ultrasound. Greg wore black jeans, a blue denim shirt, and a bemused expression.

Before the tour, they took part in a birthing class, practicing breathing exercises—"ha, ha, hoooo, ha, ha, hoooo"—and lying on a carpeted floor with a pillow between them, as though that could prepare them for the intensity of childbirth. At the instructor's urging, Greg massaged Tierney's neck. He supported her in a birthing position in which she sat with her legs spread, her knees bent, and her feet pulled toward her buttocks. "Ha, ha, hooooo," she said. Greg suppressed a smile.

During the tour, Greg and Tierney viewed a birthing room and talked softly to each other as other couples giggled and cracked jokes. They held hands. For a while, Tierney draped her arm around Greg's broad shoulders. "People are always talking about healthy babies," Tierney said quietly. "They don't even know."

They walked past a statue of the Virgin Mary outside the maternity ward, and they stared through thick glass windows that looked into the newborn nursery. Most of the couples crowded around the glass like Christmas shoppers on Fifth Avenue outside Saks. But Tierney hung back and Greg stayed with her. He smiled at the babies in their bassinets, with pink or blue knit caps on their heads and plastic name-tags on their wrists and ankles. Tierney cocked her head to one side and stared off somewhere past the bassinets. The tour moved on, leaving her briefly behind.

A few weeks later, a package arrived at their apartment. Greg's father, Bob, had refinished a handsome antique wooden bassinet then disassembled and shipped it north. Greg sat on the apartment floor, shoeless, in jeans and a T-shirt advertising a "Race for the Cure" of breast cancer. Not quite handy, better with books than tools, he struggled for more than an hour to rebuild his child's first piece of furniture.

"I'm going to have to get better at this," he said through gritted teeth. Eventually, he thought he had finished, but he had put several pieces on backward. The cradle wouldn't rock. Frustrated, he blew out a stream of air and phoned Bob to walk him through the job. With his father's patient help, the second attempt was a success.

Along with the bassinet came a pillow from Mary, embroidered with the message: "Anybody can be a father, but it takes someone special to be a Daddy."

Unlike her mother, Tierney had no qualms about preparing for the birth of her first child. Fate had already shown its hand, she figured, and so she decided to take Ann Mallin's advice and enjoy the rest of her pregnancy.

In early October, Joan, Tara, and Tierney went shopping for car seats and baby clothes at a nearby Toys "R" Us/Kids "R" Us store. They didn't buy much, spending most of their time enjoying each other's company and watching mothers with small children. Tierney focused on one harried young mother trying to corral two handsome little boys. It took all of Tierney's self-control to keep from walking over and hugging them.

In the weeks that followed, Tierney was thrown not one but two baby showers. Her work friends gave one, and the other was held at Joan's house. Friends and family jammed Joan's living room. Colored balloons and pink-and-blue streamers hung from the mantle. Presents were piled high on Joan's baby grand piano, and Tierney was showered with clothes and gifts, from a baby swing to an elephant rattle, a high-tech diaper pail to a Baby B'Gosh outfit with fish on the bib. At one point Tierney and Joan stole away from the crowd and went into the dining room. Joan hugged her baby girl and Tierney hugged her mom back, oblivious to the party in the next room and the world outside. Both cried, but not in sorrow.

Greg's work friends threw him a surprise shower in New York, providing the Fairchilds with even more clothes, toys, and blankets. "I probably would have found it hokey had all this stuff not been going on," Greg said later. "But I was moved by it. Really moved."

As the birth approached, the nesting instinct took hold. After months of consideration, Tierney and Greg bought a condominium in the same complex where they had been renting. It had only one bedroom, just like their apartment, and it needed new carpet, flooring, paint, and appliances. But the condo was in foreclosure, and that made the deal impossible to resist.

"It's a great place at a great price," Greg said.

To which Tierney responded, only half-joking: "It has a wonderful view of Taco Bell." But it would be their baby's first home, and that alone was enough to excite them. "We'll have a new place, a new baby, new everything," Tierney said.

As summer turned to fall, they returned to old routines of work, family, and friends. There also were regular visits to the obstetrician, Michael Bourque. During one, Tierney found herself scanning the waiting room, hoping to find someone facing a similar challenge. No such luck. Yet maybe she simply couldn't tell, just as most people who saw her had no idea what was happening inside her womb. The closest she came to making a connection with another expectant mother happened when a woman mentioned that Bourque was closely monitoring her pregnancy. Excited, Tierney asked why. "Because my baby is so large," the woman said. If only that was my problem, Tierney thought.

In the weeks after Tierney and Greg made the decision to continue the pregnancy, Bourque had nixed the original goal of allowing nature to take its course, possibly resulting in a December 7 birthday present for Greg. Instead, he had scheduled a cesarean section for December 3. Tierney was disappointed.

"I don't want to schedule my child's birthday," she said.

But Bourque had convinced her otherwise. Although the baby had responded to some unknown signal and turned head-down in the womb—just as Maryann Kolano, the ultrasound technician, had predicted—Bourque reasoned that the heart defect and general uncertainties surrounding the birth of a child with Down syndrome made a scheduled delivery preferable. Neonatal specialists would be standing by to deal with any emergencies, though he wasn't expecting anything he couldn't handle himself.

In the weeks that followed, Bourque monitored Tierney closely, scheduling monthly ultrasounds whose written reports became monotonous: "The fetal cranium appears normal in shape. . . . The fetal face appears normal. . . . The fetal stomach appears normal. . . . Both kidneys appear within normal limits. . . . The fetal bladder appears normal." The baby was on the small side, but in the normal range, and everything else seemed fine, with one glaring exception. Each ultrasound report repeated: "Abnormal heart."

A few weeks before the scheduled delivery, Bourque noticed that fetal growth had slowed considerably. It wasn't anything to panic about, he told Tierney and Greg, but he'd be watching it. They might have to take action if growth slowed further.

Tierney remained sanguine. But talk of growth rates and close monitoring renewed Greg's fears. It was something new to worry about, he thought, just when things had settled down. It reminded him that the risk of stillbirth was higher among fetuses with Down syndrome.

"There's a possibility that things could end up being tragic, and that's scary," he said. Even if the growth concerns proved to be unfounded, Greg was nagged by uncertainty.

"We've made a decision based on our belief that whatever the range of problems are, between us and our family we are going to be able to get through it," he said. "But still there's a fear of the unknown. If they had found some other kind of defect, like a limb missing, you know what you're getting into. They could tell you where the limb ended and where it began. They can't tell us how mentally retarded she'll be, how severe the effects of Down syndrome will be, and that's hard."


On Sunday, November 22, Tierney awoke feeling tired after a poor night's sleep. It had been hard lately to get comfortable with a beach ball for a belly. Making matters worse, in recent days the baby's kicks had reached the mulish, let-me-out stage of late pregnancy.

More than three months had passed since the August day when Tierney and Greg had decided against abortion. Tierney was thirty-seven weeks pregnant—less than two weeks remained until the scheduled delivery. Greg and Tierney spent the morning eating breakfast, reading the paper, and getting ready for Tara to drive down from Worcester to help plan the menu for a big Thanksgiving dinner. Tara also wanted a tour of their newly purchased condo, which they hadn't renovated or moved into.

When Tara arrived, they drove to West Hartford for lunch at a little Italian place called the Prospect Café. Between bites, Greg and Tara got into an animated conversation about how coworkers relate to each other. Tierney sat quietly. She wasn't interested in a discussion of workplace dynamics. She had other things on her mind: It had dawned on her that their usually active baby was unusually still. She said nothing to Greg or Tara.

They went home and watched a video of a darkly comic movie called *Search and Destroy*. Again, Tierney wasn't interested, so she took out her contact lenses and tried to relax. But her stress only mounted. As night approached, she grew increasingly certain that something was wrong. She grabbed her copy of the pregnant woman's bible, *What to Expect When You're Expecting*. She rustled through the dog-eared pages, searching for information on fetal movement. She didn't like what she read, and she placed a call to a hospital help line.

"I can't remember the last time the baby kicked," Tierney told Greg and Tara. To Greg, she said softly, "I'm worried."

# CHAPTER 12 "WE DON'T HAVE MORE TIME"

Tierney lay on her side, curled in a fetal position on a hospital gurney. Her body shook, jerking and chattering like a windup toy with an overwound spring. She drew air in shallow breaths, then huffed it out again, almost panting.

A doctor she didn't know, an anesthesiologist named Jonathan Abrams, inserted a needle through the skin of her lower back, aiming for a sweet spot between two vertebrae. Her eyes grew wide and wild. As the needle burrowed toward her spine, a strange, piercing sensation shot down her leg, as though she had stepped on a live wire. She felt afraid. Worse, she felt alone—Greg had been told to wait outside. Silently, she began to pray.

Her mind racing, Tierney thought back to the day four months earlier when an ultrasound foretold her baby's future, her husband's, and her own. It was cold in the operating room, and the memory made her shiver even more. The doctors and nurses who surrounded her took notice. They urged her to be as still as possible.

"Take some deep breaths. There's nothing to be nervous about," said her obstetrician, Michael Bourque, who happened to be on call at Saint Francis when Tierney had arrived. Tierney nodded, but she thought to herself: Sure. I'm having this emergency delivery, my baby has all these problems, but there's nothing to worry about.

It was approaching 10 P.M. on Sunday, November 22—eleven days before Tierney was scheduled for a cesarean section to deliver a baby girl with Down syndrome, a major heart defect, and uncertain prospects. As Tierney lay on the gurney being prepared for emergency surgery, those prospects were growing more uncertain by the minute. Her baby was in distress.

Two days earlier, Tierney had experienced what she would later realize was a warning sign. While out walking near home, she had felt a sharp jab in her side, like the pain of exertion and lack of oxygen that runners call a stitch. At first, the discomfort was so great it doubled her over. Frightened, she wondered if she could make it back to the apartment. To calm her nerves as she caught her breath, she reminded herself that she was nine months pregnant, and she shouldn't expect to have a marathoner's stamina.

As the pain eased and she trudged home, Tierney reassured herself by remembering a visit the previous day to Bourque's office. Although the baby's growth had slowed in recent weeks, the doctor had said he saw no cause for alarm. On Tierney's chart, Bourque had written a symbol for "positive fetal heartbeat." His only progress note had been to order yet another ultrasound before Tierney's next visit, scheduled for the following week. Before Tierney left his office, Bourque had even warned her to expect fewer kicks as the due date approached, because the baby would be taking longer naps.

But on Sunday afternoon, while Greg and Tara watched the video they had rented, Tierney had a sickly feeling that this nap was lasting too long. She told Greg she was worried, and he rushed to a pharmacy to buy a stethoscope to listen for a heartbeat. As a distraction, Tierney led Tara into the bedroom to show her the gifts from her office baby shower. Tierney liked looking at the tiny outfits and the plush toys spread out on the bed. But then she had a thought: If something terrible happened, I'd have all this baby stuff to pack up piece by piece or give away.

Standing there, afraid, her sister at her side, Tierney came to understand how her mother had felt nearly four decades earlier, when Joan declined a baby shower after her friend's stillbirth.

Greg came home with the stethoscope, but all they could hear was a gurgling noise. They realized it was folly to think they could diagnose a problem on their own, so Tierney called the Babyline, a twenty-four-hour service staffed by nurses to provide answers to worried, expectant women. The nurse told Tierney to do a fetal kick count—recording the number of movements during a thirty-minute period at a time when the fetus is normally active. Estimates vary about how many movements should be felt, but it's generally thought there should be ten or more during a two-hour period.

But Tierney had already tried that, based on what she had read in *What to Expect When You're Expecting.* During a thirty-minute period while Tara and Greg were watching the video, Tierney had felt perhaps one movement at the most. Hearing that, the Babyline nurse urged Tierney to call Bourque. It was 6 P.M.

Bourque was on weekend call for his group practice, so he called back in less than five minutes. He told Tierney to drink fruit juice or eat a candy bar, to stimulate the baby with a sugar rush—fetuses are usually most active after a mother eats. And, he told her, be sure to call back in an hour. Tierney drank two glasses of juice, nibbled at a chicken dinner that Greg had made, then ate a candy bar for dessert. While she waited for the sugar to kick in, Tierney wondered if she were being paranoid or properly cautious. Before long, Bourque called again. "I felt a little bit of movement, I think," Tierney said.

"Did you get ten kicks?" Bourque asked.

"No. I don't think so."

"Why don't you come in and we'll hook you up to the fetal monitor," Bourque said calmly. Tierney figured it would be a brief visit, a quick physical exam to check the heartbeat and to see if her cervix had started to dilate in preparation for birth. She was sure the exam would be followed by embarrassed apologies from she and Greg for making everyone worry. See you in a couple of weeks, they'd say sheepishly.

They rushed from the apartment without packing a bag, leaving the gifts and baby clothes strewn across the bed. Tara went, too, driving separately so she would have a car to pick up Joan, who would be returning that night by train from a weekend visit to Philadelphia.

It was just after 8 P.M. when they arrived at Saint Francis. To their surprise, they learned that the hospital staff was preparing to admit Tierney. While Greg filled out paperwork, a nurse directed Tierney to a wheelchair, then rolled her to a delivery room that resembled a junior suite at a Holiday Inn.

"Is this really necessary?" Tierney asked. "I wasn't expecting to stay over."

"Just in case," the nurse said as she strapped a fetal heart monitor around Tierney's abdomen. At first, the monitor picked up a steady heartbeat. Her anxieties eased.

Tierney looked over at Tara and smiled. "I guess we're ready to go," she said. Tara hugged her. They decided that Tara should leave immediately to pick up Joan at the train station. They'd catch up with each other later. They agreed that Tara wouldn't tell Joan about the hospital visit.

"Everything's fine. We'll be home soon. Why worry her?" Tierney said.

But the good news was fleeting. The baby monitor was set for forty-five minutes, to track the heartbeats over time. Almost as soon as Tara left, things took a turn for the worse. The gaps between heartbeats grew longer and longer, and soon it became clear that the baby's damaged heart was slowing to a dangerous pace.

"I better get Dr. Bourque," the nurse said.

With Bourque came a portable ultrasound machine and a young medical resident. The veteran doctor rubbed the wand on Tierney's belly, and the monitor showed that Tierney and Greg's unborn daughter wasn't moving. Also, the ultrasound revealed that the amniotic fluid that normally bathes a fetus in the womb had dried up; Tierney's body had prematurely stopped producing it. Bourque asked the resident to assess the situation.

"Since she has no fluid, I'd give her a zero for that. And I'd give her a one for movement," the resident said. On a scale of zero to ten, Tierney and Greg's unborn child was failing badly. In the antiseptic terms of medicine, a note was scribbled on the first page of Tierney's fast-growing hospital chart: "Biophysical profile poor." Though the heart was beating, if tentatively, the chance of a stillbirth was increasing by the minute.

"Your daughter wants to be delivered tonight," Bourque said.

With Greg running alongside, a birthing team rushed Tierney's gurney from the hotel-like delivery room to a far less serene operating room. She would have to undergo an emergency cesarean section. The procedure, which dates to antiquity, was long used only to retrieve babies from dead or dying mothers. Though reports of women surviving the procedure date to 1500, only in the nineteenth century did it become routine for both mother and child to survive. By the end of the twentieth century, more than one-fifth of all children born in the United States were delivered by cesarean. Tierney had been scheduled to have a cesarean delivery because Bourque thought it would be safer and easier on mother and child. Now there wasn't any choice; it was a matter of survival.

At the door to the operating room, Bourque asked Greg to wait outside and change into sterile blue-green hospital scrubs. The doctor also thought it was best that Greg not see the spinal injection that awaited Tierney.

While Greg stood guard outside, Abrams, the anesthesiologist, inserted the needle into Tierney's spine. He was administering an epidural, a common anesthetic used with c-sections that allows women to be mentally alert during delivery. Though a c-section without anesthesia is as unthinkable today as biting a bullet during an amputation, it wasn't always so. Church leaders in the nineteenth century fought the use of anesthesia in obstetrics out of obedience to the biblical injunction that women suffer in labor to atone for Eve's sin. That opposition eased only after Queen Victoria, head of the Church of England, was given chloroform during childbirth.

While he waited to be called into the operating room, Greg called Joan's house and left a message telling her and Tara what was happening. He was certain they'd rush to the hospital, and he was glad of it. Greg also called his parents and told them in a jumble what had happened. "We came to the hospital." From there, the words flowed out in a torrent: ". . . unexpected . . . distress . . . no amniotic fluid . . . the baby." Bob and Mary understood well enough: "We'll pray for you," Mary said.

About twenty minutes after Tierney was taken into the operating room, the epidural was complete and she could feel nothing below her chest. A catheter was inserted to drain her bladder, and the final preparations for Bourque's incision were completed. A nurse poked her head outside the operating room and told Greg it was OK to come in. He found a chair at Tierney's side and watched Bourque work.

Bourque made an incision across Tierney's lower abdomen, a technique known as a "bikini cut," based on the optimistic hope that the patient might be able to wear one again someday without displaying a birth scar. He sliced expertly through layers of skin, fat, and muscle to get to the womb. Bourque knew that speed was essential—the baby's vital signs were fading.

Abrams monitored those vital signs while Bourque operated. At one point, he told Bourque ominously, "We don't have more time." Frightened, Greg looked to Bourque, but Bourque displayed no sign of alarm. He just nodded.

A nurse wiped Tierney's bright red blood from the incision, and a medical resident used retractors to create a larger opening. Bourque cut deeper—through the uterus then the amniotic sac, which was intact despite the absence of fluid. Inside the sac—not moving, hovering between life and death—was Tierney and Greg's daughter.

Bourque called to Tierney: "We can see the baby's head!" He moved with a single, practiced motion, like a father lifting a child who has fallen. Through the opening he had created, Bourque pulled from Tierney's uterus a baby covered with the muck of new life.

It was 10:16 P.M. on November 22. Tierney Temple-Fairchild and Greg Fairchild had just become the proud and nervous parents of a five-pound twelve-ounce, seventeen-inch, brown-haired, not-quite-healthy baby girl.

There was no time to enjoy the moment.

Bourque snipped the umbilical cord that had sustained the baby for nearly nine months, ending not only her physical attachment to Tierney but also cutting off the rich supply of oxygenated blood that her own damaged heart couldn't provide.

"I'm not ready," Tierney groggily told Greg.

# CHAPTER 13 "HELLO, SWEET BABY, HELLO"

The birth of a child with Down syndrome is rarely uncomplicated, medically or emotionally. Most of all when the condition is unexpected. And despite the rapid growth of prenatal testing, in most cases it's a surprise. Like Ann Mallin, some parents dissolve in tears and grow depressed when they learn their new babies have Down syndrome. Some call Janet Marchese or another adoption service. Some accept the diagnosis with equanimity. And some do everything in their power to see that the baby dies.

At 8:19 P.M. on April 9, 1982, a baby boy was born at Bloomington Hospital in Indiana. He was blue, he had Down syndrome, and he was quickly diagnosed with a defect called esophageal atresia with tracheo-esophageal fistula. That meant his alimentary canal was a cul-de-sac instead of a thoroughfare to the stomach. Without surgery to correct it, milk couldn't reach his belly. There'd be no way to nourish him without intravenous fluids.

The obstetrician who delivered the baby, Dr. Walter Owens, reportedly told the parents that because of the Down syndrome, the boy would be severely retarded, a "blob" whose chances of surviving the necessary surgery were only 50 percent. Other doctors disagreed and put the success rate at 85 percent to 90 percent. Two of them, a pediatrician named James Schaeffer and the parents' general practitioner, Paul Windsler, urged that the boy be immediately transferred to a children's hospital in Indianapolis for treatment.

At 9:30 P.M., little more than an hour after the birth, the baby's parents asked for time to talk it over. A half-hour later, they decided there would be no treatment. No surgery. No intravenous fluids. They wanted to let their son die, the quicker the better, though they were told it wouldn't be quick at all. And certainly not painless.

The hospital's lawyer became involved, and so did a state judge named John Baker, who held a bedside hearing. He ruled that the doctors had offered two conflicting opinions and therefore the parents were free to choose either one. They chose the no-treatment option, Baker said, and that was their right. The judge's ruling drew widespread attention to the case. Along with the attention came couples willing to adopt the boy and lawyers eager to represent him.

The adoption offers fizzled immediately because the boy's parents refused to allow him to live with another family. The lawyers for the boy had no better luck. First they appealed the Indiana Supreme Court, to no avail. An attorney named Lawrence Brodeur made a last-ditch effort, flying to Washington, D.C., six days after the birth to appeal to the nation's highest court. But by then the baby was weak, and another Indiana court had refused to order that intravenous fluids be given at least long enough for the U.S. Supreme Court to hear the case.

Hours after Brodeur arrived in Washington, D.C., before a single justice could decide whether the full Supreme Court should hear the case, the baby died. He had begun starving the moment the umbilical cord was cut, and he had slowly starved to death. His parents hadn't named him, and so he would forever be known as Baby Doe.

The public outcry that followed Baby Doe's death prompted action by President Ronald Reagan and the U.S. Congress. On October 9, 1984, Reagan signed what became known as the Baby Doe Amendment, which expanded the definition of child abuse to include the denial of care and treatment to newborns with disabilities.

C. Everett Koop, who as surgeon general played a role in the administration's support for the law, wrote about the episode in his memoir: "I hope Americans learned anew the value of a single human life, no matter how small, no matter how handicapped. I hope Americans learned how easy and how wrong it is to ignore or deny the needs of the disabled. A child does not deserve to die just because it is retarded, or worse, might be retarded."

The Baby Doe Amendment was the first attempt by U.S. lawmakers to regulate doctors' treatment decisions at the beginning of life. But while the Baby Doe case was certainly among the most celebrated, or notorious, instances of withholding life-sustaining treatment for disabled newborns, the issue was neither new nor unique.

In fact, Baby Doe's death was consistent with long-standing practice of infanticide throughout the world. Sometimes for medical causes, sometimes for political motives, sometimes for social concerns, and sometimes for personal reasons, certain babies in certain places have been allowed, even encouraged, to die, sometimes with the explicit approval of authorities. And by no means have the practices of selective breeding, and by extension selective extermination, been limited historically to so-called uncivilized societies. Dubbed "eugenics" in the late nineteenth century by a cousin of Charles Darwin, Francis

Galton—he based the term on the Greek root for "good at birth"—
efforts to "improove" human heredity have enjoyed periods of popular support in many of the world's most highly developed countries,
including the United States.

In the World War I era, a Chicago doctor named Harry Haiselden
made himself briefly famous by advocating eugenics in widely pub-
licized statements—and actions—as well as in a film he wrote and
starred in called *The Black Stork*. Haiselden advocated ridding society
of "defectives," a broad classification in which he included people with
mental retardation, physical infirmities, and even ugliness. "To be hideous, utterly hideous, is a dreadful curse," he told a Chicago reporter
in 1915.

While Haiselden focused on defects and disabilities, other supporters of eugenics focused on broader classifications: race. The thinking
was pretty well summed up by a leading eugenicist named Madison
Grant, author of the 1921 best-seller *The Passing of the Great Race*: "Neither the black, nor the brown, nor the yellow, nor the red will conquer
the white in battle. But if the valuable elements in the Nordic race mix
with inferior strains or die out through race suicide, then the citadel of
civilization will fall for mere lack of defenders."

In a study of eugenics and race in America, author Steven Selden
pointed out that Grant was hardly considered a crackpot: "He was a
member of New York's social aristocracy, and [his book] was a popular
text read at the very highest levels of American society." It was even recommended by the *Saturday Evening Post*, based on a review written by
none other than Theodore Roosevelt, who had helped to popularize
the term "race suicide."

More recently, advocates for the disabled have sounded the alarm
that eugenics will make a comeback—or, indeed, already has—as a result of advances in prenatal testing. They base their fears on the knowledge that the only "solution" for most disorders identified in utero is
abortion. Those fears have been fueled by advances in the Human Genome Project, which by mapping the genes on all twenty-three chromosomes promises to exponentially expand the information that can
be gained from prenatal testing.

Sometimes, as in the case of Baby Doe, eugenics has mixed with infanticide. And that, too, is not a unique or aberrant impulse. Laila Williamson, an anthropologist at the American Museum of Natural His-

tory, has studied a broad range of historical and scientific literature on the subject and concluded: "Infanticide has been practiced on every continent and by people on every level of cultural complexity, from hunters and gatherers to high civilization, including our own ancestors. Rather than being an exception, then, it has been the rule."

It wouldn't be hard to imagine, then, what a committed eugenicist would prescribe as treatment for a half-white, half-black, mentally retarded infant with Down syndrome and a heart defect.

There's little evidence that Down syndrome has in recent history been a common motive for infanticide, but some prominent thinkers have made the case that it very well could be. The best known among them is an Australian-born Princeton University scholar named Peter Singer, who has written that he would allow parents, in consultation with their doctors, to kill newborn babies with certain disabilities. He has explicitly mentioned Down syndrome, spina bifida, and hemophilia. As he wrote in 1993:

> When the death of a disabled infant will lead to the birth of another infant with better prospects of a happy life, the total amount of happiness will be greater if the disabled infant is killed. The loss of happy life for the first infant is outweighed by the gain of a happier life for the second. Therefore, if killing the hemophiliac infant has no adverse effect on others, it would, according to the total view, be right to kill him. . . . It may still be objected that to replace either a fetus or a newborn infant is wrong because it suggests to disabled people living today that their lives are less worth living than the lives of people who are not disabled. Yet, it is surely flying in the face of reality to deny that, on average, this is so.

To suggest that his ideas aren't radical, Singer often points to the fact that an overwhelming majority of women abort following a prenatal diagnosis of Down syndrome. In Singer's view, newborns are not self-aware—a state of consciousness he has said takes a month or so after birth to attain. Therefore, according to Singer, a mother who chooses to end the life of a disabled, week-old infant is morally equivalent to a pregnant woman who aborts a twenty-week fetus with the same disability.

Not surprisingly, Singer is widely despised among advocates for the disabled. Among his more polite detractors is Adrienne Asch, a Wellesley College professor who holds an endowed chair in biology, ethics, and the politics of human reproduction. Asch also happens to be blind.

As Asch told Singer at a Princeton forum in 1999:

> Disability is only one characteristic of any person's life, and that is any person's life whether it is a two-day-old infant, or a twenty-year-old young woman, or a seventy-five-year-old woman or man. Along with that disability, whatever that disability happens to be, come a whole range of other characteristics. The mistake that many people make, whether it is in selective abortion or notions of withholding treatment from disabled newborns, is that the disability will stunt the life prospects of the individual and burden the family with no redeeming other benefits, with no redeeming other attributes. It simply is not true.

"You might be right," Asch continued, "that the next child—after you kill the three-week-old disabled newborn, or terminate the pregnancy of the fetus diagnosed with Down syndrome—won't have Down syndrome. That's all you know. You don't know whether they will be any happier, whether you will enjoy them, whether they will enjoy you. It's using one characteristic to make an important decision, and taking one characteristic and making it the sum total of a human being."

Security was tight at the packed debate. Outside the campus gates, six anti-Singer protesters, one in a wheelchair, wore signs that read "Singer and Hitler: Great together." But at least some Princeton students said Singer had impressed them. One sophomore told a reporter, "Every opposing argument that I could think of, he addressed in some form."

When obstetrician Michael Bourque pulled Tierney and Greg's new baby into the world, Tierney's face was screened by a sterile drape. She could hear only the faintest noise, the tiniest coo.

OK, she's alive, Tierney thought. But where's the hardy cry? Where's the healthy, powerful, wonderful first gasp of air, the scream that announces, "I'm here!" Tierney began preparing for the worst. She blamed herself.

"Did I do something wrong?" she asked Greg.

"No, nothing," he told her. Setting aside his own worries, Greg smiled and told Tierney she did great. He didn't mention that their baby's skin seemed to have a dusky blue sheen and that her movements were sluggish, as though she were drowning in molasses. On the positive side, Greg thought she had relatively firm muscle tone, not the floppy, rag doll's body they were told to expect. But before he could get a good look, their baby was gone.

A team of neonatal specialists leapt into action, taking Baby Girl Fairchild into an adjacent room. Greg followed close behind. They suctioned fluid from her nose and mouth. They cleaned, dried, weighed, and measured her, speaking to her in dulcet tones. They began assessing her health using a newborn scoring system called the APGAR scale, for Activity, Pulse, Grimace (or reflex irritability), Appearance, and Respiration. The acronym is a tribute to Virginia Apgar, a trailblazing female physician who conceived the test in 1949. Before Apgar's scoring system, babies were presumed to be healthy unless they showed obvious signs of distress. That often led to delayed treatment, sometimes at a deadly cost, for babies suffering from internal maladies. Each of the five categories on Apgar's test is scored with a zero, one, or two points, for a maximum total of ten. A seven or higher is generally considered a passing grade.

At 10:17 P.M., one minute after she was born, Tierney and Greg's baby was blue and barely breathing. Hanging onto life, her APGAR score was a two, dangerously low.

After suctioning out her mouth and nose, the neonatal team inserted a tube in her nose to force oxygen into her lungs. They placed her under warming lights, as motionless as a roast on a buffet carving station. At 10:21 P.M., five minutes after birth, Baby Girl Fairchild finally started breathing on her own, if tentatively, and her color slowly began to improve. A second APGAR placed her score at five—better, but still worrisome.

"She still hasn't had a good cry," said Dr. Hema Desilva, a neonatologist and director of newborn care at Saint Francis. Bourque had originally arranged for Desilva to be present at the scheduled December 3 cesarean, so Desilva knew in advance what to expect. He had rushed to the operating room when he heard that Tierney was there early. As he stood side by side with Greg over the baby, Desilva tried to ease the tension. "I guess she had a different idea about when it was going to happen," he said cheerfully. Greg didn't respond.

*       *       *

While Greg watched over their baby, Tierney remained on the operating table, dazed and anxious. She began shivering again as Bourque started to close the incision.

"Tierney, you're shaking like a leaf," the doctor said. "This is getting really difficult." As Bourque sewed, he comforted Tierney, praising her for recognizing the danger her baby faced: "Nice call. You saved your daughter's life."

Tierney was grateful, but doubtful, too. She knew the crisis was far from over, and she wouldn't believe anyone until she saw her baby herself or heard it from Greg. And where was Greg? Where was the baby? Was she alive?

At 10:26 P.M., ten minutes after birth, a third APGAR assessment registered more improvement—the baby's score rose to seven. That was high enough for the neonatal specialists to release her, momentarily, into Greg's care. They placed her in a see-through acrylic bassinet, and Greg wheeled it into the operating room. He brought it alongside the operating table and reached inside, lifting the swaddled child and placing her close to Tierney's ashen face. Tierney brightened, marveling at the delicate life they had created.

"Oh! She's beautiful," Tierney said.

But the combination of anesthesia and stress caught up with Tierney. Her stomach contracted and she began to vomit. For the first time, Greg was forced to juggle his roles as husband and father. He traded the baby for a bedpan and held it to Tierney's mouth.


When everyone was cleaned up, they briefly went their separate ways: Baby Girl Fairchild to the neonatal intensive care unit, Tierney to the recovery room, and Greg to search for Joan and Tara. He found them waiting nervously outside the maternity ward.

"You have a granddaughter. You have a niece," he told them in an exhausted voice. Tara gripped him in a long, strong hug. Joan kissed him.

"My baby had a baby," Joan said repeatedly.

Greg led Joan and Tara to the neonatal intensive care unit (NICU), which the hospital staff pronounced "nick-you." It was dark and quiet—a comfortable atmosphere for patients who had recently left the womb. A buzz of smooth efficiency saturated the filtered air. Nurses glided silently among seven bassinets, four of them containing tiny babies who barely dented their little mattresses. Around each bassinet was a maze of high-tech machinery and intravenous feeding tubes, oxygen tanks, and monitors that glowed and hummed and kept watch like nervous parents. Not all these babies would be going home.

A nurse led them to their daughter, granddaughter, and niece, napping in bassinet No. 5. They crowded around and marveled in unison at the baby in the tiny knit cap with tufts of hair peeking out. They admired her long fingernails and rosebud lips. Baby Girl Fairchild lay on her back, her eyes closed, her unlined face a study in repose. Her only movement was the rhythmic rising and falling of her bony chest. Tubes and monitors were attached to both arms and her left leg. Other than a tiny diaper, she was as naked as she had been when Bourque pulled her through the opening in Tierney's abdomen. Heat lamps and the devotion of her new family warmed her tender skin.

"Hello, sweet baby," Joan said softly. "Hello." There wasn't anything else to say.

They lingered a while then left. From the NICU, Joan and Tara had a quick visit with Tierney—telling her how well she did, how everything would be fine, how much they loved her, Greg, and the baby. They went home; Joan would spend much of the night praying.

Left unspoken were the continuing doubts about the baby's survival. Her serene countenance notwithstanding, her bloodstream had a dangerously high level of acid—an indicator of insufficient oxygen in her system. Another sign of oxygen depletion were her blue hands and feet, a condition called acrocyanosis. Her blood contained a frighteningly low number of platelets, which are necessary to stop bleeding. She required supplemental oxygen from a tube in her nose. Her heart rate was high, her blood pressure was low, her kidney function was questionable, and her lungs weren't working quite right. She hadn't pierced anyone's ears with a good cry. She showed signs of an infection, though the doctors weren't sure about that.

Some subtle and not-so-subtle signs of Down syndrome were also apparent. Despite Greg's optimistic observation that she wasn't floppy, she was diagnosed with hypotonia—weak muscles. The intensive care specialists also noted that she had upward slanting eyes, formally known as oblique palpebral fissures. Her weight and length were both in the twenty-fifth percentile, meaning that in a random sample of a hundred babies of the same sex and age, she would be taller and heavier than twenty-five and shorter and lighter than the other seventy-five. However, her head circumference was just below the tenth percentile—ninety of those other babies would have bigger heads. In other words, she was relatively diminutive, and, like a majority of people with Down syndrome, her head was small for her body. Also, like most people with Down syndrome, she didn't display all the physical characteristics of the condition, though she had some.

On top of all that was the hole in her heart. It wasn't clear how many of her ailments were linked to the defect, but most appeared to be the result of her difficult last hours in the womb. Bourque would later explain that Tierney's placenta had begun shutting down early, depriving the baby of nourishment. It's a relatively common occurrence in pregnancies involving babies with chromosomal disorders. Bourque said he suspected the baby would have died within a day if not for the emergency delivery.

At 1 A.M., his daughter not quite three hours old, Greg returned alone to the NICU. He stood over her, bathed in shadows, trying to digest a torrent of information about the monitors that surrounded her. He furrowed his brow and studied her heart rate, her blood pressure, and her oxygen saturation level. It seemed as though he was trying to move the numbers to their proper levels—though he wasn't sure what those were—through sheer will and new love.

"Can I touch her?" he asked a nurse. She explained that he would need to thoroughly scrub his hands and arms. He desperately wanted to, but knowing that Tierney was alone and waiting, he declined.

When they reunited in the otherwise empty recovery room, Greg told Tierney all he knew about their baby's condition. They told each other how grateful they were that Bourque was on call that night. They called George and Allison, as well as Tierney's aunt Margaret, Joan's sister, to share the news and accept congratulations and good wishes.

Lying on a gurney, Tierney felt pleased she had realized there was a problem. But she couldn't help wondering if her active lifestyle was partly to blame, and she wished she had called Bourque even sooner. "Did I reach too high? Did I do something? Did I not rest enough?" she asked, not expecting an answer. "Should I have called on Friday, when I felt that pain in my side? Should I have called earlier today? What would have happened if I didn't call at all? Would the baby have died?"

To themselves, both Tierney and Greg wondered: Will she die anyway?

Greg helped a nurse wheel Tierney's gurney from the recovery room to one of the hotel-like delivery rooms, where Tierney would recuperate for several days. Eager to get her situated, Greg pushed the gurney at top speed, making Tierney nauseated again.

"I'm going to have to recover from that ride," she joked. But then the emergency c-section, the gravity of their baby's condition, and her exhaustion lowered Tierney's spirits. She was in no mood for humor.

It was nearly 2 A.M. when they got settled in Tierney's room, and soon they were drifting toward sleep. Tierney tried to get comfortable in the bed while Greg scrunched his body on a foldout chair. Before shutting their eyes, they formally gave Baby Girl Fairchild a name, one that they had agreed on a few weeks earlier.

Tierney and Greg had spent the last months of pregnancy puzzling over possible names, adding and deleting prospects on a list posted on their refrigerator. Both were drawn to unusual names, names that wouldn't be shared by three or four owners in a kindergarten classroom.

Something clicked when Greg spotted Lake Nyasa—a huge body of water in Malawi—while scrolling through a computerized encyclopedia. Fiddling with the spelling and dropping the "s," they came up with Naia. They pronounced it "Nye'-uh," which rhymed with "papaya."

Before settling on Naia, they debated whether to give an uncommon name to a child with developmental challenges. On top of everything else, did she need people mispronouncing her name? Tierney understood that issue well. Her name was frequently abused. Some people pronounced it "Tyranny." Misspellings were common. Sometimes people didn't know if her first name was Tierney or Temple, or if she were a man or a woman. But Tierney and Greg cast aside those doubts. They chose Naia. It was the first step toward treating her the same as they would any other child, whenever possible.

Only later would they learn their baby's name was more appropriate than they ever imagined. With a slightly different spelling, Naia was a Swahili verb meaning "decide." As a noun, it meant "purpose."

For a middle name, they chose Grace. For Tierney, it evoked the hymn "Amazing Grace." It had the added benefit of honoring a relative of her father's; Ernie had an aunt named Grace who had died in childhood. Maybe that would touch him, help him establish a link to his granddaughter.

For Greg, the baby's middle name reflected a desire to heal the wounds that surrounded their decision. "For me, grace is the concept of forgiveness," he said later. "This has not been easy on our family. I believe, or I wish, that the baby will do more to raise people, to change people's expectations and beliefs. She provides an opportunity for people to have grace. To mend bonds that were strained."

## CHAPTER 14 "WE HAD TO GIVE HER THE CHANCE TO MAKE IT"

When day broke, Tierney slept late while Greg went home briefly to walk Onyx and pack a suitcase with clothes and toiletries for them both. When he returned to Saint Francis, Greg gingerly helped Tierney into a wheelchair and rolled her down the hall to the NICU. A nurse admitted them through a security door, and they were met by one of several new doctors in their lives, a boyish, dark-haired pediatric cardiologist named Seth Lapuk.

Lapuk brought them to a small, sterile conference room away from the NICU bassinets. He perched on a padded stool and elaborated on what they already knew about the array of problems facing their daughter. An echocardiogram had confirmed the heart defect, and Naia had been started on a drug called Dopamine to raise her persistently low blood pressure. Her oxygen saturation level—a measure of the amount of oxygen in her blood—was well below the 90 percent mark considered a minimum for safety. As a treatment for that, doctors were alternating between a tube in her nose and a hood over her head, to make sure she received a heavy dose of oxygen with each breath. It seemed to be helping, Lapuk said warmly. But there were new issues to worry about.

Their baby had a condition called thrombocytopenia—a dangerously low number of platelets. A healthy child should have a platelet count of 150,000 to 450,000. Naia's count at birth was 76,000. Within hours, it had dropped to 40,000 and she was given an emergency transfusion. That had brought the platelet count up to 144,000, but there was no telling whether it would level off or plummet again. The fluctuating platelet count might be a sign of a liver problem, or perhaps it was something else entirely. It was too early to tell.

Lapuk explained it all in a soft voice, trying to be optimistic without being unrealistic. Tierney, wearing a pink bathrobe over a white nightgown, slumped in her wheelchair. Her eyes drooped from painkillers, exhaustion, and the litany of medical problems facing the daughter she had yet to hold in her arms. Greg sat in a chair next to her, his chin resting heavily on his fist.

"When do you think she'll be able to come home?" he asked.

"We don't know," Lapuk said.

After a silent, awkward moment, Lapuk changed the subject by telling them a story from his boyhood.

He was playing in his family's garage, trying to reach a button mounted high on the wall that would raise the electric garage door. He arranged a teetering stack of boxes under the button and started to climb. He was halfway to the top when his younger brother came in and saw what he was doing. Without a word, the younger boy went to a car parked in the garage, reached inside, and hit the remote. The door rose while Lapuk watched in astonishment. Lapuk's younger brother has Down syndrome.

"Don't underestimate what your daughter might do. Expectations with these children are often lower than they should be," Lapuk said. "You don't know what can happen." Later, Lapuk would add an unexpected flourish to one of his medical notes on Naia's condition, referring to her as a "delightful, beautiful baby."

Encouraged by Lapuk's story, Greg pushed Tierney's wheelchair out of the conference room and over to Naia's bassinet.

"That's our baby," she said, leaning her head against Greg's side. It was the first time Tierney had seen their daughter outside the delivery room.

Greg had scrubbed this time, so he took the opportunity to touch Naia. He couldn't lift her—tubes and monitors were in the way—so he stroked her chest, his hand as big as her torso. She took rapid, shallow breaths, trying to deliver the necessary oxygen to her hungry cells.

"It's OK, little girl. It's OK," he said.

"She looks good," Tierney said in a hopeful voice.


The next day, in Tierney's hospital room, three books sat unopened on a table by her bed. One was a sequel to *What to Expect When You're Expecting,* called, *What to Expect the First Year.* It was a book about month-by-month development and challenges for children who don't have Down syndrome or heart defects, and it would be of limited use to them. The second book was a memoir on race called *Life on the Color Line,* about the struggles of a man whose mother was white and whose father was black. Third was the Holy Bible. On the television high over Tierney's bed, Martha Stewart was turning ordinary household items into a domestic masterpiece. The sound was on mute. A bouquet of pink, purple, and white flowers from Joan brightened the room. A camera sat on a rolling table, waiting for a happy moment to record.

Greg had already visited Naia in the NICU, and he didn't like what he had seen. He thought her problems and treatments had multiplied overnight, her odds of survival grown longer. The nurses tried to be upbeat, but Greg thought they were trying too hard to convince him that she would pull through. After the visit, he returned to Tierney's room so downhearted that all he could do was curl up on the foldout chair and seek the solace of sleep. He woke an hour later, feeling as tired as he had when he lay down.

"You know, the baby might not make it," he told Tierney, his voice cracking with emotion. And if Naia dies, he said, some people will think: "You see, you should never have had this baby. We were right. It was tragic for the baby, it was tragic for you, and you should have terminated months ago and saved everybody this huge problem."

"And," Greg continued, "as traumatic as that will be for us, I think, yeah, it will make those people feel better because it will confirm what they were thinking all along." Greg's voice faded to a whisper. He held his head in his hands. He didn't name names, but Tierney knew he was talking about members of her family.

Propped up by pillows in her hospital bed, she nodded in understanding. But none of that mattered to her. Regardless of the outcome, regardless of what people might say, regardless of what they might think, she was certain they had made the right decision.

"The baby is doing well enough that she deserves a fighting chance, and she deserves her own opportunity," Tierney said. "It's not like she's on a respirator. She's breathing on her own. Yes, she's got some challenges and she might not make it, but this was the right thing to do. I'm convinced of that. We had to give her a chance." Around her neck was her "hope" necklace from Greg, which she hadn't removed since arriving at the hospital.

Tierney's beliefs were reinforced by another baby they had seen in the NICU, a child who looked like Naia in miniature. The baby's grandmother sat in a rocking chair, whispering encouragement to the frail infant in her arms. The woman's focus had been complete; a half-hour passed and she never looked up, never acknowledged the nearby presence of Tierney, Greg, and several nurses. The baby's mother had been in a car wreck that triggered early labor, and the little girl was born at twenty-six weeks—fourteen weeks premature. She weighed just one-and-a-half pounds, and her tiny lungs were poorly formed. Brain damage was a possibility. It occurred to Tierney that the baby was roughly the same size that Naia had been when she and Greg were deciding whether to continue or abort.

"They are spending a ton of energy saving this baby," Tierney said, "and this baby is worth saving." For a moment, it wasn't clear if Tierney meant the other woman's child or her own. Either way, the point was the same. Gulping air between words, Tierney added, "We had to give her the chance to make it. And if she . . . can't . . . she . . . can't."


A half-century earlier, a mother of a young girl with Down syndrome received a brief, formal, typewritten letter. "Dear Mrs. Lott," it began. "If you feel that your baby is improving under her present care you probably are wise to follow the present treatment. I am sure I do not need to tell you that many physicians feel that for the good of the family, as well as the baby, institutional care is more desirable. I am sorry that I have nothing more constructive to offer."

The letter was dated June 23, 1947, and it was signed Paul de Kruif. He was a bacteriologist from the University of Michigan who had gained fame and fortune as a popular interpreter of modern science. Much of his celebrity came from his best-selling 1926 book, *Microbe Hunters,* in which he lionized pioneering microbiologists including Pasteur and Leeuwenhoek. Somehow, a backwoods Mississippi woman named Jewel Lott had obtained de Kruif's home address and had written to him seeking advice.

Jewel Lott's letters to medical and scientific luminaries like de Kruif began shortly after her daughter, Brenda Kay, was born in 1943. All of her letters asked essentially the same question: How can I help her? Most of the responses were brief and unhelpful. Most contained the word "sorry." One was from the pediatrician in chief of the Johns Hopkins Hospital in Baltimore, Dr. Francis F. Schwentker, who began, "I am sorry that we have no successful treatment for cases of mongolism." Dr. Marian M. Crane, chief of the Child Development Research Branch of the U.S. Social Security Administration, wrote, "Dear Mrs. Lott: I am sorry to report that no progress has been made in finding any method of treatment for children with mongolian idiocy, and it seems very doubtful whether any progress in this direction is to be expected in the near future."

Jewel Lott brushed aside one "sorry" after another and kept writing. She wrote to the Naval Medical Research Institute, to private doctors, to anyone she thought might have even a nugget of information that could help Brenda Kay. In time, she learned that she pretty much had to ignore the experts—most of all the ones who recommended that she send Brenda Kay away—and rely on herself. Jewel did so for decades, until her death.

With her mother's help, Brenda Kay lived a relatively long and rewarding life, eventually moving into a group home in California. A fictionalized account of their lives formed the basis of the best-selling 1991 novel *Jewel,* written by Jewel Lott's grandson, the author Bret Lott. Once, when he asked his grandmother to describe her greatest failing in life, Jewel said, "I thought I could fix things, but I realized too late I couldn't."

Yet, as Jewel Lott demonstrated, a mentally retarded child's best chance for a successful life depended on having at least one person on her side who was stubborn, devoted, self-sacrificing, and demanding. It was that way for Brenda Kay, and Tierney and Greg were determined it would be that way for Naia Grace. Much had changed about the treatment of people with Down syndrome and other forms of mental retardation between the births of Brenda Kay and Naia Grace. But the necessity of an iron-willed advocate had remained the same.

In the early years of the United States, mental retardation was treated as a family or local issue, an unfortunate, inevitable, irrevocable flaw of nature. In the vernacular of the time, a village might have a drunk, a loon, and an idiot, and all would be tolerated as long as their behaviors remained within a not-too-disagreeable spectrum.

For people with mental retardation—"the village idiot"—that generally meant no breaking the law and no acting in ways that disgusted or frightened the local population. Their disabilities were usually met with pity and acts of kindness, though there was also thoughtless derision, occasional loathing, and random acts of cruelty. In the eighteenth century, these individuals were likened to the character in the nursery rhyme "Simple Simon"—fairly useless souls who thought they could catch whales with fishing poles and carry water in sieves.

By the mid-1800s, according to the sociologist and historian James W. Trent Jr., the view of mental retardation evolved into a social or state "problem." For the next century, societal responses were focused on eliminating it from view, one way or another. If a newborn had physical ailments, there was the Baby Doe option of denying care. If the baby was otherwise healthy, there were institutions whose purpose was largely to segregate and control persons with mental re-tardation, though some sought to teach work skills that could be used in the community or at the institutions. The keepers of the institu-tions used methods that ranged from enlightened to benign to bar-baric. But while their methods were often debated, the existence and efficacy of the institutions were rarely challenged.

None other than Dr. Benjamin Spock suggested in 1946 that babies with Down syndrome be institutionalized immediately: "If (the in-fant) merely exists at a level that is hardly human, it is much better for the other children and the parents to have him cared for elsewhere." Spock either didn't know or didn't care that there was no way to know at birth what developmental level a child with Down syndrome could achieve. Spock's position evolved over time, but the sentiment he ex-pressed persevered.

In 1968, an ethicist and euthanasia enthusiast named Joseph Fletcher argued in the *Atlantic Monthly* that there was "no reason to feel guilty about putting a Down's syndrome baby away, whether it's 'put away' in the sense of hidden in a sanitarium or in a more responsi-ble lethal sense. It is sad, yes. Dreadful. But it carries no guilt. True guilt arises only from an offense against a person, and a Down's is not a person." Even John Langdon Down, when describing the condition as Mongolian idiocy a century earlier, recognized those in his care to be "people."

Fletcher, who taught at the Episcopal Theological School in Cam-bridge, Massachusetts, also wrote that real guilt should be reserved for "keeping alive a Down's or other kind of idiot, out of a false idea of ob-ligation or duty, while at the same time feeling no obligation at all to save that money and emotion for a living, learning child."

Fletcher might have been strident in his beliefs, but he wasn't far outside the mainstream. Rather, he was expressing a set of widely, if mistakenly, held assumptions about the humanity and potential of people with Down syndrome and other forms of mental retardation. Thirty years after Fletcher's piece in the *Atlantic*, despite enormous advances in treatment and understanding of mental retardation, Tierney's father used almost precisely the same logic when he first heard about the prenatal diagnosis.

In the past 150 years, mental retardation was viewed sequentially "as a disorder of the senses, a moral flaw, a medical disease, a mental deficiency, a menace to the social fabric, and finally as mental retardation," as Trent wrote in his history of mental retardation in the United States. It was only in the 1970s that people who were mentally retarded—following the trail blazed by blacks and women—began to be generally viewed as members of society entitled to rights and respect. Not coincidentally, it was around the same time that institutionalization was largely abandoned as a "treatment" for mental retardation, though that development had as much to do with cost-saving measures by governments as it did with concerns about civil liberties.

The case against institutionalization was made frequently and forcefully in the years before Naia's birth. Rarely was it more eloquently expressed than by a woman with Down syndrome who could not speak.


As a child in the 1940s, Judith Scott was misdiagnosed as severely mentally retarded. In fact, she was severely hearing impaired. It wasn't so much she couldn't understand people. She simply couldn't hear them. She was institutionalized at age seven and spent the next thirty-six years locked in human warehouses. Hidden away, she grew from a sweet little girl into a short, heavyset, middle-aged woman with blue eyes and extraordinary untapped potential.

In 1986, after it became clear that Scott's faulty hearing was a significant part of her disability, her fraternal twin sister, Joyce Scott, removed her from institutional care and brought her to a supervised group home in Berkeley, California.

Judy Scott began spending her days at the Creative Growth Art Center in Oakland, which served the mentally, emotionally, developmentally, and physically disabled. It took a year for her to shed the torpor of institutional life, but then she began to create wondrous, cocoonlike sculptures from yarn, string, twine, sticks, paper towels, and other materials of varying color, weight, and textures.

She would steal items—a diagnosis of kleptomania was added to her chart—and incorporate her pickings into her pieces. She would bind together pairs of stolen items in what one critic described as a "provocative yet almost certainly unconscious allusion to twinship." Another critic said her works "call to mind internal organs, primitive fetish objects, limbless mannequins as well as the blobs and squishes of contemporary abstract art."

In time, Scott's sculptures became larger and more elaborate, eventually catching the attention of Dwight MacGregor, an art historian and authority on "outsider" art. In a treatise that spawned several international exhibitions, MacGregor described her work as "masterpieces in an unfamiliar and deeply private language." He continued:

> As well as being mentally handicapped, Judith cannot hear or speak, and she has little concept of language. There is no way of asking her what she is doing, yet her compulsive involvement with the shaping of forms in space seems to imply that at some level she knows. Unmistakably, she is working, and working hard. Her formidable concentration surpasses that of most professional artists. Is it possible she is obsessionally involved in an activity that is without meaning? Does serious mental retardation invariably preclude the creation of true works of art?

Whatever the answers—MacGregor certainly deemed the work "art"—the market spoke with a clear voice: Scott's pieces sold for more than $150,000 in 2001. Her galleries took their standard 50 percent commission, the Oakland art center took one-quarter, and Scott received about $35,000, which was held for her in a trust. That is, except for the money she spent on colorful scarves that she wore carefully wrapped on her head.

"What I find so amazing and remarkable about Judy is that she survived everything," her sister told a reporter. "And she not only survived, she has come to show that someone who has been written off by society, one of the throwaways, can come back and show us that they are capable of being remarkable."

\*       \*       \*

On Naia's fourth full day of life, Thanksgiving Day, Joan delivered a turkey dinner to the hospital. Before eating in Tierney's room, Tierney and Greg said grace, which had added meaning as Naia's middle name. Their mealtime prayer had always included a vow to help those in need. Tierney realized they'd be keeping that promise in their own home. "I'm really supposed to be helping somebody less fortunate, and it's going to be my baby," she said.

Tierney had largely recovered from the cesarean, and she was preparing to go home with Greg. Naia's condition was slowly improving, though she wasn't ready to leave the hospital. It bothered Tierney to be leaving without her, but there wasn't any choice.

Before Tierney was discharged, she and Greg had a visit from their geneticist, Robert Greenstein. After examining Naia and talking medicine a while, Greenstein asked about their families and offered some advice. "I remember you had some pressure regarding your decision," he said. "Try to put the earlier comments out of your minds. Don't hold it against them. The most important thing is what they're doing now. Just as you needed an adjustment period, they needed one, too."

As the hospital days passed, Naia clung more fiercely to life. She shed more of the IVs, monitoring devices, and other medical appendages that had sprouted from her body like tentacles. She began getting visits from the pediatrician Greg and Tierney had chosen, Dr. Della Corcoran. On first meeting Naia, Corcoran gushed, "She's beautiful. She's so adorable."

Naia's greatest immediate medical challenge was getting enough oxygen, and somehow her tiny lungs and her small, defective heart began figuring out how. The doctors and nurses on the Saint Francis staff worked literally around the clock to wean her from the plastic hood and the nose tubes that delivered oxygen in high doses.

On December 1—her ninth day of life—Naia was taken off oxygen completely. She was able to maintain an oxygen saturation level above 90 percent all on her own. Tierney chatted and sang happily that day as she lifted Naia from the bassinet. Still, Tierney's eyes were red from tears and lack of sleep.

A second persistent problem was Naia's platelet count, but that, too, was improving. When Naia was five days old, it had dropped to its lowest recorded level, 25,000, or one-sixth the minimum her body needed. A second emergency transfusion had been ordered, and the count had risen to 91,000 the next day. It had dipped again to 69,000, but then it had climbed on its own, eventually reaching a relatively healthy level of 145,000. Finally, Naia's bone marrow had kicked into gear and had begun producing enough platelets to sustain her. Nevertheless, questions about her liver function remained unresolved.

For the most part, though, Naia's systems began working as required. Her kidneys were functioning properly. Her blood pressure crept up, making it no longer necessary for her to take Dopamine. The high acid level in her blood was corrected with treatments of sodium bicarbonate, a refined version of the baking soda in Tierney and Greg's pantry. The doctors diagnosed another condition, called hyponatremia, or low sodium in the blood. But that, too, was corrected, with intravenous fluids.

Fears that Naia was brewing an infection turned out to be unfounded, but she remained on the antibiotic ampicillin for her first week, just to be sure. She passed her first eye exam, but failed her first hearing test. She would need to be tested again in a few weeks to see if she was hearing impaired—nearly 50 percent of people with Down syndrome have hearing problems. It was something else for Tierney and Greg to worry about. Impaired hearing would add to the communication challenges and delays Naia likely would face. They might have to teach her sign language, after learning it themselves, that is.

While Naia's bodily systems were improving, weight gain remained a challenge. By her sixth day outside the womb, she had reached a hospital high of six pounds, five ounces, a gain of nine ounces from her birth weight. But then she began slipping backward. On December 2, her tenth day, she had fallen to five pounds, 14.6 ounces. The next day it was five pounds, 14.4 ounces, and the next it was five pounds, 14.2 ounces. The downward trend was a harbinger of troubles to come.

Yet, for the moment, things were generally looking up. When Naia was six days old, her doctors had decided that her condition had improved enough to supplement intravenous feedings with breast milk.

Until then, Tierney used a pump to collect her milk, storing it for eventual use in bottle feedings. On her first try at the breast, Naia didn't take much, and she tired quickly, but it pleased Tierney just the same. Tierney would come to the hospital at least three times a day for as long as Naia remained there, to hold Naia in the crook of her arm, open her shirt, and nourish her as best she could.

The day after Naia's introduction to breastfeeding, she was introduced to Tierney's father. It was Sunday, November 29, and Ernie seemed ready to live up to his promises of support. Before going to the hospital, he and Greg went to look at the new condo, so Ernie could share his knowledge of home repairs. Afterward, Ernie went shopping with Tara to buy a changing table for Naia. They also tried out rocking chairs, and Tara thought Ernie wanted to fill a grandfatherly role. Maybe Greenstein's thoughts about an adjustment period had been right.

On their way to the NICU, Greg told Ernie about Naia's medical problems and prepared him for the frail infant in the acrylic bassinet. Ernie seemed engaged, asking questions and listening closely to Greg's explanations. They both washed at a sink just outside the NICU, and they went in together to see Naia. Greg tenderly picked her up, and Ernie said she looked good. Sensing an opportunity, Greg asked his father-in-law if he wanted to hold her.

"No. Not this time," Ernie said. The visit ended soon after.

Afterward, Greg and Tierney gave Ernie the benefit of the doubt. They reasoned that his reluctance to hold Naia was innocent, reflecting his fear of detaching one of her tubes or otherwise harming such a fragile baby. "Some men are just uncomfortable picking up tiny babies," Greg said. "I know there were some fathers in there who clearly didn't feel at ease doing it. This could be an intimidating situation for a guy who is uncomfortable with babies. Or, you can go with Option Two, and he's uncomfortable with this baby, period. We don't really know."

On December 4, Naia's doctors decided that she had beaten the worst of her immediate problems and was ready to go home. She had been in the hospital for twelve days, eight more than planned.

The cost was $14,100, not including several individual doctors' bills. Prices at Saint Francis ranged from a high of $1,233—the daily charge for Naia's NICU bed—to a low of $2.10 for the sodium bicarbonate for the acid in her blood. There were thirteen charges of $23.86 each for platelet counts; $214.28 for a short-term ventilator; $68.42 for an electrocardiogram; $2.67 for a five-hundred-milliliter vial of ampicillin; $262 for a portable chest X ray; $5.25 for artificial tears; and on and on for five single-spaced pages.

A separate hospital bill for Tierney's care at Saint Francis came to $4,600, also not including certain doctors' bills. Tierney's hospital costs included $1,722.73 for her cesarean section; $616 per night for her room—reduced to $474 the first night because she arrived after 1 A.M. She was charged $72.21 for use of a fetal monitor; $66.84 for use of a breast pump; and $4.02 for two tablets of four-hundred-milligram Motrin.

The combined bills for Tierney and Naia were more than three times the cost of routine mother-and-newborn care at Saint Francis. Greg and Tierney's copayment costs were $900. The balance was paid by the health insurance Tierney received through her job at United Technologies.


Discharge day was surprisingly warm for December, with temperatures topping sixty degrees. Sunlight glinted off the hospital's ten-story Patient Care Tower, and the rosebushes outside Saint Francis clung to their rich, red petals. Greg's parents had taken a train from Virginia to meet Naia and escort her home. While waiting for Naia to undergo one last tune-up—making sure her fluid levels were right, her blood pressure was acceptable, her oxygen saturation was in the nineties—Mary Fairchild expressed her hopes for the future. It sounded like a cross between a promise and a prayer.

"I think a lot about how the world will treat Naia," she said. "But the people who love her will be so heavily weighted on her side that how the world perceives her will be totally irrelevant."

"I know it will be challenging for Greg and Tierney," Mary continued while Bob nodded in agreement. "I wish more than anything they could have had the healthy child they were hoping for. They didn't, and that hurts a lot. But I admire them, and I know they will always want the best and do the best for Naia. That will never change."

After a final briefing from doctors, Greg and Tierney emerged smiling. Just a few days earlier, they didn't know if Naia would ever leave the hospital. Finally, for at least a few moments, they could imagine they were like any other young couple, bringing home their healthy new baby.

Despite the unseasonable warmth, Naia was bundled for a blizzard, tucked under a pastel-colored crochet blanket—a gift from Saint Francis, made by hospital volunteers. At her side was a black-and-white stuffed dog. Tierney and Greg had read that babies are best stimulated by bold, black-and-white images, so they had filled her bassinet with them. They reasoned it was never too early to start helping Naia's brain to develop.

Naia yawned and looked around, unfocused, at the lights on the ceiling, at her parents, at her paternal grandparents. A nurse wheeled Naia's bassinet, but Greg kept one hand gripped protectively on the side, as if it might roll away.

They arrived in the parking lot, and the Honda was there waiting; Bob had pulled it up to the entrance and installed an infant car seat that doubled as a baby carrier. Greg lifted Naia from the bassinet, his sleeves rolled up, his biceps tense, his lips pursed. He held her like a cracked piece of porcelain whose glue had not yet set.

Naia fell asleep on the short drive home, and Greg carried her into the apartment, still bundled and buckled in her removable car seat. Gingerly, he placed the seat on the floor. Tierney bent down to their daughter. She unwrapped Naia from her suffocating swaddling, and in a soft, singsong voice said, "I'm a sleepyhead."

Tierney, Greg, Bob, and Mary stood in an awkward circle around Naia, arms at their sides. Eventually, Mary suggested that they transfer Naia from the car seat carrier to the wooden cradle that Bob had sent. They did so, and then Greg looked to Tierney.

"OK. Now what?" he asked.

"I don't know," she answered, smiling.

Naia latched onto Tierney's breast, her eyes rolling back in sleepy serenity, her body more relaxed with each sip of milk.

"Yes. You're a good eater, Nai-nai," Tierney whispered, cradling her baby on their living room sofa.

Greg was setting the table for a take-out Chinese dinner. A small Christmas tree with a gold garland—a gift from George and Allison— waited expectantly nearby. Snow flurries brushed against the apartment window. A jazz CD played softly.

But this was no blissful family tableau.

Naia's skin had a distinctly yellow cast. Tierney's mouth was a tight line. Her eyes were bloodshot and her neck muscles danced under the collar of her white turtleneck. Greg was unshaven, drowsy, funereal in all black clothing.

During the ten days since she had come home from the hospital, Naia had stubbornly failed to thrive. It was December 14, and she was twenty-three days old. She weighed five pounds, fourteen ounces— the same weight as when she had left Saint Francis. In her three weeks of life, Naia had gained just two ounces, the weight of one chicken egg, minus the shell.

She was burning up the nourishment she took in just trying to stay alive. Her damaged heart was struggling to pump enough oxygen to the rest of her body. Her liver wasn't working properly. She was brewing a urinary tract infection. She was sleeping too much, eating too little. Her system was so fragile that a cold could kill her, so nearly all her trips outside were her near-daily visits to doctors.

Having decided to continue the pregnancy knowing their child would have Down syndrome and a heart defect, having soldiered through the difficult birth and frightening first days of Naia's life, Tierney and Greg were discovering a truth of parenthood: No matter how tough it's been, it can always get tougher. The problems kept piling up. More even than they had allowed themselves to imagine.

"We're in that grind of always worrying that there's something else we need to worry about," Greg said.

And there was good reason to worry. With each passing day, Naia's body was in a more urgent race with itself. Despite weakness and lethargy, Naia needed to quickly gain enough weight to survive the heart surgery she needed for a chance at a full and healthy life. If she gained the weight, she might win the race. But if her heart began to fail before she was strong enough for the operation, the surgery itself might kill her.

The first goal in Naia's life was deceptively simple: eight pounds. That was how much her doctors thought Naia should weigh before they put her through the stress of opening her chest to repair her heart. It was an increase of just over two pounds from her current weight, but that seemingly small amount was misleading. Imagine a ninety-pound woman trying to bulk up to one hundred twenty pounds, while running ten miles and swimming fifty laps a day, then feeling too tired to eat. Eight pounds seemed months away for Naia.

With her growth rate stalled, Tierney and Greg faced difficult new choices. First among them was whether to end breastfeeding and switch exclusively to a bottle, using breast milk that Tierney collected with a breast pump. Already, when Greg fed Naia breast milk from a bottle, she finished more quickly, was less tired afterward, and seemed to drink more than when she nursed directly from Tierney.

Naia's pediatrician, Della Corcoran, had even begun dropping hints about ending Naia's reliance on breast milk altogether and switching her to a fortified, high-calorie formula more likely to hasten weight gain. Breast milk and regular formula each contain about twenty calories per ounce; Corcoran thought Naia should be bumped up to a formula that would provide twenty-seven calories per ounce.

Greg and Tierney wanted to do what was best, but it seemed odd that breastfeeding—usually the best choice for babies—might be placing Naia at greater risk. It was especially hard for Tierney. She was eager to breast-feed, believing it would help Naia flourish despite her challenges. "She's getting a bonding experience from me, which I love and I'm sure is good for her," Tierney said after Naia finished nursing for the night. "But why am I doing this if it comes at the expense of her gaining weight, which I know is the most important thing right now?" Sighing, she added, "It's just all so hard."

The question of breast milk or formula would vex them for several more weeks. But it wasn't the only challenge that Naia, Tierney, and Greg faced on the road to eight pounds.

\*      \*      \*

Eight days later—December 22—Naia was one month old. A visit to the doctor's office took the place of a celebration. Greg and Tierney put tiny white booties on Naia's feet and dressed her in a hooded pink outfit. It was designed for a newborn but seemed three sizes too large.

Before seeing Corcoran, Greg and Tierney sat with Naia in the waiting room and listened to a mother laughingly complain about how big and heavy her daughter was at birth. Her baby was the same age as Naia, but twice the size. Greg and Tierney offered the woman thin smiles but said nothing. Comments about Naia's size—"Is she a preemie?"—were common when Tierney and Greg braved the potential for illness and exposed Naia to the world.

Matters only got worse when they went into the office to see Corcoran, who was thirty-three years old, petite and attractive, the wife of a cardiologist, the working mother of two young sons. The doctor delicately placed a squirming Naia on a countertop infant scale. Greg and Tierney watched intently, barely breathing. Worry lines creased Tierney's forehead. Her "hope" necklace stood out like a beacon on her white shirt. The scale tilted then stopped.

No change. Naia weighed five pounds, fourteen ounces. Tierney threw up her hands up in frustration.

Corcoran knew a change had to be made, and she tried to break the news gently. You've been working hard and doing great, she said, but Naia's failure to gain weight means the end of pure breast milk. Tierney could nurse Naia twice a day, but four other feedings would come from a bottle of breast milk mixed with a high-calorie formula called Pregestimil. Corcoran explained that Naia's slow growth was likely a result of her heart's failure to pump enough oxygen-rich blood, without which her body lacked the fuel it needed to gain weight. The fortified formula would boost her growth and weight gain, the doctor thought, despite the heart defect.

Tierney was upset but tried not to show it. She knew Naia needed those calories. She dutifully recorded Corcoran's instructions in a small brown notebook she had begun carrying to keep track of Naia's numerous doctors' visits and lengthening list of medical problems. A smaller version of the notebook was posted on their refrigerator, as part of a complicated schedule of feedings and medication that ruled their daily lives.

Corcoran also noticed that Tierney and Naia shared a common yeast infection called thrush—it was on Tierney's breast and inside Naia's mouth. She prescribed a topical antifungal medication called nystatin for both. Naia needed it four times daily; Tierney would use it twice daily. Again, Tierney wrote it down in her book.

Since the previous week, on orders from her cardiologist, Naia had been taking a heart medication called Lasix. Defects such as Naia's can lead to a buildup of salt and fluid in the body, a condition that compounds heart problems. By encouraging urination, Lasix helps to improve heart function.

During the examination, Corcoran added an unintentional insult to the injury of Naia's newly diagnosed ailments. Affectionately, Corcoran referred to her as "my little peanut."

Tierney recoiled.

"What's the matter?" the doctor asked.

"We don't use the word 'peanut' for her," Tierney said, calm but cool. She explained that the word had negative racial connotations in the South, where Greg grew up.

Innocently, Corcoran said she called all her infant patients peanut. But she apologized and promised not to refer to Naia that way again.

The doctor punctuated the visit by saving the worst news for last: Naia was jaundiced, a clear sign of liver problems and the cause of her yellowish skin tone. Jaundice—from the French word "jaune," for yellow—is relatively common among newborns, regardless of whether they have Down syndrome or heart defects.

The yellowish skin tone comes from an excess of a substance called bilirubin, which is released during the breakdown of red blood cells. The liver is supposed to process the bilirubin and send it to the intestines for excretion from the body. Jaundice occurs when the liver is unable to process the volume of bilirubin being created. Sometimes jaundice is related to breastfeeding and it clears up on its own, with no lasting effects. Sometimes a newborn's liver simply needs extra time to catch up developmentally, and again, the jaundice resolves by itself. Sometimes it results from a benign, hereditary condition called Gilbert's syndrome, in which mild jaundice develops during times of stress. And certainly Naia was under stress.

But there was another kind of jaundice, a serious, more complicated type that can lead to severe brain damage and even death. To find out which kind she had, Naia needed to undergo blood tests and see a specialist.

Worried and discouraged, Tierney and Greg left Corcoran's office and drove immediately across town to Connecticut Children's Medical Center, where Naia would undergo blood tests to check her liver function. Before the tests, Greg and Tierney went to the hospital pharmacy to fill Naia's new prescriptions from Corcoran. While sitting in the cramped waiting area, a little boy walked over to them. He had an awful, hacking cough, but his mother did nothing to shoo him away from Naia.

Tierney looked to Greg with pleading eyes, fearful that—to make matters worse—Naia might catch a deadly germ.

"Don't worry," Greg said quietly, shielding Naia as best he could until the boy got bored and walked off. "He was far enough away."

Tierney nodded, but her face betrayed her deepening anxiety.

As they waited for nearly an hour for the prescriptions to be filled, Greg had to walk repeatedly from one service window to another, filling out forms and answering questions. Each time, he picked up Naia's portable car seat and carried her with him.

When Tierney suggested that he leave Naia with her, Greg said, "They might not believe me. They might think I don't have a baby."

When he walked off again with Naia, Tierney said to no one in particular, "The life of a black man in America."

Medicine in hand, they went to a small room on the hospital's second floor. It was gaily decorated with hanging mobiles and cartoons of Barney and Tweety Bird, but it was hardly a happy place. The attempts to draw blood went poorly. The phlebotomist, Debbie La-Belle, poked Naia several times in an unsuccessful search for a vein. Naia screamed in pain. Her parents grimaced and spoke softly to her, but they didn't intervene.

While waiting for Naia's cries to end, Greg and Tierney noticed a poem pinned to the back of the door, placed there by a hospital worker whose son had nearly died. Shoulder to shoulder, they read its rhyming couplets, growing sadder with each line. The closing stanza read:

> *We'll love him while we may . . .*
> *But shall the Angels call him*
> *Much sooner than we planned,*

*We'll brave the bitter grief that comes,*
*And try to understand.*

Finally, LaBelle's needle hit its mark and Naia's blood was drawn. Tierney and Greg scooped her up, held her close, and brought her home. But that wasn't the end of it; it would be weeks before questions about Naia's liver problems would be answered.

In the first two months after Naia's birth, medical problems and routine care dominated Greg and Tierney's time and thoughts. Naia's first Christmas was a low-key affair. Gifts ran along the functional and decidedly unfestive lines of a bottle sterilizer. But there also were piles of new baby presents that had poured in during the past few weeks, from clothes to cards to cookies, courtesy of family, friends, and colleagues.

Greg and Tierney had nothing to compare it with, but they wondered if all new parents received so many gifts. "This thought has crossed my mind: Is part of the outpouring an expression of sympathy? I don't know. I just don't know," Greg said.

The year ended on two sour notes. First, Greg was in a car accident when another driver ran a stop sign and crashed into their Honda. He was unhurt, but the car took it hard and would be out of commission for weeks. Then they had to cancel their plans to attend a New Year's Eve house party when the hostess told them her children had been fighting the flu.

Bringing home a bug was too great a risk, and they had worked too hard to keep Naia germ-free to chance it on a party. For a brief time after Naia came home from the hospital, Tierney had even worn a surgical mask while breastfeeding to avoid sharing a cold with her daughter. "Mommy looks crazy!" Tierney had told Naia when she wore it. She had dropped that practice quickly, but her hands remained chapped from frequent washings.

Tierney also frequently found herself stressed by people who thought nothing of touching Naia—innocently patting her head, or playing with her delicate little hands—without realizing that they could pass her a life-threatening bug. "I try so hard to do what's best for her," Tierney said, "but at some point I have to realize that I can't try any harder, and if she's going to catch my germs or someone's germs, she's just going to catch them." But that casual approach didn't feel right, and Tierney knew it. Later, she told Greg, "It's probably best for us to just hunker down and stay inside together."

So the new year rolled in with Tierney and Greg dozing in front of the TV. Naia, jaundiced, not gaining weight, was in her bassinet. There were no champagne bottles or silly hats in sight.

In the rare quiet moments between feeding, diapering, medicating, and sleeping, Tierney and Greg found time to consider the decision they had reached nearly five months earlier.

One such discussion was triggered when Greg came across a *Newsweek* magazine lying around the house. It was nearly two years out of date, but they had never read it. Deep inside, Greg noticed an article on birth defects and prenatal screening. It contained this matter-of-fact statement: "Down syndrome in theory is completely preventable, in the sense that there is a reliable test for the extra chromosome known to be its cause, after which the pregnancy can be terminated."

Greg and Tierney knew that already, but the next line came as a shock to them: Ninety percent of women who learned they were carrying a fetus with Down syndrome chose abortion. Despite all their reading, Greg and Tierney had somehow never before come across that statistic. At last, they had an answer to the question Greg had tried to ask Tierney's obstetrician, Michael Bourque: "What do people do?"

"There's no changing our decision, not that we'd even want to," Greg said. "But 90 percent? It's human nature when you do something to look around and see what other people have done. But to hear that you're so in the minority. . . . That's nine out of ten. You have to wonder, 'What do the other nine people know that we don't?'"

Greg realized that in the months since the decision, neither he nor Tierney had heard of anyone else who had continued a pregnancy after learning the child would have Down syndrome. Yet the more he thought about it, the less Greg considered it odd that their choice placed them in such a small minority. "That shouldn't surprise you," he told Tierney. "You probably wouldn't do the same thing that 90 percent of other people would do in most cases, anyway."

That made Tierney think about their decision to marry across racial lines. "Well, I guess that's true about both of us," she said.

It dawned on her that, based on the 90 percent figure, almost everyone they had told about their decision would have made the opposite choice. Tierney realized it was even possible that, unknown to her, some people she had told might have aborted pregnancies in similar circumstances. She wondered how people reached that decision, and how they felt afterward.

Around the same time Tierney and Greg were deciding whether to continue their pregnancy, an expectant couple a hundred miles away in southeastern Massachusetts received a phone call from their obstetrician. You're thirty-five, the doctor told Kimberly Bento. That puts you at higher risk for some problems, like Down syndrome. You should schedule an amnio.

Kim said she'd consider it, but she put it out of her mind as soon as she hung up the phone.

Kim was outgoing and pretty, with short blond hair, diamond stud earrings, and an easy manner. Her husband, Dino, was forty-two, handsome, with glasses, salt-and-pepper hair, and the look of an ex-football player with a healthy appetite. A native of Brazil, Dino had immigrated to the United States with his family when he was fourteen. He retained a strong accent from his homeland, and he held onto what he called a Brazilian way of looking at certain things. They were both middle children in close families, each with older and younger brothers. Kim was raised Episcopalian, though she wasn't very religious. Dino was a lapsed Catholic.

They had met thirteen years earlier at work, at one of Massachusetts's last remaining institutions—"residential facilities" was the modern, preferred term—for people with mental retardation. After working her way up from recreation therapist and service specialist, Kim had become a "quality enhancement specialist" at the state-run Wrentham Developmental Center. It was her job to make sure the facility adhered to the voluminous regulations that protected residents' rights and guaranteed them appropriate services. Dino was an occupational therapy assistant, providing hands-on care for some of the most profoundly retarded among the center's 337 residents.

All the residents were adults, the youngest in their thirties, the oldest in their eighties. Most had spent all or nearly all of their lives in places like Wrentham, brought there by parents or guardians in the years before home care and community inclusion became the preferred model for the mentally retarded.

Wrentham had received no new admissions since the late 1970s, but in recent years, the center had absorbed residents from several other facilities that were closed during the trend toward deinstitutionalization. Nearly all the residents who remained were considered unable to function elsewhere. A small number had Down syndrome, perhaps twenty or so, but most had major mental delays of unknown origin. The number of residents with Down syndrome had been larger once, but they tended to be among the ones who could adapt to group homes and other less restrictive, noninstitutional settings. So, they had been moved out into the community.

Founded in 1907, the center looked more like a college campus than a stereotypical, Victorian-era asylum. Its sixty-six one- and two-story buildings were spread among trees on six hundred well-tended acres. Some residents had the mental capacities of infants and needed near-constant care, but others who were higher functioning were free to walk the grounds and earn money and self-respect by working at the facility's bottle and can recycling center.

The bureaucracy at Wrentham sometimes frustrated Kim and Dino, but they enjoyed working with the residents. "They're wonderful," Kim said one night in the living room of their comfortable suburban home. "They're all individuals, all different, some challenging, but all worthwhile."

Over the years, Kim had developed certain favorites. One was a man in his sixties with Down syndrome who had attended a breakfast program she ran for hearing-impaired residents. Nearly a decade after the man's death, Kim had lost none of her affection for him. "He was funny, happy. He had a lot of friends. He was one of those guys people gravitated towards," she recalled.

The breakfast program was supposed to help sharpen residents' skills with sign language, but the results with Kim's special friend sometimes seemed as much like comedy as therapy. "He would say, 'Pass me the milk,' but he would sign, 'Pass me the butter.' So I'd hand him the butter." The man would laugh and call her silly—didn't she know the difference between milk and butter?—and Kim would laugh, too. Eventually he'd make the sign for milk, and only then would she hand it over.

Kim and Dino's eight years of marriage had produced one child, a four-year-old daughter, McKayla. She was bright and sweet, the kind of child who weans herself from the bottle, toilet trains herself, and goes right to sleep when asked. "When you have one like that, you want to have more, more!" Kim said, snapping her fingers for emphasis.

They began trying to have another baby when McKayla was about eighteen months old. Nothing happened for more than two years. They were starting to consider fertility treatments when Kim learned she was pregnant.

They didn't want to know the baby's gender, so they decided to pick names for both. No boy's name seemed quite right, but they settled on one for a girl: Olivia Odilia Bento. Olivia was a name they both liked, and Odilia was Dino's mother's name.

In mid-July, the obstetrician called to suggest an amnio, and Kim let it slide off her radar screen. Why risk miscarriage after trying so long? Plus, she figured, their jobs had prepared them for just about anything. Whatever happened, happened.

"I had always thought to myself, 'That's no problem for us,'" Kim said. "Mental retardation? I can handle that. I know how to go about getting the services, getting the help, whatever my child would need." Mostly, though, she and Dino were optimists, and they figured their second child would be as healthy as them, as healthy as their first. Though she didn't want an amnio, Kim continued to receive up-to-date prenatal care, including ultrasounds and an alpha-fetoprotein (AFP) test—part of the triple screen.

On Monday, August 31—three weeks after Greg and Tierney had reached their decision—Kim and Dino got another call from their obstetrician. Kim's AFP test had registered an elevated risk of Down syndrome, the doctor said. Kim should make an appointment with a genetic counselor at Women and Infants Hospital Prenatal Diagnosis Center in Providence. There was nothing to worry about yet, the doctor said, adding that it might be a false-positive reading. But Kim needed to have an amnio if she wanted to know for sure.

Three days later, Kim and Dino met with the genetic counselor, Jackie Halliday, who was herself pregnant at the time. Halliday calmed their fears, explaining the AFP results and urging them to take things step by step. "She said there was a 6 percent chance of Down syndrome," Kim said later. That was considerably higher than the usual odds, but Kim saw a silver lining. "I said, 'No, that means there's a 94 percent chance of a healthy baby.'"

Feeling confident, Kim underwent the amnio the following Tuesday, September 8. Part of the sample was set aside for a FISH test, for quicker if slightly less accurate results. As part of the exam, the doctors also used a more advanced ultrasound machine, just as Tierney's doctors had done during her amnio.

If the AFP test was the first sign of trouble, the advanced ultrasound was the second: there appeared to be a defect involving the baby's ureter, the tube that transports waste from the kidneys to the bladder. Kim was there with a friend who was a nurse. Dino didn't handle hospitals well and had remained at work. Kim's friend said later that she knew from the ultrasound that it was serious, but Kim wasn't ready to accept that. "I thought, 'OK, they'll need to watch the ureter.' No problem," she recalled.

Three days later, Kim and Dino were eager to start packing for a weeklong getaway. They were heading to an oceanfront cottage that Kim's parents owned in Boothbay Harbor, Maine. It was their version of Greg and Tierney's summer trip to Martha's Vineyard, and the circumstances were about to become even more similar.

When they arrived home from work, a message from their obstetrician was waiting on the answering machine. Call today, the message said, or stop by the office. No appointment necessary. It was the kind of message no woman ever wants from her obstetrician, and Kim knew what it meant. When she called, the doctor got right to the point.

"I have news about the baby, and it isn't good," the doctor said. The FISH results had come back. "The baby is a girl, and she has Down syndrome. Do you want to come by and talk?"

Devastated, Kim decided instead to call Jackie Halliday, the genetic counselor. "What are the chances the test could be wrong," Kim asked through her tears.

"Don't get your hopes up," Halliday said.

"Don't worry about it," Dino said afterward, trying to cheer his wife. "It's going to be all right. This isn't 100 percent."

"No. This is it," Kim answered.

She called her parents, Ann and Russell Myers, who lived nearby. Neither tried to influence them, but Ann Myers—who also worked at the Wrentham Developmental Center, as director of physical therapy—captured what her daughter and son-in-law were feeling: "No matter how you look at it, it's a loss. It's the loss of a normal, healthy child." She promised her support, no matter what they decided, as did Kim's father, Dino's parents, their extended families, and their close friends.

Kim's first instinct was to stick with her belief that, with their experience and positive outlooks, she and Dino could handle a mentally retarded child. "I'm keeping this baby no matter what," Kim said that night. But deep down, she could hear a voice saying, "I want this over."

Dino was leaning hard toward abortion. He spent every working day with people who could do little or nothing for themselves, some of whom had physical disabilities as well as mental ones. "Think about what our lives would be like. Think about the quality of the baby's life. The suffering," Dino said. "Look at children who are cross-eyed. Look at all the abuse they take. Think about how much worse *this* would be." Later, Dino would say his cultural background influenced his decision as much as his job had: "I'm Brazilian. If you're not normal looking, it's a struggle."

Dino also pointed out that no one could tell them how mentally retarded their child would be, and that uncertainty was difficult to bear. "We're in a business where we see things," he said. "You don't have to look very far to see what this could be like."

The conversation, and the tears, continued on the drive to Maine, and all day at the cottage. They talked out on the porch, with Dino rubbing Kim's belly and McKayla playing nearby. They talked about how much the baby would love coming to Maine, how much she would love her big sister. But the more they talked, the more those thoughts were outweighed by what they envisioned would be a lifetime of struggle for their child.

Kim began moving toward Dino's position. The more she thought about the baby inside her, the baby she loved, the baby she felt kicking, turning, the less Kim could imagine her as an adult. She would be a child forever, Kim thought.

"There was my answer," she said. Kim went alone out onto the rocky beach and had a good, long cry. "I knew Dino was right," she said later. "I came to understand that it would be better for us to suffer"—from ending the pregnancy—"than for her to suffer her whole life." She also felt it would be unfair to McKayla. "She wasn't asking for this child. If something happened to us, it would make it her responsibility, and that really wasn't her choice. How would that impact her life?"

Their first day back from Maine was Tuesday, September 22. Kim went to the doctor to begin preparations for the end of her pregnancy. She was twenty weeks along, halfway to full term. Rather than have a routine second-term abortion, in which a fetus is often dismembered as it is removed from the uterus, Kim decided with help from Jackie Halliday that she wanted to undergo an early delivery, called an induction, which would render the fetus stillborn but keep it whole. It would be a more arduous process, involving an overnight hospital stay, but it was what Kim wanted.

The next morning, Dino stayed with McKayla while Kim's parents drove her to the hospital. They arrived at 7 A.M., and the doctors at Women and Infants gave Kim the drugs that would start the birth process. She spent nearly eleven hours in what she would call her "labor of love," knowing it would end in death.

As planned, Olivia Odilia Bento was stillborn at 5:40 P.M. on September 23. She was tiny—her footprints on a hospital form are the size of a man's thumbprint—and she weighed barely one pound.

During the twenty minutes that Kim spent with Olivia, she held her, talked to her, kissed her, cried over her. She said hello, and she said goodbye.

Kim's parents came into the delivery room and took Polaroid pictures. They show Olivia's body covered by a quilt the size of a handkerchief with a star-shaped design, a gift from the hospital. A white knit cap covers her head. The only visible parts of her body are her delicate hands and her face, its fine features covered by dark bruises from the delivery. She looks like she's asleep. Kim thought Olivia looked like Dino.

A female vicar came and baptized the baby, but Dino stayed away. He would be haunted by that decision. Years later, talking about it reduced him to sobs. "I'm going to say this quick, because it's hard," he said. He paused, fighting to get the words out. "That's the only regret I have in my whole life. I should have held her, given her a kiss, and now that's not going to happen. We made the right decision. I'm sure of that. But I should have given her a hug and kiss."

Like any perceptive preschooler, McKayla knew something was going on at the time, though she didn't understand. She had been expecting a baby, too, and Kim and Dino had to explain why there would be no brother or sister. "The baby had broken parts, and she went to heaven," Kim told her.

Two days after the induction, Olivia was buried in a lakeside cemetery among generations of Kim's family. Both sets of Olivia's grand-parents came to the service, along with Kim and Dino's brothers and their families, as well as the couple they had chosen to be Olivia's god-parents. When the service ended, Kim knelt and kissed the tiny cof-fin. McKayla did the same. As a fuller understanding dawned on her, McKayla joined the adults in tears.

They lowered the box into the ground, setting it down gently atop the long-interred coffin of Kim's great-grandmother, Mary Shute Lin-coln. On the huge family tombstone, Olivia's name was carved, along with the single date of her birth and death.

The days after were awful, but Kim, Dino, and McKayla clung to each other, and each day became that much easier. They returned to their jobs, to their lives, and slowly they regained equilibrium.

"I know God gave us this difficult decision because He knew we would make the right decision and give her back to him," Kim told herself.

Three months later, the unexpected happened: Kim became preg-nant again. This time Kim didn't hesitate to have an amnio, and it showed a healthy fetus. It was another girl. When they told McKayla, she had a single request: "Can Olivia be the middle name?"

The following August, Kim gave birth to an impish blond baby with big blue eyes. They named her McKenna Olivia Bento, and they were certain that Olivia's soul had found a home inside her. "This is good. She's in a healthy body," Kim said. Added Dino: "We lost Olivia, and God said, 'Well, here's McKenna.'"

Kim and Dino pay regular visits to Olivia's grave. They never miss her birthday. Dino sometimes imagines what Olivia would have been like, playing on the beach in Maine, or dancing and singing with her sisters in a Christmas play.

In their home is a pink-and-yellow box covered with images of angels. Inside, they keep Olivia's pictures—the Polaroids as well as the ultrasounds—the sympathy cards they received, her obituary and death notices, the little quilt with the star, a *Ladies' Home Journal* with a story about another woman's decision to terminate, and the hospital form with Olivia's footprints. All they have of her.

One night, McKenna watched as her mother gingerly went through the box, refreshing painful memories of a decision she remained certain was right for them. "I'm good now," Kim said, "but back then you don't think you're going to live through the day. You just sob."

Turning to McKenna, scrunched in a ball on her lap, Kim said: "When you're bigger, I'm going to have a story to tell you. About your other sister."

# CHAPTER 16 "SHE'S NOT PINK"

"I've been preparing myself mentally that at some point she will just stop gaining weight and start failing," Tierney told Greg. "I've been worst-case-scenario Tierney lately."

It was January 14. Naia was nearly eight weeks old. She weighed just six pounds, eight ounces. The pages in Tierney's rapidly filling medical notebook recorded Naia's weight changes in ounce-by-ounce measures. She had gained only twelve ounces since birth, ten of them in the past three weeks, mostly because of orders by pediatrician Della Corcoran to add even more fortified formula to Naia's feedings. Eventually, the formula would be mixed as thick and rich as a double milk shake. Naia was a pound and a half away from her goal, and time was growing short. Surgery would be necessary sooner than expected.

Naia's heart could barely keep pace with her body's hunger for oxygen. To compensate, she took deeper and deeper breaths. With each, her skin sucked up and under her ribs, making her chest look like a child-size xylophone. Naia's cardiologist, Dr. Hank Leopold, began teaching Greg and Tierney to look for signs of congestive heart failure, where the heart is unable to pump blood with enough force to the body. One sign is a bluish tint to the skin.

Greg and Tierney had always expected that they and their child would be aware of black and white. Now, because of Naia's medical problems, they also had to worry about the yellow of jaundice and the blue of heart failure. To top it off, a fifth skin color had unexpectedly entered the mix: pink.

Just before Christmas, Tierney had taken a picture of Naia to a photo shop across the street from their apartment to order reprints for faraway family and friends. A few days later, Greg picked them up and brought them home. Tierney pulled them out of the envelope and exploded.

"Greg, they lightened Naia's picture!" she fumed. "She looks a lot whiter than she did in the original."

Tierney marched across the street with the original photo. She went to the counter and confronted the man who had taken her order.

"I don't understand why you did that," she said.

"You wanted her to look like that?" he said, looking at the original.

"Well, *that's* what she looks like!"

"I'm sorry," he said. "I just looked at your complexion and figured that she would look like you. It's just that most babies are pink, so I made her pink."

"She's not pink," Tierney said.

He agreed to redo the photos. No charge.

During the early weeks of the new year, Naia's heart remained a priority, but her liver problems caused more immediate fears. The tests taken in December came back showing that her bilirubin level was more than ten times higher than normal. And yet, the cause of her jaundice remained a mystery.

After two weeks of near-daily visits, Naia's liver specialist, gastroenterologist Jeffrey Hyams, tentatively concluded that Naia had one of the more dangerous types of jaundice. He suspected it was a blocked tube connecting the liver to the small intestine. Another possibility, though, was a less serious inflammation of the liver called neonatal hepatitis.

Hepatitis could be treated with drugs, but a blockage likely would require surgery. There also was a possibility that Naia's liver could fail completely, requiring a transplant. In the meantime, Hyams told Greg and Tierney there was a good chance Naia would need a liver biopsy, a surgical procedure in which cells from the liver would be surgically removed for extensive tests and microscopic analysis.

When added to the looming heart surgery, the prospect of liver surgery, a transplant, or even a biopsy frightened and depressed Tierney and Greg. Hyams also diagnosed a urinary tract infection, which required Naia to take another antibiotic, amoxicillin. The infection might be contributing to the jaundice, Hyams said, so they might see some improvement when the antibiotic took effect. He also prescribed vitamins K and E, and a multivitamin called Polyvisol. The information filled another page in Tierney's medical notebook.

Early in the new year, Hyams wrote a progress note to Naia's pediatrician. After detailing Naia's condition, he discussed his concerns about her lack of weight gain and added ominously: "She is now six weeks old and we will need to start to make some decisions. . . . If things do not pick up, we may need to consider nasogastric tube feedings." And then, in the oddly formal language of one doctor communicating with another, "Thank you for the opportunity to continue to participate in her care."

After more days of fear and uncertainty—"So much for a relaxing maternity leave," Tierney said—she and Naia went to Hartford Hospital for a procedure in which a chemical dye would be injected into Naia's body then traced as it moved through her system. If the dye didn't pass from her liver to her intestine, a life-threatening blockage would be the most likely culprit and surgery would be almost certain.

When Tierney arrived at the hospital, she began reflecting on the relative nature of sickness. "You focus on your own problems, your own daughter, and then you look around at a place like this or Children's Hospital and you get sad because it's all very sick children. And then I think about all the things that we could be going through, and I feel very fortunate."

To perform the test, a technician placed Naia on a padded gurney, using straps to immobilize her under a machine that would track the dye. Tired and hungry, Naia screamed and struggled, but eventually she surrendered to sleep. Tierney also succumbed to stress and exhaustion, nodding off in a chair at Naia's side, her head down on the gurney just inches from her daughter's.

By the time Tierney awoke, the test was already over. Knowing that Tierney was anxious about the result, the technician gave her the first morsel of good news in what seemed like ages. The dye had passed cleanly into Naia's intestine. She didn't have a blockage after all. Tierney left the hospital the happiest she had been in weeks.

"What are you doing back so soon?" Greg asked when they got home.

"We're done!" Tierney said. "Our prayers were answered."

Naia's jaundice remained an issue, but Hyams concluded that she most likely suffered from simple neonatal hepatitis. It was an ailment of uncertain cause—possibly an infection, possibly some link to Down syndrome or the heart defect—that would resolve with medicine and time. No surgery, no biopsy, no transplant needed. By the middle of January, Naia's bilirubin level had indeed begun to fall—it was still five times the normal level, but it was heading steadily downward. Soon, her skin would begin to lose its yellowish hue.

\*     \*     \*

Another piece of good news came from the follow-up hearing test, which had been ordered after Naia had failed her newborn audiology exam. She passed the second test, on January 19, scoring in the normal range of hearing in both ears. She would continue to be watched for signs of impairment, but there was no reason to think she'd fall below the typical range of Down syndrome delays in speech and language development.

Despite the positive turn of events, the constant medical concerns and near-daily doctors' visits were taking a toll on Greg and Tierney. A casualty of their worries about the heart, the weight, and the jaundice was Tierney's effort to breast-feed. By mid-January, she was no longer even pumping her milk and mixing it with the formula. Tierney told herself she did the best she could. The enriched formula was Naia's best hope.

"The big thing is, I need to get my daughter's weight up. If this is what needs to happen, then that's what we'll do," she told Greg, a trace of disappointment in her voice.

No longer nursing, Tierney could again enjoy an occasional glass of wine, and she no longer passed up the deli meats that she had avoided out of fear that harmful preservatives would reach Naia through her breast milk. But these small indulgences carried as much guilt as pleasure. Her daughter was struggling, and no longer could Tierney feel as though her breast milk might help to heal her.

For several days after she stopped breastfeeding, Tierney's breasts remained painfully engorged. Half in jest, she tried a folk remedy of putting cabbage leaves in her bra. It didn't work—not that she really expected it to—but there was an unexpected side benefit: Greg ended up cooking her a dinner of delicious cabbage rolls.

When breastfeeding ended, fifteen glass bottles were left in the freezer, each filled with four or five ounces of breast milk that Tierney had pumped during the weeks after Naia came home from the hospital. Tierney didn't want to dilute the thick formula that was supposed to help Naia gain weight, yet she couldn't bear to throw away the precious liquid. The bottles of breast milk would remain in the freezer for months, until they spoiled.

\*　　　\*　　　\*

Back in August, when Greg and Tierney had chosen to have Naia, the most vocal opponents had been Tierney's father and brother. After Naia's birth, Ernie and George began trying in their own ways, with varying degrees of success, to heal the rift.

In the first weeks after her birth, Ernie had expressed himself mostly with gifts, sending her a playpen for Christmas along with pants, booties, a yellow sweater, and several body suits. Tierney suspected the outfits were the work of Ernie's girlfriend, whose daughter ran a company that sold clothing for undersized babies.

On January 5, Ernie was on the tail end of a business trip when he stopped in Hartford on his way home to New Hampshire. He arrived at 5 P.M., just as Greg was making one of Ernie's favorites for dinner: shrimp pizza. Ernie seemed in a happy mood, joking that he was "making a whistle stop."

He walked over to Naia's cradle and peered inside. "How's she doing?" he asked.

"She's gained some weight, which she needs. So that's good," Greg said.

"That's good," Ernie echoed.

"Do you want to hold her?" Tierney asked.

"No, thanks. Another time," Ernie answered.

They sat down to dinner and talked about other things.

After her father had gone, Greg tried to ease Tierney's disappointment. He reminded her that one of her maternal uncles had boasted that he hadn't touched any of his five children before they were six months old. "Maybe he's just like that," Greg said. At other times, though, Greg and Tierney wondered whether Ernie's attitude reflected something more than what he had said about having a baby who'd be a burden to society and themselves. They wondered if Naia's problems stirred painful memories of his own.


Ernie had a younger brother named Norman, his only sibling. Four years apart, the two were devoted to each other. When Tierney was born, Norman became not just her uncle, but also her godfather. He was bright and inventive, a kind and funny man. With light brown hair and broad shoulders, Norman Temple was handsome. But only from one angle. The left side of his face was deformed, his nose crushed like kneaded dough. There was a skin-covered lump of protruding bone on his forehead. His left eye was small and misshapen, sightless and prone to oozing discharge.

When Norman was a teenager growing up in New Hampshire, a surgeon attempted to repair some of the deformities by sewing his hand to his face—a primitive form of skin grafting. Norman spent several tortured weeks that way. It was just one of several unsuccessful attempts to grow new skin that could be used to reshape Norman's face, none of which met with much success.

Tierney once asked her father about Norman's condition, and all Ernie said was the family never knew why he was born that way. There was talk of forceps used at birth, but really, no one knew.

It is only speculation, but it's possible that Norman's deformities were symptoms of a condition called Goldenhar syndrome. The congenital condition was named for a French ophthalmologist who described it in 1952, nearly two decades after Norman was born. The syndrome is a form of hemifacial microsomia, in which the tissues on one side of the face are underdeveloped. The deformity occurs once in every thirty-five hundred to forty-five hundred births, and in most cases includes a narrowing of the opening of an eye, benign tumors inside the eye, and underdeveloped upper and lower jaws, which results in facial asymmetry. There often are skeletal malformations as well.

Doctors are uncertain why Goldenhar syndrome occurs, but environmental factors have been suspected. An apparent cluster of cases in babies of Gulf War veterans was investigated, but no clear link was found. Another theory suggested that it results from a vascular accident in the fetus at an early stage of development. Such an accident might cut the blood supply and produce blood clots in the tissues that are supposed to develop into the face. Although it has yet to be proven, there are suspicions that some cases of Goldenhar syndrome might be inherited. Some researchers think the disorder might result from a rare interaction of many genes, with environmental factors mixed in.

Oddly enough, there are several intriguing similarities between Goldenhar and Down syndromes. There's no scientific evidence that they're anything but coincidence, and the differences exceed the similarities. Nevertheless, people with both conditions tend to have what are called epicanthal folds of skin at the inner corner of the eye, as well as a narrowing of the eyelid folds called palpebral fissures. People with both syndromes have a significantly increased incidence of congenital heart defects, including holes in the heart. Hearing problems are relatively common with both syndromes. People with Goldenhar and Down syndromes tend to have a single crease on the palms of their hands, as opposed to the more typical two creases. And finally, mild mental retardation occurs in 5 to 15 percent of people with Goldenhar syndrome.

Norman had no mental problems, and no known heart or hearing disorders, but he was affected by his facial deformities his entire life. For years, he fixed televisions from the home he shared with his father. Eventually he found a job outside the house and worked his way up to engineer for a nearby manufacturing company, a notable achievement given his lack of a college degree.

Norman dreamed of visiting Hawaii but never did. His life revolved around the rural New Hampshire town of Twin Mountain, where the Temple family traced its roots to the nineteenth century. He had a girlfriend for a time, but he never married. He played piano and loved show tunes and classical music, and he would take long hikes in the mountains that surrounded his home.

Growing up, Ernie had always looked out for his kid brother, and he cared for Norman before Norman's 1989 death from cancer at age fifty-four. A decade later, Tierney retained fond memories and missed Norman, whom she had called "Unc." "Unc was the best. He was just a very sweet, loving person who was really fun," Tierney recalled tearfully. "He was able to make light of difficult things, make fun of himself, make us feel really comfortable at times when we just didn't. He definitely knew how to make other people feel special." A photo from when Tierney and her siblings were small shows their uncle Norman sitting on the floor with them, happily watching them at play.

Tierney's mother also looked back fondly on her late former brother-in-law. "He was a very secure man, despite everything," Joan recalled. "He was someone who wouldn't turn his back on anyone. He was a very accepting person. Without a doubt, Norman would have accepted Naia."

Early in Tierney's pregnancy, before anyone knew about Naia's Down syndrome, Ernie made a comment that had struck Tierney and Greg as strange but unimportant. In retrospect, though, the comment took on an entirely different meaning.

It had been a warm day in the previous spring—two months before they learned that the fetus Tierney carried had Down syndrome. Greg and Ernie were sitting on the small wooden deck outside the Hartford apartment, kicking back, feet up, enjoying the day and, by all indications, each other's company. Greg casually asked Ernie if he had any advice or concerns about his unborn grandchild.

"Well, you're both physically fit, and you both have good genes," Ernie said, as Greg recalled. "That would be the only thing that would concern me. But there's no reason to think you two wouldn't have a healthy child. If it happens, it would be a fluke."

After Naia's birth and Ernie's repeated standoffishness, Greg and Tierney thought back on that conversation. They became convinced that Ernie had been trying to reassure himself as much as them. "It's like that was the ultimate test for him, his ultimate fear," Greg said. Finishing his thought, Tierney added: "And now it's come true, like a self-fulfilling prophecy. And it's difficult for him to accept."

Maybe that's why he couldn't bring himself to touch Naia. Or maybe it was something else entirely.


The next day, George and Allison stopped by on their way to join Ernie in New Hampshire. The visit couldn't have been more different.

George scooped up Naia and raised her high in the air, as though she had just scored a winning touchdown. Allison held Naia in her arms and fed her a bottle of high-calorie formula. Soon it was time for bed, and George stepped confidently into the role of favorite, and only, uncle. Naia was wide awake, so George knelt by her cradle, rocking her back and forth.

"It's time to go to bed," he told her. He talked softly to her, and he rocked and rocked until she fell asleep. Afterward, the adults gathered around the kitchen table.

"I'm sorry," George told Greg and Tierney. "I wish I had never said anything."

"You did what any brother would do," Greg said. "Your sister was dealing with a problem. You had medical personnel available at your whim. So you asked them their opinions on the situation, they gave them to you, and you came to us with it. I don't hold that against you. The part that disappointed me was when Tierney called you afterward, to let you know the information was wrong or biased, and you got defensive. That's when she needed you to capitulate and admit you were wrong."

"OK," George said. "But I still regret having said what I said originally."

As the conversation continued, it became even clearer to Greg and Tierney that had circumstances been reversed, George and Allison likely would have been among the 90 percent who chose abortion. But there was nothing to be gained from arguing that point, and Greg and Tierney were ready to move on.

Slowly but surely, the heavy diet of formula took effect. By January 28, Naia weighed six pounds, thirteen ounces. On February 11, she was seven pounds, four ounces. On February 26, she was seven pounds, eight ounces. Despite the improvement, Greg and Tierney became fixated on how much larger other babies seemed in comparison to Naia. They eased the tension by joking that they should organize a betting pool among their friends to see who could guess Naia's weight or bilirubin level on a given day.

Finally, by mid-March, when she was nearly four months old, Naia reached her first goal: she tipped the scale at eight pounds. Yet her growth rate remained troublingly slow, and her heart defect continued to tax her body. Hope began to fade that surgery could wait until late spring. It needed to happen by April 1.

In the meantime, despite all her challenges, Naia was growing into an individual in her own right. She seemed to recognize her name. She was starting to like baths, best of all when someone sang "Rubber Ducky," endlessly, while washing her. She had a favorite toy, a stuffed red Elmo doll from *Sesame Street* that she carried everywhere. She followed boldly colored objects with her eyes. She decided that her right thumb tasted better than her left one. She sang out in little yelps. She smiled an innocent, toothless smile. Greg melted whenever she gave him one. She had problems, but she was a beautiful baby. Their beautiful baby.

One late winter day, Greg told Tierney: "I think Naia is beginning to look a lot like me."

"She's cuter!" Tierney said.

\*　　　\*　　　\*

When Naia was two months old, Tierney ended her maternity leave and returned to work in a new position. She was promoted to a job managing executive education programs for United Technologies' Pratt & Whitney division. She arranged a schedule that allowed her to work from home some days. Most everyone at work knew about Naia's condition, and her new bosses promised to give her the flexibility she needed. And for the first time in months, Tierney resumed jogging.

Greg continued to work at home on his doctoral dissertation, whose working title was "Getting Beyond the Rhetoric: Social Embeddedness and Investment in the Inner City." During Naia's difficult first seven weeks of life, he completed only about eight pages. But once the jaundice began to resolve, a better routine developed, and he started cranking out as many as twenty-five pages a week. He also continued to oversee daytime care of Naia—with some unexpected help.

While visiting Hartford shortly after Naia's birth, Greg's mother had noticed one of the city's ubiquitous Starbucks outlets. There were no Starbucks in rural Virginia, and Mary wanted to know what all the fuss was about. She asked Greg to stop the car. She went inside for a grande-mocha-shade-grown-something-or-other and quickly decided it was just about the best thing she had ever tasted.

Not long after, she mentioned in passing that if Greg and Tierney needed help with Naia, she'd be willing to move temporarily from Virginia. The offer took Greg by surprise. He remembered how uncomfortable his mother had seemed when she visited him years earlier in Manhattan.

"We got on the subway and she wouldn't talk. She just sat there, not talking. I didn't know what was going on, so I said, 'What's wrong with you?' She shushed me and said, 'I don't want anyone to hear us.' I mean, this is on the New York subway, and she's shushing me!"

But Greg also knew that Mary had a healthy sense of adventure. And he knew how committed she was to helping Naia. But he didn't say any of that when they talked about her moving to Hartford. Instead, Greg teased: "It's really so you can have all the Starbucks coffee you want, isn't it?"

Shortly before Tierney's maternity leave ended, Mary resettled temporarily in Hartford. While Greg and Tierney remained in their old, rented apartment, Mary moved into the condo that Greg and Tierney had bought in the same complex just before Naia was born. The renovations were nearly complete—Greg and Tierney had installed a new parquet floor, refinished the cabinets, and given the place a complete once-over—so Mary had a lovely one-bedroom unit all to herself.

Soon Onyx the poodle moved over, too, to sleep at the foot of Mary's bed and keep her company. Bob remained in Virginia to take care of their house and their German shepherd, but he began making plans to join Mary in Hartford after Naia's surgery.

Mary described Hartford as "the big city," and she worried about crime. "I lock my door here, though I don't at home," she said. "But I like having a little grocery store so close, just across the street." In time, Mary would explore the neighborhood, join the local Y, take her first aerobic classes, and find little boutiques where she could buy Naia treats like tiny rattles sewn into baby booties.

Though Mary's devotion to Naia was complete, and Greg and Tierney were grateful for her help, the proximity exposed some intrafamily tensions involving space and boundaries. "I won't lie," Greg said once. "Having your mother close, yet having your mother not in your house, is a nice thing. Everybody can go home when they need to."

It was March 16, and Naia's growth had stalled again. The operation was scheduled for March 29, and Greg and Tierney drove to Connecticut Children's Medical Center for a tour of the hospital's surgery suite. Despite the setback on growth, Tierney was feeling confident about Naia's prospects. Doctors were telling them to expect her to have more energy after the surgery, as well as more personality—though they liked her personality just fine as it was.

"I am ready for Naia to be the Naia that I know she's going to be afterward," Tierney said. "Only occasionally do I think that maybe something will go wrong and she's not going to be with us, or she's going to be with us in a different state."

But Greg's worries were intensifying. "It's major surgery," he said. "I've never even had my tonsils out, or my appendix." He also hated to think about Naia going back into intensive care. "It's the idea of her having all that stuff attached to her. It's depressing." He sighed. "It's definitely going to create a big physical distance. She's going to be lying there in this bed and with this thing and that thing on her, and this respirator and all that business. I'm looking forward to being done with that."

Lately, more out of fear than logic, Greg had been wondering if they could delay the surgery for a decade or more. "We were told when we first met with Dr. Leopold that there are a number of children who had this same defect and never had the surgery until their late teens. So, it's a little flirtation in my mind. Not one that I necessarily think is right, but I think about it. We're talking about the risk of mortality here. It's that simple."

Near the end of their hour-long hospital tour, Tierney and Greg walked into the intensive care unit. There was a commotion at the end of the hall. Five doctors in long white lab coats huddled together, talking in low tones with grave looks on their faces. Just outside the doctors' circle, a young couple stood limp, sobbing and rocking and making feeble, futile efforts to comfort each other.

No one explained to Tierney and Greg what was going on. But no one needed to. The tour guide hurriedly steered them the other way.

## CHAPTER 17 "I DIDN'T GET MY KISS FROM NAIA THIS MORNING"

A doctor in blue surgical scrubs held out Naia to her worried parents. "Give her a kiss," said Dr. Craig Bonnani, director of anesthesiology at Connecticut Children's Medical Center.

Tierney and Greg took turns touching their lips to Naia's soft cheeks. They looked at each other with watery eyes and a shared thought: He's telling us to say goodbye. Bonnani said nothing. He either didn't sense their anxiety or didn't want to make it worse. When Greg and Tierney finished their kisses, Bonnani left with a bouncy walk, holding Naia like a football in the crook of his arm. Naia was calm, quiet. She seemed sleepy. Doctor and patient headed down the hall to an operating room.

Over the next five hours, if everything went according to plan, Naia's plum-sized heart would be stopped. Her blood would be circulated by machine, and mechanical lungs would do her breathing. Her chest would be sawed open, and her malformed heart would be rebuilt to support her growing body. Her life would begin anew.

That is, if everything went according to plan.

It was Wednesday, March 31, the day of the surgery Tierney and Greg had known would be needed ever since they made their decision about the pregnancy eight months earlier. They knew the odds were good, but now they also knew Naia, and abstract talk of odds had little meaning anymore. The life of their four-month-old daughter was at stake. As they watched Bonnani walk away with her, all they could do was wait, and wonder, and pray they had made the right choice.

"She'll be OK," Tierney said to no one in particular.

"She'll be OK," Greg repeated, wiping his eyes.


The night before, Mary Fairchild had given Naia a leisurely bath, letting her splash around on her stomach as though she were swimming. Naia loved the water, and Mary loved bathing her—the smells, the smiles, the satisfying warmth of a clean baby snug in a fresh towel. Afterward, Tierney gingerly clipped Naia's fingernails and placed her in a battery-powered swing. Oblivious of what awaited her, Naia swung back and forth, back and forth, until her eyelids grew heavy.

The phone rang. It was George, calling to offer best wishes and to give Tierney a hospital pager number for Allison, just in case.

Two days earlier, Tierney had spoken with Ernie. "Don't worry," Ernie had said. He would remain in New Hampshire during the surgery. He'd visit later.

Before Naia fell asleep, Tierney read to her from a children's book of prayer. On one page was a pastel drawing of a little girl bear in bed, a blanket pulled up to her chin. Next to the drawing was the "When I'm Afraid Prayer":

> *I'm scared, God,*
> *So please help me,*
> *And keep me in your care.*
> *I always feel much safer,*
> *Just knowing you are there.*
> *Amen.*

After reading it aloud, Tierney closed the book and tucked it safely into Naia's cradle. She kissed her goodnight. Greg did the same.

With surgery just hours away, Naia was the only one who slept peacefully. Greg and Tierney's anxieties had been increased by two extra days of waiting; the surgery had been scheduled for March 29, but a sicker child, a newborn, bumped Naia off the schedule. Greg sat bolt upright in the bed at 3:30 A.M. after dreaming they had overslept and missed the operation. Tierney woke three times just to check the alarm.

They dressed at dawn—Tierney made sure to wear her "hope" necklace outside her black turtleneck, like an amulet against harm. They drove in silence and arrived at the hospital at 6:30 A.M. A half-hour later, they settled into the preoperation holding area, a hive of activity filled with doctors, nurses, parents, and sick children.

While the adults scurried around, most of the children were still —little ones in cribs, big ones in beds—all wearing hospital gowns adorned with cartoons of Bugs Bunny, Daffy Duck, and Tweety Bird. One father rode his toddler son around the room on a miniature all-terrain vehicle. The mother sat on the boy's bed, trying to muster a smile. Her sad eyes made an indelible point: Despite all the effort to make it seem like a children's playroom, this was a scary place, filled with fears of the worst possible loss. The parents tried not to show it, but even the youngest children seemed to sense it.

Twenty-six children were scheduled for operations that day. "For the most part, they're healthy kids coming in for day surgery. Pretty minor stuff," said nurse Fran Macoomb.

Naia, facing major open-heart surgery, was an exception. She was also the smallest child in the room. Though more than four months old, she weighed eight pounds, eight ounces, and was twenty-two inches long, lighter and smaller than some hardy newborns. Naia was in only the fifth percentile for growth among children with Down syndrome — on average, ninety-five out of a hundred children her age with the disorder were bigger than she. It wasn't even possible to compare Naia to children without Down syndrome — she fell far below the bottom rung of their growth chart.

At 7:30 A.M., phlebotomist Debbie LaBelle came to Naia's crib to draw blood to match her type for a transfusion and for other routine presurgery tests. Tierney cringed when she saw LaBelle; two months earlier, LaBelle needed to poke Naia repeatedly, and painfully, to take blood from one of her weak and tiny veins. Other people who took blood from Naia seemed to have an easier time of it.

Just as Tierney feared, LaBelle again had difficulty. Naia's cries rang through the preop room as LaBelle tried to find a vein. Greg gripped the metal bars of the hospital crib. Tierney closed her eyes. When La-Belle finished, Greg sat with Naia in a rocking chair next to her crib, whispering all the things a father says to a daughter when he's scared and she's too young to understand. He held one of her hands. Her other hand clutched her stuffed Elmo doll.

The hospital's veteran nurses kept watchful eyes on the parents of children facing surgery, to see which ones might need extra help. None were worried about Greg and Tierney. "I'm impressed," nurse Terri DeSocio said out of their earshot. "They're really together, and they seem to have a real grasp of what's going on."

At 7:45 A.M., Bonnani arrived, picked up Naia, and made his request for kisses.

Operating Room 3 is a twenty-by-thirty-foot room bathed in artificial light. On the morning of Naia's surgery, it was filled with trays of gleaming steel surgical tools covered by sterile blue cloths. Naia's name and admission number were scribbled on a white board hung on a wall over an old-fashioned desk that seemed incongruous in the ultra-modern surroundings. Nearby was a bank of flashing monitors, one of which would show Naia's oxygen saturation, the level of oxygen in her bloodstream.

A backlit screen on one wall displayed X rays of Naia's chest, front and side views, taken two weeks earlier. To a trained eye, the X rays revealed an enlarged heart, a side-effect of Naia's malformation. The X rays also offered a fuzzy look at the defect itself, the hole inside her heart, called an endocardial cushion defect or a complete atrioventricular canal defect.

The defect allowed blood that was saturated with oxygen to mix with blood that was depleted of oxygen. Mixed blood acts on the body like watered-down gasoline in an engine, causing it to sputter and stall. Another way to understand the defect is to imagine a busy restaurant with two swinging doors to the kitchen, one for waiters coming in and the other for waiters going out. If waiters used the wrong doors, efficiency would be lost and crashes would be inevitable. Naia's defect also forced her heart to work overtime to supply the oxygen her body craved, adding extra stress to an already weakened system.

Near the X-ray light board was a heart-lung machine that would breathe for Naia and circulate her blood during the operation. And right in the middle of the room was a padded table where Bonnani gently placed Naia. Surrounded by all the equipment, all the activity, she seemed even tinier than usual.

Naia lay on her back, naked, content at first to watch Bonnani and two nurses assisting him. "She's just happy," Bonnani said. One of the nurses, Cookie Eckel, briefly pulled down her face mask and kissed Naia on the cheek. "I just can't resist," she said. Eckel looked up at the oxygen saturation monitor. It read 84 percent. "Normal would be in the nineties. It's a good thing she's here," Eckel said.

Naia's calm was shattered when Eckel and the other nurse pinned down her arms so Bonnani could cover her face with a plastic mask. Through it flowed an anesthetic gas. Naia cried, fighting to get free.

"Hey, you *are* strong!" Eckel told her. "You're a wiggle worm."

Fifteen seconds later Naia was deeply, unnaturally asleep. Bonnani gripped Naia under the chin, gently bent back her head, and inserted a breathing tube down her throat. He placed gauze pads over her closed eyes and taped them shut. In her stillness, she bore a disturbing resemblance to a corpse with coins on the eyelids. One of the nurses inserted a catheter. Eckel stroked Naia's temple and whispered in her ear. As they worked, a fan blew warm air over Naia's exposed body to ward off any chill. A pad under Naia's back forced her chest to arch upward, giving the surgeon the best possible angle to work.

"How're you doing, sweet cakes?" Eckel asked Naia. "You sure look comfortable." In fact, she looked anything but.

At 8:02 A.M., in walked Dr. Lee Ellison, pediatric cardiac surgeon, the hospital's director of cardiovascular/thoracic surgery. He was tall and lean, with brown hair and a loose-limbed stroll. He wore scrubs and stylish white clogs. Though he had been carving with a scalpel for more than three decades, since beginning his surgical training at Boston City Hospital in the mid-1960s, Ellison carried himself with none of the stereotypical bluster of old-time surgeons. Rather, there was a quiet confidence, a low-decibel voice of authority. Gary Cooper in a John Wayne role.

He began by measuring Naia's bony torso. To guide the cut he planned to make, Ellison used a thin marker to draw a four-inch line down the center of Naia's chest. As he worked, a song began to play on a radio speaker overhead. It was the 1960s hit "Never My Love," with a lyric every cardiac surgeon must relish:

> *You wonder if this heart of mine*
> *Will lose its desire for you*
> *Never my love*
> *Never my love*
> *. . . you know that my whole life depends on you*

As the song played, the room began to fill. Eventually nine people surrounded Naia: Ellison, Bonnani, and a second surgeon, Dr. Chester Humphrey; one scrub nurse; one circulating nurse; a nurse anesthetist; one physician's assistant; and two perfusionists, the medical technicians who would run the heart-lung pump that would keep Naia alive while her heart was immobilized. They stepped quickly, darting around the room in pairs and threesomes.

In his last acts of preparation, Ellison painted Naia's chest with a brown antiseptic liquid called Betadine, then draped over her body sterile blue cloths large enough to sheet a queen-sized bed. Only a candy bar-sized patch of skin on her chest was visible, but that was all

Ellison needed. He looked at the sterile field through custom surgical glasses with tiny binoculars that resembled the loupes of a diamond cutter.

At 8:44 A.M., Ellison grabbed a gleaming scalpel and pulled the blade slowly down the line he had drawn on Naia's chest. The line turned red with a thin ribbon of blood. The incision made, the blood wiped away, Ellison took a small power saw from the surgical tray at his side. He revved the motor and the sharp teeth moved back and forth. He brought it down carefully onto Naia's chest. The blade sliced quickly and cleanly through her exposed breastbone.


While Ellison worked, Greg and Tierney took refuge in the hospital cafeteria. It was a round room with forty-foot-high walls painted to re-semble a fantasy galaxy. One of the painters had been a *Star Trek* fan; a tiny starship *Enterprise* soared among the stars in an inconspicuous spot.

They talked about the weather, the war in Kosovo, the coffee—it was no Starbucks blend—and the sunlight that poured through the cafeteria's soaring glass ceiling. For long periods they sat silently. In their hands, each held a piece of polished marble shaped like an egg—worry stones that were gifts from a friend. The conversation turned to an off-and-on discussion they'd been having about Naia's future, a dis-cussion that presumed the surgery would succeed. In recent weeks, Greg had concluded that as prenatal testing became more routine and sophisticated, the number of people with Down syndrome would al-most certainly decline. He based that prediction on the 90 percent abortion rate among women who knew in advance. The prospect of fewer children with Down syndrome worried him.

"There's safety in numbers," he said. "When there are other children in the school system who are different, when Naia isn't the only one, it makes it easier in terms of advocacy. I'm not saying, 'Gee, I wish people all over the world would go out and have a child with Down syn-drome.' But I will confess that I have a question in my mind about what would happen if the critical mass didn't exist for us to have sup-port in advocating for Naia. The more kids there are like her, the easier it makes it for people to understand why the things we're suggesting are important, and why they need to be done."

Spinning out related scenarios, Greg thought it was conceivable that prenatal testing might lead to a new wave of eugenics. "I don't want to get all *Brave New World* here, but as a society we've decided that all children should be inoculated for diphtheria because we want to eliminate it. What's to prevent people from saying that we should have a policy to test for Down syndrome because we want to eliminate that, because children with a disability like Down syndrome are too much of a weight on society?"

Even if it were never adopted as an official policy, Greg thought, the result would be the same if it were commonly accepted as the "right" thing to do. "Let's say doctors begin to believe that this is an important thing, and so they recommend it and it becomes institutionalized. It would just become part of what happens whenever someone comes in who's pregnant in a situation like this."

Without knowing it, Greg was echoing a preeminent philosopher of biology, Harvard professor emeritus Ruth Hubbard, who had written several years earlier: "In this liberal and individualistic society, there may be no need for eugenic legislation. Physicians and scientists need merely provide the techniques that make individual women, and parents, responsible for implementing the society's prejudices, so to speak, by choice."

Greg also wondered if advances in genetic therapy might eventually allow doctors to remove or repair the extra chromosome that caused Down syndrome. That thought carried its own complications. "As I sit here now, I'm not sure I'd want that," he said. "I'll bet money that twelve years from now, if someone walked up to me and said, 'Would you change who Naia is?' the answer would probably be no. Part of what I love about Naia might be directly related to the fact she has Down syndrome."

Tierney was intrigued by the idea of eliminating certain genetic flaws, particularly while a baby was in the womb. "In the papers last week there was a story about a child who had spina bifida corrected to some extent in utero," she told Greg. "If it's fixable, then why not? Why wouldn't we want every opportunity for everything to go right? It's not that I wouldn't appreciate Naia for exactly who she is. But it could become similar to whether or not my child has polio. Of course you'd fix that."

"The question," she added, "is what if you were having another baby? If we got divorced and you married somebody else, and you were having your second family, and you and your wife got the diagnosis of Down syndrome. And then you were faced with the decision of whether to repair it in utero. What would you do?"

It was a good question, and Greg knew it. He thought for a minute then said: "I'm not sure I can answer that yet." To decide about another child, he explained, he would have to balance what he loved about Naia that was related to her having Down syndrome, against the advantages and opportunities she missed because of the condition. He also would have to weigh the costs in his own life, and he didn't know what those might be.

"OK," Tierney persisted. "Let's talk about something that would change who you are. What if somebody told you that you didn't have to be black?"

Greg took a breath, nodded, and leapt in: "I think the answer is the same one I gave when we first talked about this, about our decision to have Naia. The issue isn't that I would want to change, or that I wouldn't want to have experienced what I've experienced. The real issue is discrimination. It's not about changing me, my race, or my child's race. And so maybe it's not about changing Naia so she doesn't have Down syndrome. It's about believing you can change the impact that it has. You have to believe you can change the impact it has on the people around you and your child."

"There are always easier exits you can choose that take you away from discrimination," Greg continued. "But you need to have a well within yourself that says, 'Yes, I know that people are going to discriminate against me and my child. But I have to believe that I can deal with that discrimination over time. I will be able to diminish it.'"

The coffee was growing cold, and there was no word on how the surgery was going. They sat in silence, waiting.

At 10:50 A.M., a woman with a familiar face entered the cafeteria, smiling and heading toward their table. It was Karen Mazzarella, the cardiology nurse who eight months earlier had spoken some of the first encouraging words about their unborn child's prospects. She arrived with an update from Operating Room 3.

"Everything is going fine. Smooth as silk," she said. "You always like to have a very dull surgery."

Greg's shoulders relaxed. Tierney exhaled. They touched hands.

At that moment, Naia's grandmothers entered the cafeteria together. When they heard Mazzarella's report, Mary and Joan reveled in the news, making grandmotherly plans for Naia's future. Mary said she would be enrolling Naia in a swimming class called "Water Babies," and Joan said she was looking forward to springtime walks in the park.

Joan also voiced mock frustration with her granddaughter. "I didn't get my kiss from Naia this morning," she said. "I want to get it."


After sawing through Naia's breastbone, Ellison carefully spread it apart to expose her pericardium, a tough, double-walled, leatherlike sac that surrounds and protects the heart. With a practiced hand, he cut through it, setting aside a piece of the pericardium the size of a half-dollar for use later during internal repairs.

With the calm that comes from twenty-five years of holding life in his hands, Ellison prepared to put Naia on the heart-lung machine. He had been a surgeon almost as long as the extraordinary tool had been in use.

The heart-lung machine was designed in 1953 by a Philadelphia surgeon named John Gibbon and first used during the repair of a congenital defect similar to Naia's. Although an African-American surgeon named Daniel Hale Williams was credited with the first open-heart surgery sixty years before that—in an emergency procedure to save a stabbing victim—the heart-lung machine developed by Gibbon ushered in the modern era of open-heart surgery.

After checking with Bonnani to be sure that Naia was fully anesthetized, Ellison inserted plastic tubes with metal ends into the veins that brought blood to her heart. The tubes would divert her blood to the heart-lung machine, where it would be oxygenated then returned to Naia's aorta for distribution to her body, bypassing the heart muscle altogether. Although the machine was well tested and the surgical team lavishly trained, there was significant risk attached to the blood diversion. Throughout the operation, Ellison and the others needed to take special care to prevent air from entering Naia's circulatory system. Even a tiny amount could travel to her brain and cause a paralyzing stroke.

Ellison's next step was to stop Naia's heart, so he wouldn't have to make precise cuts and sew delicate stitches on a moving target. That, in essence, was the brilliance of the heart-lung machine, though its star was dimming. Surgeons had begun developing daring new methods of operating on beating hearts that eliminated the risks of the heart-lung machines; when the new techniques worked, they also hastened recovery. For the moment, though, Ellison was relying on the tried-and-true method.

He injected a solution into Naia's coronary circulation system that paralyzed her heart muscle. At the same time, he cooled Naia's heart with ice. The choreographed maneuvers worked as intended. Naia's heart slowed then grew eerily still. In precise medical jargon, Ellison called it "an excellent cardiac arrest." In less controlled circumstances, it would be called sudden death.

Twenty minutes after Ellison made the initial incision, the only thing keeping Naia alive was the heart-lung machine. In addition to its work as a pump, the machine continually cooled Naia's blood, lowering her body temperature to 82.4 degrees Fahrenheit. Just as people could survive relatively long periods at the bottom of a frozen pond, the cold would bring Naia's system to the point of suspended animation, limiting the risk of brain damage.

His preparations completed, Ellison began his repairs. He cut through the right atrium, the chamber where depleted blood enters the heart to begin the process of being saturated with oxygen and pumped to the body. With the blood drained, the beating stopped, and the heart opened for inspection, Ellison could clearly see the hole in the center of the brownish-red muscle. The defect was precisely as pictured by the ultrasound image made while Naia was in the womb.

Ellison cut a piece of white Dacron cloth to roughly the size of a Chiclet. That's how much he needed to patch the lower half of the hole, between the left and right ventricles. He sewed the Dacron patch into place, and then used forceps to pick up the piece of Naia's pericardium that he had set aside earlier. With it, he patched the upper half of the hole, between the left and right atria. In time, the heart's lining would grow over the patches and they would become permanent parts of Naia.

As he sewed each patch into place, Ellison used deft suturing techniques to convert the single large valve Naia had at birth into two separate valves. Each valve would have to open and close thousands of times a day, to allow blood to flow in and out of the chambers.

As the internal repairs neared completion, Ellison asked the perfusionists to begin raising Naia's body temperature by warming the blood before returning it to her circulatory system. He sewed closed Naia's heart, sucked out any air that might have seeped inside, and allowed blood to fill it once again. The warm, red fluid counteracted the paralysis. Ellison watched with satisfaction as the rebuilt muscle grew pink. It shivered for a moment as the body's electrical impulses returned. It began pumping on its own, quickly falling into a steady rhythm.

Ellison's next concern was whether the hole was closed and the new valves worked properly. He tested his work with an echocardiogram, a machine that uses sound waves to monitor heart function. It showed that Naia's hole was closed completely. However, as Ellison suspected, the rebuilt valves allowed a small amount of blood to flow backward whence it came. Ellison wasn't concerned about it; he called it "a trivial leak" that was unlikely to affect Naia's recovery or health.

In his surgical notes, he wrote: "The repair was felt to be satisfactory." In fact, he felt even more confident, describing it in conversation as "an excellent result." He was fairly certain Naia would need no more heart surgery in the future.

Ellison sutured closed the pericardium, then used stainless steel wires to rebuild Naia's sawed-open breastbone. The wires would remain visible in X rays for the rest of her life. He stitched her skin back together, taking special care to make the scar as straight and small as possible, so it would virtually disappear in time. Just as Mazzarella had said he would.

At 11:35 A.M., while Ellison was patching and sewing, Greg, Tierney, and their mothers moved from the cafeteria to a comfortable waiting room near Operating Room 3. Toys were scattered around, along with poignant memorials to children who didn't survive. A wall plaque was engraved with a lost child's name and a passage from a favorite children's book: "In memory of Jason Michael Cianci. Love you forever, love you for always. As long as I'm living, my baby you'll be."

They were alone in the room, and as they waited no one mentioned the memorials. The grandmothers chatted about how wonderful Naia would be when she got better. Tierney recounted details from the first stroller ride she had given Naia, only a week earlier, when the weather warmed enough to risk taking her outside. Lost in thought, Greg watched a television set mounted high on a wall.

At 12:55 P.M., Ellison walked in. Everyone stood for the surgeon's arrival. He smiled. "She's all done," Ellison said. "We did exactly what we talked about, and so far everything looks just right."

He explained Naia's need for a blood transfusion and more sedation. He described the breathing tube in her throat and mentioned that the rebuilt heart valves showed small signs of leakage, but nothing troublesome.

All Tierney and Greg heard was that their daughter was OK.

"That's great," Greg said. The tension drained from their faces, their bodies. They embraced.

"Yay for Naia!" Tierney called out. "Naia the great!"

The outburst tickled Ellison. "We're all in this together," he said. He would never say so, but in the previous five hours, Ellison had done his part once again to lengthen the average life span of people with Down syndrome.

On his way out of the waiting room, Ellison turned back toward the happy family. He warned them not to be alarmed by Naia's appearance. "Just treat her like you're at home," he said. "Just smooch her."


A half-hour later, Naia's parents and grandmothers were escorted to Room 306 of the pediatric intensive care unit. There were no doors to the twelve rooms on the PICU, only glass sliders that made the hallway look like a huge aquarium.

Naia lay on her back, her eyes closed. She had lines attached to all four limbs, her torso, and her head. She looked like a crumpled marionette. A breathing tube brought air to her lungs. A drainage tube removed blood from her chest. An intravenous line supplied nutrition to her depleted system. A nasogastric tube snaked from her nose to her stomach, to empty it of digestive juices. A catheter drained her urine. An arterial line in her wrist checked her blood pressure. A pulse oximeter measured the oxygen level in her blood. Its monitor read 96 percent, just where it belonged.

Ellison's warning notwithstanding, the sight of Naia made them cry. Greg touched her fine hair. Tierney followed doctor's orders and kissed her. Then Tierney stood close to her mother, resting her head on Joan's shoulder. Greg huddled with his mother, talking quietly and wiping his eyes.

A nurse, Wendy Lord, arrived to check Naia's pupils and adjust the monitors. Mostly for modesty's sake, she put a doll-sized diaper on Naia. Lord wore a Black Dog T-shirt, the unofficial symbol of Martha's Vineyard. It seemed a lifetime had passed since Tierney and Greg's vacation on the island in the midst of deciding about the pregnancy.

Dr. Seth Lapuk, the cardiologist whose brother had Down syndrome, dropped in for a quick check on Naia and some encouraging words for Tierney and Greg. A few minutes later, surgical nurse Cookie Eckel came by to see how Naia was doing. "She's one feisty little lady," Eckel told Greg and Tierney. Eckel explained that the surgery was flawless, and necessary. "She had a big hole in there. You got your money's worth."

Greg and Tierney couldn't help but smile.

By coincidence, Eckel said, the newborn whose emergency surgery had delayed Naia's operation by two days was in the next room. Greg and Tierney looked in and saw him, at barely five pounds small enough to make Naia look robust. His surgery had gone well, and he lay silently on the hospital bed, tugging absently on the ear of a soft Eeyore doll.

Eckel left and Tierney's mother decided it was time to take care of unfinished business. Tears streaming down her face, Joan bent low and touched her lips to Naia's forehead. "Grandma loves you," she whispered.

## CHAPTER 18 "IT'S LIKE HER BIRTH, WHEN SHE DIDN'T CRY"

Considering the alternative, hospital days are best when they're tedious. For the most part, that's what Naia and her family experienced after her surgery, though there were occasional unwanted bursts of excitement.

Doctors and nurses monitored Naia on a near-constant basis, fine-tuning her medications and continually recalibrating the machines that surrounded and sustained her. Tierney and Greg kept vigil, sometimes with relief from Joan, Mary, or Bob, who had come by train from Virginia.

For three days after the surgery, Naia was oblivious of everything going on around her. A steady morphine drip kept her in a deep sleep. Then, on the third day, Tierney sat at her bedside, reading aloud, and Naia stirred at the sound of her mother's voice. It was a brief awakening, but it did them all good. "It's great to see her eyes—even half-mast!" Tierney told Greg, who was outside the room and had missed the big event. They called their mothers to share the news.

Joan sensed something in Tierney's voice, so on her next visit to the hospital she brought a stack of photographs of Naia. One showed Naia alert and smiling up at Tierney. Tierney placed it by Naia's bed, as a reminder and a visual prayer.

To comfort both Naia and herself, Tierney brought in a tape player with a recording of classical lullabies that Naia enjoyed listening to at home. The soothing tunes wafted through the halls of the intensive care unit. One of Naia's nurses was planning to be married later in the spring, and she grew so enchanted by Pachelbel's "Canon in D" that she decided to have it played at her wedding.

Easter Sunday arrived four days after the surgery, and Naia remained in intensive care. Greg and Tierney had been told to expect her to be moved to a standard hospital room just two days after the operation, but her recovery was taking longer than anticipated. She remained on a ventilator, sedated by morphine, and she was fighting a 102-degree fever. Her blood pressure was low. There was no telling how long the recovery would take.

Most troubling of all, Naia was resisting attempts to get her to breathe on her own. Each time the doctors turned down the respirator—hoping her own breathing system would get the message and kick into gear—she barely responded. She'd take a few tentative breaths then quit. So the ventilator continued to do the work for her.

Easter began for Naia with a visit from a man in a bunny suit. He left a basket of toys and a blue-and-yellow quilt sewn by Girl Scout Troop 988. Beforehand, nurse Claire Hibbs had told Tierney that they shouldn't tell Naia the bunny was coming; she might get too excited, and they didn't want that. It was one of countless ways, large and small, that the nurses signaled to Tierney and Greg that everything was going to be OK. Someday Naia would indeed be old enough, well enough, and alert enough to know the joy of a visit from the Easter Bunny. On this day, though, Naia slept through the bedside performance.

Lee Ellison, the pediatric cardiac surgeon, came by shortly before noon to remove the drainage tube from Naia's chest. He also ordered an end to the morphine—it was well past time for Naia to wake up.

Five hours later, he returned to remove the breathing tube and to end her reliance on the respirator. Greg and Tierney stood by, watching, hoping, expecting Naia to scream when the tube came out. But when Ellison pulled it from her throat, there was only silence. Naia remained deep in a morphine-induced sleep, and her parents began to fear the worst.

"It's like her birth, when she didn't cry," Tierney said, her eyes filled with tears.

Ellison tried to calm them, urging both to "look at the big picture." He pointed to the machine monitoring respiration: though she was sleeping, Naia had begun, finally, to breathe for herself, if tentatively. Greg and Tierney relaxed, but not for long.

Twice in the following two hours, Naia's breathing diminished and her oxygen saturation levels fell to the eighties, significantly lower than where they belonged. Each time, alarms began blaring, and Greg and Tierney stood nervously aside as nurses came rushing into intensive care Room 306.

During one episode, it was feared that Naia's tongue had folded back into her throat, blocking the passageway. A nurse suctioned out her throat and Naia began to wheeze; soon the crisis passed and she began breathing smoothly again.

Just as when Naia was in the neonatal intensive care unit after her birth, Tierney and Greg became fixated on the monitors—oxygen saturation, blood pressure, respiration rate, heart rate—readying themselves to press the emergency call button at the first sign of danger.

At 8:30 that night, Tara came by to offer encouragement and to give Naia a small, painted wooden cross. Tierney displayed it in a prominent place near Naia's bed.

An hour later, they got a call from George's wife, Allison, who reassured them that a slow, sluggish awakening from several days of morphine sedation wasn't surprising, and based on all that she had heard, Naia would be fine. It was good to have an anesthesiologist in the family, and Allison's call calmed them.

As the night wore on, it troubled Tierney and Greg that Naia continued to sleep. Ellison conferred with her other doctors then ordered an antidote for the morphine called Narcan. It took effect quickly and Naia began to stir. Then she started to thrash, pulling at the tubes in her nose and on her foot.

The nurses switched the oxygen saturation monitoring line to her left hand, instead of her right, so she could suck her favorite thumb. When she didn't put it in her mouth immediately, Tierney worried that she had forgotten. But thumb and mouth eventually connected, and after a few scary moments Naia settled down. After more than an hour awake, Naia fell into a normal sleep.

Early that evening, Joan brought Greg and Tierney an Easter dinner. But it wasn't until 11:30 P.M. that they felt comfortable leaving Naia long enough to eat it in a nearby parents' room. It was the second major holiday meal they had eaten in the sanitized confines of a hospital—the first had been Thanksgiving, after Naia's birth—and they hoped it wouldn't become a habit. Before eating Joan's lamb, Swiss chard, mashed potatoes, and black olives, Tierney and Greg gave a prayer of thanks that included a plea for Naia's continued healing.

They returned to Naia's room and Tierney tenderly wiped tiny saliva bubbles from Naia's lips. She pressed the play button on the tape player and an ethereal nocturne by Chopin filled the room. Tierney and Greg curled up in chairs and joined Naia in sleep.


Hours after their Easter prayer, the news began to improve. Naia woke at 9 A.M. and gave her parents a groggy smile. The monitors showed all her rates were right where they belonged. By early afternoon, Tierney was able to hold Naia in her arms for the first time since they had handed her to Craig Bonnani for the surgery five days earlier. It was two hours of bliss.

With her rates stabilized, Naia could finally move from intensive care to a standard inpatient room of her own. Late that afternoon, they gathered their belongings, rode the elevator to the seventh floor, and settled into Room 708.

As the days passed, Naia's strength gradually returned. Her voice was scratchy from irritation caused by the tube that had been down her throat, but she was beginning to coo and cry the way she used to. She started to take a bottle, though her sore throat made eating a challenge. Overall, though, her discomfort seemed to be lessening.

At the suggestion of Hank Leopold, Naia's cardiologist, Greg and Tierney began taking Naia on short walks around the hospital to let her look out the window and see the world. When they returned from one such walk, they got a piece of unexpected good news: Naia's liver problems, which had bedeviled them for much of the winter, were completely resolved. Her bilirubin level, once more than ten times normal, was just right.

Another happy surprise was buried in the hundreds of pages of medical records generated by Naia's surgery. Despite her health problems, Naia had achieved almost every developmental milestone expected for babies her age—and not just babies with Down syndrome. She could fix her eyes on a moving object. She gave social smiles. She could lift her head from a prone position. She babbled. She turned her head to follow sounds. She was on the brink of rolling over.

Several times during their hospital stay, Tierney, Greg, and Naia were visited by families whose children faced similar surgeries. The visits were invariably arranged by Karen Mazzarella, whose job title of cardiology nurse came nowhere near describing the scope of her involvement with patients.

One visitor was a woman whose three-month-old daughter was scheduled for heart surgery the following month. Alexandria was a big baby, with a shock of brown hair and the signature facial characteristics of Down syndrome. Her mother wondered at first if Naia actually had the disorder—"Isn't she cute!" she marveled. "She doesn't look like she has it."

Just before leaving, the woman turned to Tierney and innocently asked, "Is Naia on Nutrivene-D?" It was a question with a long and complicated history.

In 1940, the father of a child with Down syndrome sought treatment from a Michigan chemist turned medical doctor named Henry Turkel. At the time, relatively little was known about the cause of Down syndrome—the extra twenty-first chromosome wouldn't be located for nearly two decades.

Turkel thought it might be a disorder of deficiencies. He concluded that Down syndrome could be improved by supplementing or replacing certain bodily ingredients that were missing or in short supply. He came up with a mixture of vitamins, minerals, hormones, fatty acids, digestive enzymes, amino acids, antihistamines, and a diuretic. Turkel called his formula the "U-Series," and prescribed it to patients with Down syndrome for the next few decades.

Though there was no independent, scientific proof, Turkel and the families of some of his patients claimed that his formula increased intelligence and "improved" the appearance of children with Down syndrome.

Eventually Turkel retired, handed off his formulas to another doctor, and moved to Israel. That's where a Louisiana woman named Dixie Lawrence Tafoya tracked him down in 1991. Her adopted daughter, Madison, had Down syndrome, and Tafoya had dedicated herself to helping Madison overcome her mental and physical challenges.

A woman of great energy and boundless self-confidence, a natural promoter somewhat prone to exaggeration, Tafoya ran an adoption agency that specialized in finding homes for disabled children. By her dramatic account, she located Turkel in Jerusalem during a bombing raid and learned about his formulas while military ordnance exploded in the background.

When Madison was twenty-eight months old, Tafoya started her on the "U Series," to little effect. She began tinkering on her own, revising the formula to create what she called an improved mix of more than forty vitamins, minerals, and amino acids, among other ingredients. Tafoya gave the new formula to Madison and saw what she called remarkable improvements. She wanted to share her success with the world, and the world—or at least television producers—couldn't resist the story of a Southern-housewife-turned-adoption-provider-turned-adoptive-mother-turned-homebrew-chemist-turned-Down-syndrome-crusader.

In January 1995, the ABC television show *Day One* aired a flattering fifteen-minute segment on Tafoya and what she called her program of "Targeted Nutritional Intervention" (TNI). By that time, Tafoya had dubbed her formula MSB Plus and had arranged for it to be produced and sold by a Canadian company. In 1996, she tinkered some more with the formula, signed a new deal with a Baltimore company called International Nutrition Inc., and named the new product Nutrivene-D.

In the meantime, Tafoya had read an article about a drug called Piracetam, a so-called smart drug popular in Europe and Japan that supposedly improved communication between the left and right sides of the brain. Piracetam also had been investigated as a possible treatment for Alzheimer's disease, stroke, and dyslexia, prompting one doctor to describe it as "a drug in search of a disease." It lacked Food and Drug Administration approval, so Tafoya said she obtained it outside the United States and tested it on herself for a month, taking what she called huge "attack" doses. Satisfied by the apparent absence of ill effects, she started giving Piracetam to Madison, though in much smaller doses.

On the *Day One* show and in numerous other interviews, Tafoya made impressive claims for Nutrivene-D and Piracetam. At six years old, she said, Madison "understands complex instructions and follows them probably better than most 'normal' six-year-olds." Though Madison was speech-delayed, she was in a mainstream class in a private school and performed on the level of her classmates without an aide, Tafoya said. Tafoya also claimed Madison was a computer whiz with an impressive attention span, a budding athlete, and a confident swimmer. The changes Tafoya saw were physical, too. During Madison's first three months on the formula, she told one interviewer, her daughter "went from having a flat face, typical of Down syndrome, to almost normal. It was such a dramatic change that some people who had not seen her in a while did not recognize her."

Tafoya also frequently told the story of how thirty-three-month-old Madison had refused to give up her diapers, but then toilet-trained herself five days after starting Piracetam.

Tafoya's claims, along with the enthusiastic testimonials of other parents, caused a commotion in the tight-knit world of Down syndrome, where word of possible treatments raced from support group to support group, over telephone lines and through Internet chat rooms. Some of the debate was philosophical, focusing on whether Down syndrome should be considered a "disease" for which someone might find a "cure." Or, as most medical authorities maintained, a "condition" that could be improved by hard work and early intervention, but, like eye color, genetically irrevocable.

Though Tafoya became a hero to some, her credibility took hits when she accused parents who didn't use her formula of "failing their children." It also didn't help when reporters pointed out overstatements in her claims. Nevertheless, some parents took the position that there was no evidence Nutrivene-D or Piracetam harmed their children, so that alone made it worth a try. Some parents also felt frustrated that so much Down syndrome research was devoted to prenatal testing and early dementia at a time when they were searching for ways science could immediately improve their children's lives. Tafoya, a vocal critic of the limited research being done on nutrition and Down syndrome, offered hope — even if some called it false hope.

Tafoya's formula plus Piracetam wasn't the only drug or vitamin potion on the market, and some came cloaked in the imprimatur of scientific research. In the 1980s, a doctor named Ruth Harrell came up with a formula that she said raised IQ scores and resulted in "physical changes toward normal" among children with Down syndrome and other mental deficiencies. However, a later study by other researchers using more rigorous controls found no benefit from the treatment and also turned up some unpleasant side effects. Also on the market was a mixture called "Hap Caps," based largely on Turkel's original "U-Series." It, too, never passed scrutiny by independent scientists. Overall, though, much of the attention focused on Tafoya, whose competitors had neither her personality nor her compelling personal story to help market their products.

And so, Nutrivene-D and Piracetam grabbed the popular attention. By some accounts, in the late 1990s more than ten thousand people with Down syndrome were taking Nutrivene-D, many of them adding Piracetam as well. And it wasn't cheap. A three-week supply of Nutrivene-D, based on dosage for a seventy-pound child, cost $75, or about $1,300 a year. As for Piracetam, it was only available with a prescription in the United States, and few doctors were prescribing it for

Down syndrome. So most users purchased it overseas or through Internet and mail-order pharmacies. One such pharmacy charged $53.90 for a nine-week supply for a seventy-pound child, or about $311 a year. Because the purported effects lasted only as long as the treatment, Nutrivene-D and Piracetam were lifelong commitments for believers. In her defense, Tafoya insisted she had no financial stake in either product.

Although satisfied customers raved about the results in television and newspaper interviews, skeptics seized on the apparent exaggerations by Tafoya and the absence of scientific proof for her claims. In 1996, the American College of Medical Genetics felt compelled to caution that there was "no scientific evidence that treatment can improve the mental functioning of people with Down syndrome."

In a landmark study conducted at the University of Toronto, researchers reported they found no significant difference in mental function between children with Down syndrome who took Piracetam and those given a placebo. Even more troubling, some of the children given Piracetam showed side effects including aggression, irritability, and poor sleep. The lead researcher, Dr. Nancy Lobaugh, said the behavioral side effects suggested that the drug had a stimulant effect similar to being "wired" on coffee, and parents might mistake that for improved mental function.

"We did not identify even a single case that would suggest the possibility that Piracetam therapy generally improved cognition," the researchers wrote. Even the company that licensed Piracetam, UCB Pharma of Belgium, urged against its use in children with Down syndrome.

While much of the focus was on Piracetam, megadoses of vitamins didn't fare much better with independent scientists. One group of researchers concluded: "In no instance did the megavitamin therapy result in an increase in intelligence, motor performance, or communicative abilities, or change the appearance of the children or adults studied. Unfortunately, some professionals continue to offer false hope to parents by promising changes with this therapy."

Questions about the therapies proved difficult terrain for Down syndrome advocacy groups. They were torn between wanting to encourage new treatments and not wanting to endorse unproven, expensive, and possibly harmful ones. It was a dilemma they had dealt with previously. In the 1980s, a treatment called sicca cell therapy, which involved injections of fetal calf cells, was briefly popular as an alternative treatment for Down syndrome. That approach only began to disappear when studies found it had no proven benefits and potentially life-threatening risks.

Ultimately, two of the most authoritative and widely respected advocacy groups, the National Down Syndrome Congress and the National Down Syndrome Society, issued carefully worded statements saying they could not support the use of nutritional supplements or Piracetam. "Despite large sums of money which concerned parents have spent for such treatments in the hope that the conditions of their child with Down syndrome would be bettered, there is no evidence that any such benefit has been produced," the National Down Syndrome Society said in a statement. The National Down Syndrome Congress suggested a proven alternative: "Early intervention, thoughtful educational programming, good health care, and optimistic expectations remain the core of best supports."

From the very start, Greg and Tierney had their doubts about alternative therapies. Steeped in academia, serious and respectful practitioners of the scientific method, they discussed Nutrivene-D and Piracetam with Naia's geneticist, Robert Greenstein. With his help, they concluded that the approach was unproven, potentially risky, and, not for them.

Greenstein didn't force his opinions on them. "Some people feel better about themselves when they give their children the formulas," the geneticist said.

"So," Greg responded, reading between the lines, "you mean it makes the parent feel better, even if it doesn't necessarily help the child?"

"Well, isn't that important, too?" Greenstein answered.

Not for Greg and Tierney, it wasn't. When Alexandria's mother asked if Naia was taking Nutrivene-D, Tierney told her simply, "No, she's not."

On April 9, it was time to go home. A planned five-day hospital stay had stretched to ten, and Greg and Tierney were eager to reclaim their lives. The twenty-one-page, itemized bill for the hospital stay added up to $39,067.67—paid for by Tierney's insurance, with a small deductible. The biggest charges were $10,125 for Naia's five days in intensive care, $6,862.50 for the surgery, $6,739.69 for medical-surgical supplies, $3,760 for her care on the seventh floor, and $2,755 for the medications she needed.

A final physical exam pronounced Naia in good condition, with no fever, healing surgical wounds, and a weight of eight pounds, eight ounces — the same weight at her arrival. And, of course, a rebuilt heart.

"The next time we see her, we want her to have fat cheeks and chubby thighs," said nurse Claire Hibbs, who had come to see them off.

Greg and Tierney were buoyant. They happily signed forms, collected a fistful of prescriptions, and gathered Naia's belongings. She was theirs again, to care for in their own home, as a family. They could even begin thinking ahead to a future with their baby that didn't involve sickness or surgery.

On the elevator heading down from Naia's room, Tierney mentioned offhandedly, "Maybe we'll start trying to get pregnant again in the summer." Greg nodded, smiling. Tierney and Greg spent the elevator ride staring at Naia, who was snuggled in pink-and-green footy pajamas. There was something different about her.

It was the silky ribbon a nurse had tied to a lock of her hair. It was the shine that had returned to her eyes. And it was the open-mouthed smiles she showered on passersby like rice at a wedding. Most of all, it was her coloring. Naia's skin had taken on a healthy glow.

It was neither the white of her mother nor the black of her father. Not the yellow of jaundice or the blue of heart failure. It certainly wasn't the pink of a photo clerk's baby ideal. It was her own unique color.

## CHAPTER 19 "NAIA IS A MIRACLE
## JUST AS SHE IS"

His basket filled with food and diapers, Greg ambled toward the
Stop & Shop checkout line. It was morning, and the store wasn't
crowded. He could have chosen any line, but he was drawn to one in
particular. He placed his groceries on the moving belt and looked past
the cashier to a smiling young woman at the far end of the counter.

"Hello," Greg said.

The young woman looked up from her work as a bagger. "Hi," she
said sweetly.

Greg wished he could tell her all the things in his heart. He wished
he could ask a hundred questions about her life, her job, her family.
How she got to work each day. Where she lived. What she did for fun.
He wished he could ask about the friends he hoped she had. He wished
he could tell her about his six-month-old daughter.

He said none of those things. It would have seemed odd, intrusive.
So he left it at hello. When her work was done and his groceries were
neatly packed, Greg said, "Thanks." He gave her a warm smile. She
smiled back.

The bagger's name was Sarah, and she had Down syndrome.


The date was June 3. After all the uncertainty, all the fears, all the medical problems from an emergency birth through open-heart surgery,
Greg and Tierney had begun settling comfortably into life with Naia.
Still, a day rarely went by that didn't include reflections on the choice
they had made. Greg's grocery store encounter reinforced his and Tierney's certainty about their decision ten months earlier. They knew it
wasn't the right choice for everyone, but it was for them.

"In retrospect, it doesn't seem like a big deal. This hasn't crushed us
or demolished our relationship or affected anybody in our family in a
negative sense," Greg reflected after seeing Sarah. "All the issues that
were big issues pale now. Naia has a cold and it's nothing. It's very
much a day-to-day, raising a child situation, like anybody else."

Of Sarah, he said: "It felt really nice to see she's not closeted in a facility someplace. She's out working, in a productive way, as a member

of society. Maybe this is evidence that the days when you didn't see any adults with Down syndrome in the community are at their end."

He and Tierney knew there might be unforeseen problems ahead, obstacles that couldn't be corrected by doctors, prayer, effort, or time. But with Naia growing stronger, more active, and more inquisitive every day, the hurdles seemed lower.

"It's important for us to have high expectations," Tierney said. "I'm preparing myself that there will be developmental delays. It's our job to help Naia through her challenges. How well we do that will determine how she pursues life as an adult."

For all their willingness to face the hard work ahead, Tierney and Greg knew it was too early to predict how independent Naia would be. It would be years before anyone could fully gauge how the extra chromosome would affect her mental and physical development. And yet, there were reasons for optimism.

Two months after the surgery, the positive results were as visible as the tender rolls of fat that had sprouted on her once-frail body. Along with the high-calorie formula she drank, Naia had begun eating mushy cereal from a spoon. Soon she would graduate to squash and mashed carrots. As Greg's mother put it, "Of course she has no problem eating. She's a Fairchild."

She had the energy to laugh more often, and with more vigor. And, her cries were no longer the weak mews of a kitten. They were full-throated yells.

"Now that her heart's fixed, the highs are higher and the lows are lower," Greg said. "Just like with any other kid, I guess."

With each passing day, Naia came more into her own. She played a flirtatious game of peek-a-boo with visitors, staring at them until they made eye contact, then quickly turning away. She rolled over and used her pudgy arms to propel herself forward on her stomach. She used this precrawl to pursue her new favorite diversion: Onyx the poodle. Naia couldn't catch her yet, but she was getting closer by the day.

Naia's developmental leaps were partly traceable to state-funded visits from therapists with Connecticut's Birth-to-Three system, which provided early intervention for children with disabilities. The program traced its roots to a 1975 federal law—the Education for All Handicapped Children Act—that guaranteed school-age children with disabilities a free and appropriate public education in what was described as the "least restrictive environment." As related laws were passed, they were eventually grouped together under the Individuals with Disabilities Education Act (IDEA).

Stripped to its essence, IDEA was built on a single, fundamental principle, articulated in its preamble: "Disability is a natural part of the human experience and in no way diminishes the right of individuals to participate in or contribute to society. Improving educational results for children with disabilities is an essential element of our national policy of ensuring equality of opportunity, full participation, independent living, and economic self-sufficiency for individuals with disabilities."

To advocates, that statement was a perfect complement to a better-known American sentiment: "We hold these truths to be self-evident, that all men are created equal, that they are endowed by their Creator with certain unalienable Rights, that among these are Life, Liberty, and the pursuit of Happiness."

Building on the 1975 law, Congress in 1986 encouraged states to create support systems for infants and toddlers with disabilities, as well as their families. Services varied by state, but the Connecticut program that served Naia—administered by the state Department of Mental Retardation—was considered a model.

Individual Family Service Plans were designed for each child, and service coordinators oversaw teams of therapists working together to lessen mental and physical delays. Families whose incomes were below forty-five-thousand dollars a year received the services free. After that, charges were assessed on a sliding scale, starting at twenty-five dollars a month and rising to more than one hundred seventy dollars a month for families with incomes above two hundred thousand dollars. Private health insurers also contributed to the cost.

Naia's team included Mary Halloran, a developmental therapist who saw Naia weekly and marveled at her every accomplishment. "Naia is doing beautifully," she wrote on a May 9 progress report. "Today she rolled, played with her feet and played with her hands at her midline. She's experimenting with sounds and is very aware of what's going on around her."

Halloran was a jovial, motherly, middle-aged blond woman who threw herself into her work, rolling on the floor, clapping hands, and lavishing Naia with affection. "Amazing!" she would cry. "If you trained her, you couldn't get it any more perfect!" When Naia held her pinky in the air while sucking her thumb, Halloran joked, "My, she's well bred!"

Greg and Tierney supplemented the work being done by Halloran, occupational therapist Wilma Ferkol, and physical therapist Bonnie Herrin. Nearly every day, they did exercises to improve Naia's mobility and strengthen her muscles.

"If she had a leg problem and the doctor said you have to massage her legs every night with liniment, you'd do that. I have this child who needs these exercises, and so I do them with my child," Greg said. "It might just be that's what parenting is all about, for us or for anyone with children. There's always something else to be working on with your kid."

"It's not that we're going to be able to work our way out of these deficits," he added. "But we'll do whatever we can to be further down the road."

During one therapy session, Greg winced when Wilma forcefully encouraged Naia to use the muscles in her stomach to sit up, a milestone she had yet to achieve. Naia wasn't quite crying, but she wasn't happy, either. Wilma noticed Greg's discomfort.

"You don't want to be abusive, but you don't want to stop immediately, either," Wilma told him. "You want to establish discipline. With these children, some people think you don't need to be disciplined. That just isn't true."

Afterward, Greg said, "I don't want to be a parent who doesn't push Naia because she has Down syndrome, and I don't want to overcompensate and push her too much just because she has Down syndrome. I'm trying to find a balance."

As for Naia, her balance came soon enough—she was sitting up on her own a couple months before her first birthday. It was an accomplishment, though the timing reflected Naia's physical delays. Most babies sit up between five and seven months, and 90 percent can sit by eight months; Naia was among the remaining 10 percent.

\*       \*       \*

The improvements in Naia's life extended to her medical outlook. Tierney's little brown notebook took on a decidedly different tone. When cardiologist Hank Leopold listened to Naia's heart six weeks after the surgery, he said, "Sounds good." Tierney happily wrote that down. Two weeks later, gastroenterologist Jeffrey Hyams examined Naia for lingering signs of jaundice. "Looks great," he said. Tierney wrote that down, too.

One by one, her medicines became unnecessary. When she first came home from the hospital, Naia was taking Lasix twice a day, Digoxin twice a day to improve the heart's pumping ability, a blood pressure medicine called Captopril three times a day, vitamin E twice a day, and a multivitamin with iron once a day. By her first birthday, she would need just one medicine, Captopril, along with her multivitamin. With her weight rising, she no longer needed special formula. And just as cardiac surgeon Lee Ellison intended, the scar on Naia's chest had begun to fade.

Trips to the doctor became less frequent and less momentous. "We take her into the waiting room now, and everybody there is all nervous," Greg said. "We're like, 'Hey, it's just a couple of shots.' After all Naia's been through, that's nothing."

No one expected Naia to be free from medical concerns. Sight and hearing problems are common among people with Down syndrome; glasses were likely in Naia's future. More ominously, there were the heightened risks of leukemia in childhood and Alzheimer's-like dementia after age thirty-five. There was also the possibility of more heart surgery, to transplant the valve of a pig or a cadaver if problems arose in the valves that Ellison had built. But the likelihood of that lessened as time passed and Naia's heart continued to work well.

In general, Greg and Tierney's focus changed almost from the moment they brought Naia home after surgery. No longer fearful about her survival, they introduced her to the world. Naia became a girl about town, visiting parks, stores, restaurants, and the homes of family and friends.

"What a cute baby!" strangers often said. In the parking lot outside a bagel store, one woman went on at length about how beautiful Naia looked in a little brown outfit. "What a wonderful skin tone she has!" the woman said.

If only she knew the whole story, Greg thought. But all he said was, "Thank you."

Some people noticed Naia's petite size and asked if she was premature. Rarely did anyone ask about Down syndrome. A few who did left Greg cold with their comments. "Some people want to share the 'I knew someone . . .' story. That's OK. I don't mind that," he said. "The worst are the ones who are like, 'I know about this because there was this kid in my neighborhood back in 1943, who rode a special bus to a special school, and let me tell you all about your daughter.'"

He didn't say so, but to himself, Greg thought, You don't really know. You aren't informed. You haven't read anything about this, and you're coming across as ignorant. Greg and Tierney suspected most people either didn't realize Naia had the condition or thought she had only a "mild" case.

Even Naia's pediatrician, Della Corcoran, wondered aloud during one visit if Naia might have the rare, less severe form of Down syndrome called mosaicism, in which not all cells are affected by the extra chromosome.

"No," Tierney told the doctor. "We've had it tested. She has full-blown Down syndrome."

"Well, she doesn't look it," Corcoran said.

In fact, the facial features common among children with Down syndrome were relatively subtle on Naia. Her eyes didn't slant sharply upward, and they didn't have pronounced skin folds at the inner corners. Her tongue only rarely jutted forward out of her mouth. Whenever it did, Greg and Tierney used a behavioral technique they learned from the Birth-to-Three therapists—they would gently touch Naia's chin and, reflexively, she would pull back her tongue and close her mouth. Soon it became unnecessary.

There was no known link between the severity of Down syndrome–related features and the extent of a person's mental retardation. However, Greg and Tierney believed the less Naia exhibited those features, the less discrimination she might encounter. The notion left them with mixed emotions.

"I know she's cute, and I think she would probably be just as cute to other people if she had those features. But would she?" Tierney wondered. "I don't know."

"People have this expectation of what they're going to see," Greg said. "They have a visual idea of what Down syndrome is. They don't know what it is medically, genetically, but maybe they met a child once or saw that show *Life Goes On,* and for the rest of their lives that's what it means to them."

Greg could well have been describing himself when he first learned that his unborn child would have Down syndrome. He saw the issue differently now, and he considered comments about Naia's relative lack of Down syndrome features as value judgments. "They're clearly saying how pleasant it is that she doesn't have those eyes. Pleasant for us and pleasant for them, because they don't have to feel uncomfortable when interacting with our child."

It was a short leap to see parallels to racial discrimination. "I have no doubt that people who don't like black people will let me know very quickly, one way or another," he told Tierney. Whenever that happened, he reacted accordingly, deciding whether to steer clear or confront them head on.

"But when you're part of an invisible minority, you don't always have that knowledge of where they stand, and that's not always an advantage," he said. "People might have unreasonable expectations of Naia, based on her appearance. When they talk to her and find out about her condition, they'll have to readjust, and that might be difficult, for her and for them."

Without knowing it, Greg was stepping into a long-running controversy about "improving" the appearance of people with Down syndrome.


Beginning in the 1970s, some German and Israeli doctors began advocating plastic surgery for children with Down syndrome. Their thinking was summed up by one plastic surgeon who wrote: "It is a challenge for the aesthetic surgeon to make good-looking people more handsome. But it is even more rewarding to 'normalize' people who are isolated because of their ugly facial expression. . . . Children with Down's [*sic*] syndrome are frequently concealed from the public by their parents. The children suffer from two disadvantages: Their mental abilities are limited and they have ugly facial features."

The proposed solutions to such "ugliness" fell into two general categories. First was a procedure called tongue reduction or partial glossectomy. Proponents said removing a section of the tongue had the combined advantages of improving speech, reducing drooling, minimizing mouth breathing, and increasing "general attractiveness."

The second type was called facial reconstruction, in which surgeons minimized the classic features of Down syndrome. They inserted cheek implants and built up nasal bridges to reduce the "flatness" of the face, removed fat from the neck, and reshaped the eyes by removing epicanthal folds and reducing the slant of palpebral fissures. Some surgeons also lifted downturned lower lips. Sometimes, facial reconstruction was combined with tongue reductions.

Surgery advocates tended to quote Aristotle—"Personal beauty is a greater recommendation than any letter of introduction"—and touted the health and aesthetic benefits. "You are not doing the parents or these kids a favor by keeping them looking different," Dr. Leo Rozer, an Australian doctor who was an early advocate of the procedures, told a reporter. "In our society, appearance is everything."

Parents who chose surgery said they didn't want their children to be judged based on Down syndrome appearances, and claimed their other children enjoyed the benefits of not being stared at during family outings.

"We're always going to have bigots, and we're always going to have racists, and we're always going to have those who don't care for people who are different from the mainstream," said Carol Schwenk, who brought her son for eye reshaping surgery at age three. "I'll do anything I can to help Robert."

But skeptics suggested that such parents were motivated at least in part by self-interest. And not all parents felt good about the surgery afterward. Janet Tataryn wished she had never decided to have her four-year-old son, Matthew, undergo tongue reduction surgery. "I think I got caught up in this fantasy, but I really regretted doing it and I would never put Matthew through it again," she told a reporter.

Other parents echoed Greg's concern that by removing the features of Down syndrome, they might be setting up their children for failure because society might have unrealistic expectations of them. Even some plastic surgeons warned about that effect. "Denial of an underlying intellectual or social problem may lead to the child not receiving appropriate remedial teaching and psychological help. This in turn may actually retard the child's psychosocial development," warned one.

No studies demonstrated improved social functioning or speech intelligibility among children who underwent facial reconstruction or tongue reduction. But, in subjective measures, parents generally said they were pleased with the results. In that sense, plastic surgery shared a treatment niche with Piracetam and Nutrivene-D: proven benefits for children were elusive, but it made some parents feel better.

In the absence of tangible results, some medical ethicists strongly condemned the surgery. Writing in the *Journal of Medical Ethics,* a retired London pediatrician named R. B. Jones called it "mutilating surgery" that constituted child abuse and was comparable to female circumcision: "In that facial surgery in Down's syndrome is often equally major, painful, and always therapeutically unnecessary, consideration should be given to outlawing it also." Down syndrome advocacy groups neither supported nor opposed plastic surgery, viewing it as an individual choice that warranted thorough investigation—with help not just from a plastic surgeon but also from a psychologist and a speech therapist. Privately, though, some leading Down syndrome advocates said what needed fixing wasn't the faces of their children. It was society's attitudes about them.

That feeling was shared by a majority of parents whose children had Down syndrome. An unpublished survey by a Brandeis University graduate student found that 90 percent of 265 parents polled had no plans to pursue plastic surgery for their children with Down syndrome. Nearly all said they would consider it to improve their child's health, but more than 80 percent said they considered it "inappropriate" for any parent to choose plastic surgery for their children with the primary goal of increasing "social acceptance."

Greg and Tierney's exposure to plastic surgery came largely through a Discovery Channel documentary called *Skin Deep,* about a Kansas couple's decision to have their three-year-old son undergo facial reconstruction.

"Is it really worth it?" Tierney said after seeing the show. "It's not like heart surgery, something you have to put your child through. You don't have to do it, and your child is in a tremendous amount of pain. And, your child can't choose whether he or she wants it."

Greg focused on a discussion among the Kansas family members about how the surgery might minimize discrimination against the boy. "I'm not in a position to judge anybody else," he said. "But that's not reason enough for me to want Naia to go through this."

\*       \*       \*

With Naia's medical outlook improved, Tierney and Greg decided it was time to formally include her in their spiritual lives. Both had drawn heavily on faith in the previous year, and both had thought deeply about how they defied the stereotype of faithful people as passive about life.

"You know what I mean," Greg said once, "the idea that you're just sitting back and waiting for God to tell you what to do." To the contrary, their beliefs had supported them, given them the strength they needed to take a leap into the unknown—indeed, they had called it a leap of faith. "The thing about faith is it's a base, a sense of stability," Greg added. "That doesn't mean you're sure that things are going to work out. But you're not as fatalistic."

On the sunny morning of June 12, the Fairchilds drove fifteen minutes to the Church of Saint Timothy in West Hartford. Naia Grace was seven months old. It was the day of her christening.

Tierney and Greg didn't worship regularly at the parish, but the choice was both appropriate and symbolic. A circle was being closed. They had gone to Saint Timothy's two days after the ultrasound that found the heart defect. They had hoped to see the Reverend Henry Cody, an old family friend, but he wasn't there; instead, the priest on the pulpit that day was a stranger.

As they had sat together that Sunday morning the previous July, sad, frightened, and unsure what to do—they had heard a sermon about unexpected miracles. They appreciated the message then, but over the ensuing months its meaning had deepened. "Naia is a miracle just as she is," Tierney told Greg. "That's something I feel every day."

As they walked from the parking lot to the brick church, all done up in their Sunday best, Naia let out a stream of happy gurgles. Angelic in a white satin dress with puffy sleeves and a scalloped hemline, she played with her feet, tugging at green-and-white rosettes on her dainty socks. A white ribbon held a lock of her fine hair. The sun was warm on her cherubic face, and the breeze carried the sweet scent of new-bloom flowers to her nose.

From her perch in Tierney's arms, Naia yelled up at the trees and the azure sky. Her high-pitched chatter drew the attention of six handsome young men in morning suits who had gathered outside the church for a wedding later that day. They looked over toward Naia and smiled. Greg and Tierney smiled back; Naia babbled on.

Tierney and Greg had chosen as godfather Kyle Rudy, their old friend from Saks Fifth Avenue. Kyle had recruited them both to the store and had been with them the day they met. They had remained close even after Greg and Tierney left New York, and Kyle would prove a loving and generous addition to Naia's life.

They chose Tierney's sister as godmother. Tara's initial doubts about continuing the pregnancy had been replaced by consistent support and deep affection for her one and only niece. Tara and Tierney were part of each other, and Naia had become a third link in an unbreakable chain.

Father Cody was eagerly awaiting their arrival—this time he made certain he was there; no substitute priest would get this honor. He met them just outside the heavy wooden door, a casting director's dream of a beefy, bespectacled Irish-American priest in a long white robe. "Naia Grace, the Christian community welcomes you with great joy," he said, ushering them inside.

They gathered around a baptismal font at the side of the chamber. Greg held a tall white candle and Tierney held Naia. Father Cody took a shallow golden cup shaped like a scallop shell—the symbol of James the fisherman, who had given his life for Christ—and blessed her with sacramental oil and water. He placed his hand on her forehead and announced that Naia had been reborn through baptism: "She is now called a child of God, for indeed she is."

Father Cody read from a prayer book that seemed written just for Naia. "The parents have generously invited the child into this world by giving a share in the life of their own bodies," the priest read. "This invitation will be prolonged with every mouthful of food, every drop of medicine, and every inch of shelter they provide."

Naia's grandmothers took pictures. Father Cody remarked that Naia "was a lot easier to get along with than a lot of the babies who come in here."

The grandmothers laughed. Greg beamed. Tierney cried, for joy.

## CHAPTER 20 "DA-DA!"

Tierney and Greg's lives remained hectic—days filled with Naia, Tierney's job, Greg's dissertation and his search for a job as a university professor, their families, and their friends. And, whenever time permitted, each other. Neither was complaining. Life was easier than it had been for a very long time.

But just when things seemed to be calming down, the Fairchild family had to face an unexpected new challenge.

It was Wednesday, June 23, and Greg and Naia were relaxing in the apartment, waiting for Tierney to come home for dinner. Greg had finished working on his dissertation for the afternoon and had picked up Naia from the condo occupied by Mary. It was one of Mary's last days helping with Naia's care before she returned home to Virginia. Tierney and Greg weren't eager to see her go, but they were looking forward to claiming the condo as their own.

At 5:30 P.M., the phone rang. "Greg," Mary said, "the back porch is on fire."

She hung up, called 911, knocked on the doors of the other units, and ran outside. A spectacular fire had engulfed a nearby vacant factory building called the Hawthorn Center, a gathering spot for vagrants that had been scheduled for renovation as a drug rehabilitation facility.

Embers took flight with the wind, landing on the building that housed the condo where Mary had been living—Greg and Tierney's future home. When it was over, what wasn't ruined by fire or smoke was spoiled by water. Most of the losses were covered by insurance, but the place was in shambles. The ceiling had collapsed, the windows were broken, and the floors were a wreck. It would take nine months to rebuild.

Greg, Tierney, and Naia were about to become homeless; the lease on their current apartment was expiring, and there was no hope of renewal.

When they recovered from the shock, Tierney and Greg realized their best option was to put their belongings into storage and move in with Joan, in Tierney's childhood home in nearby Avon. Joan would take over the hands-on grandma role from Mary. Soon they would also hire a part-time nanny, a loving woman named Minnie Jones who made Naia's baby food from scratch. Joan's cat would be a challenge to Greg's allergies, but that seemed minor compared to all they'd been through.

"Last July we found out about Naia. In November was the emergency c-section. In December, we buy a house. In January, Greg's in a car accident. A new job for me in March. Then, the heart surgery. And now the new house we bought burns down!" Tierney said. "Nothing surprises me anymore. And when the next big thing happens, I'm at the point now where I think we could handle just about anything."

Maybe there was a benefit to all their trials. "We've learned that we really are the people we thought we were when we married," she said. "Sometimes it takes a long time to learn how you'll react together in a crisis. I think it's safe to say now we know exactly who the other one is, how we'll react together, how we'll work it out."

Greg agreed. "You learn quickly that as long as you're right with the person you're with, even if other people around you don't agree with what you're doing, it's OK. They can hop off the train, because we're going on without them."


Summer faded to fall, and Naia's progress continued. On November 19, days before her first birthday, she received an encouraging assessment from the Birth-to-Three therapists. "Naia's strength has improved greatly over the past few months," it said.

Under cognitive development, the report read: "She visually explores and takes in much of what is happening in her surroundings. Naia is very aware of sounds in her environment, particularly the dog barking, phone or doorbell ringing. She typically likes to explore toys with her hands and sometimes with her mouth. She is fascinated with her own hands and will watch their movement. . . . She is especially attentive to cause and effect toys that produce music or voices. . . . Her biggest distraction is her dog. She will stop what she's doing to crawl after the dog. This has been a wonderful motivation for movement."

Under communication, the report read: "Naia has made consistent progress in her language development. She is very attentive to the speaker, carefully watching his/her face. She shows awareness of the tones of people's voices, especially that of excitement. . . . Naia vocalizes quite a bit during play. Because of her low muscle tone, she tends to keep her mouth in an open posture. However, she is usually able to keep her tongue in her mouth."

Under social/emotional development: "Naia is a very friendly little girl who greets her visitors with a broad smile and vocalizations, often 'Hi?'" Despite the good news, however, there were signs of developmental delays. Using standardized scoring methods, the therapists estimated Naia, at twelve months, was at the level of a nine-month-old without Down syndrome in terms of gross motor skills, a seven- to eight-month-old for fine motor skills. She was on the level of a six-month-old in terms of "visual reception"; a ten-month-old for "expressive language"; and a nine-month old for "receptive language."

Even more upbeat was Naia's one-year medical exam. After routinely depressing visits to doctors during the first months of Naia's life, this one was downright festive. Greg joked around, wearing Naia on his head like a hat. She laughed and tugged at his hair. Pediatrician Della Corcoran burst into the room with outstretched arms and a hearty "Happy Birthday!"

"I'm astounded by Naia's development," Corcoran said, taking special note of Naia's newly acquired ability to pull herself to a standing position, a precursor to walking.

While the doctor spoke, Naia sat on an infant scale, her back straight, her eyes bright, wearing only a diaper and a sassy expression. She babbled to Corcoran and showed off her first two teeth.

"If I didn't know she had Down syndrome, I wouldn't make a referral to Birth-to-Three," Corcoran said. When Tierney suggested that Naia's progress was at least partly a result of early intervention therapy, Corcoran expressed doubt. "This isn't Birth-to-Three," the doctor said. "This is Naia."

Adding to Greg and Tierney's delight, Naia weighed seventeen pounds, ten ounces, and had reached twenty-eight inches tall. She had gained nearly twelve pounds and had added more than ten inches since birth. This baby who flirted with death, who arrived for surgery eight months earlier brushing the bottom of the Down syndrome growth chart, had made a stunning reversal. She was in the fiftieth percentile for weight and the seventieth percentile for height among girls her age with Down syndrome. Naia had even grown her way onto the standard growth charts for typically developing children. She was on the low end, but she was there.

On their way out, a woman in the waiting room struck up a conversation. She asked how old Naia was, and whether she seemed close to walking.

"Pretty close," Greg said proudly.

The woman's son—who had no apparent disabilities—was fifteen months old and had shown no interest in standing. "Oh well," the woman said, a little defensively, "twelve months is early to walk, I think."

Greg and Tierney finally left a doctor's office smiling.


Looking back, they couldn't help but remember the pain of the prenatal discovery and the difficult days that followed. But almost without exception, that pain was replaced by pleasure. When they thought about the two weeks from discovery to decision, the back-and-forth of whether to abort, they felt confusion, a shared bewilderment: "How could anybody not want Naia?"

"At this point," Greg said, "it's like I don't know what the big deal was to have a child with Down syndrome. I'd say there were challenges, but it's not like there was some big weight brought down on us."

"I think a lot of people look at it like, 'Life is tough enough. Why would you want to add anything else to it?'" Greg continued. "They have enough problems. They want to watch the game on Saturday, and anything that takes away from that experience is inherently bad and should be removed. We don't see it that way."

It had been only sixteen months earlier, but the summer of their decision seemed like ancient history. At times, it felt as though it had happened to someone else.

"That was an intense time, wasn't it?" Greg said to Tierney one afternoon, chuckling at the memory. "You took off from work that entire time, right? Yeah, that was a fascinating two weeks."

And yet, they were grateful to have learned about Naia in advance. "The diagnosis she got in utero is exactly what happened," Tierney said. "Being prepared for her to have special needs allowed us to adjust our expectations, to deal with the grief and to reach acceptance. When she was born, we were ready. We were ready to celebrate Naia."

"I think the big issue in these situations is the fear of the unknown," Tierney added. "I've learned that life and parenting are about being flexible with your expectations. In terms of where we are now, I have to be open to the idea that Naia's health might change again, or she might start tongue-thrusting again, or she might be a troubling teenager for reasons involving Down syndrome, or maybe not because of reasons involving Down syndrome. And it's up to us to work through it as it comes."

No longer did Tierney wish their decision had been what she had once called "clear-cut"—involving a congenital disorder so severe she would have automatically chosen abortion, or so minor they wouldn't have faced a decision at all. "People would love to take the hard parts of life away from you," she said. "They want everything to be OK. No pain. I've come to the point where the experience is actually an enlightening one. It's not a great experience, but it's something that will equip me for the next one we face."

On Sunday, November 21, Greg and Tierney threw a party to celebrate Naia's first birthday. It was unseasonably warm, a bright autumn day in Connecticut, just as it had been on the day she was born. Tierney baked a cake using her grandmother's recipe and topped it with pink frosting. "Happy Birthday Naia," was spelled out in green. In the center was a rainbow-colored candle shaped like the number "1."

Joan's house was filled with presents from family and friends—piles of clothes and books, dolls and stuffed animals, toddler toys and a tiny xylophone. A few days later, a package of clothes would arrive from Ernie, who couldn't make the party.

Before the guests arrived, the party began with some unintentional Naia mischief. She grabbed Joan's leg to pull herself up, and Joan's pants came down around her thighs. Blushing, Joan screamed. Naia laughed.

As the party got under way, Naia positioned herself in the midst of her presents, pulling at the shiny wrapping paper and taking an occasional lunge at Onyx the poodle. She wore a pink-and-white knit sweater, black pants, and tiny white sneakers that could have dangled from a rearview mirror. Wisps of fine brown hair lay on her smooth forehead, and she smelled of talcum powder and baby shampoo. Atop her head was a Winnie the Pooh party hat. That is, until the elastic string snapped the tender skin on her neck. She cried and tore it off.

Using the couch for balance—instead of her grandmother's pants—

Naia pulled herself to a standing position. She stood that way for a minute, looking around until she spotted Tierney. When she knew her mom was watching, she started to laugh.

Tierney and Tara stood close together, beaming at Naia and wearing their matching "hope" necklaces. Tierney hadn't worn hers quite so often lately. She had traded hope for something more concrete, an amber locket that opened to reveal tiny photos of Greg and Naia. And Tierney might soon need a bigger locket. Undaunted by all they'd been through, she and Greg had begun making plans for another child. They thought Naia would make a great big sister.

Greg came over to Naia while she stood against the couch. She didn't notice him at first, but then Greg took her hand. Surprised by his touch, Naia looked over to him. Realizing who it was, she let out a squeal: "Da-Da!"

Her hand in his, she took one step. Then another.

# Part III

## CHAPTER 21 "WE HAVE THE ENCYCLOPEDIA, BUT WE DON'T HAVE *HAMLET*"

G rapes, Mommy. . . . Please." It came out sounding like, "Gapes, Mummy. . . . Peas." But Tierney understood.

"You're still hungry? You want grapes, Naia?"

"Yes, Mummy. Gapes."

"It's late, Naia. I'll give you three grapes."

"No! Five gapes. *Five* gapes!"

It was a kitchen showdown. Tierney looked at Naia. Naia stared back. Not far off, a baby gurgled. A mantle clock ticked loudly.

Someone had to blink or all hell might break loose.

"OK, Naia," Tierney said, her voice thick with exasperation leavened by pride. "Five grapes."

As strong-willed as her parents, as challenging as any toddler—with a healthy appetite, a healthy heart, and a healthy sense of childhood entitlement—Naia knew she had won again. Gracious in victory, her voice sweetened: "Thank you."

"You're welcome," Tierney said, handing over the loot.

Naia gobbled the grapes, then held her empty hands triumphantly in the air: "All done!"


Nearly two years had passed since the birthday party at Joan's house. As Naia approached her third birthday, she was straddling the line between babyhood and big-girldom. Her achievements were more apparent than ever, though some of her challenges were more evident, as well.

Testing by professionals and the inevitable backyard comparisons to other children revealed that Naia had many of the anticipated developmental delays of Down syndrome. But those same formal and informal measures also demonstrated that Naia was clearly among the more high-functioning children her age with the condition. And Tierney and Greg—while never denying the implications of her extra chromosome—were more certain than ever that it was too early to accept limits on what she might accomplish.

Like all parents, they had goals for their daughter, and they hoped to make them Naia's goals, too. Short term, the goals were many and varied, from clearer speech and strengthened muscles, from better fine motor skills to improved coordination. Long term, there was one goal, the hope all caring parents share for their children: a productive, happy, and independent life.

During the two years between her first birthday and her third, Naia had climbed the first rungs of that ladder. She had moved from crawling to dancing, from tentative steps to bursts of running, from a few simple words to a vocabulary with several hundred. Her words were sometimes hard to make out—Naia sounded like "Yaya"—and her sentences were short, mostly two- and three-word combinations. But she could make herself understood.

She could count to twelve, higher with help. She had gone from sucking a bottle to feeding herself with a spoon, from soiling her diapers to seeking out the toilet. When she made it to the bowl in time, she earned stickers on a potty rewards poster attached to the refrigerator.

She knew her colors, the names of different shapes, and major parts of her body. She sang songs—"Wheels on the Bus" and "Ring around the Rosie" were favorites. Sometimes she skipped words, or mixed things up, but she knew the hand and body motions that went with the tunes. She loved "All fall down." And yet, because of weakness in her trunk muscles, her gait was stiff and she couldn't jump.

Although she wasn't as verbal as most of her typically developing peers, Naia followed along patiently and intently—better than many other three-year-olds—when her parents and teachers read picture books aloud. She knew the letters of the alphabet, and she liked to crow about it.

"What's after 'E'?" Tierney asked one day. "F!" Naia answered. And when she spotted a sign in a store, she called out: "Mommy, look— M!"

"That's right, Naia," Tierney said. "What's the first letter of the next word?"

"T!" Naia yelled. Right again.

To increase her communications skills, Naia's speech therapists taught her sign language, reinforced at home by Tierney and Greg. She often used the sign for "all done"—sweeping her hands aside, like birds in flight—and she added more signs on a regular basis, including "please," "eat," "more," "read books," and "play."

Naia loved music and would bang the keys of an electric piano and sing a tune known only to her. She mastered simple computer games. She played with puzzles, though delays in her fine motor skills made that difficult. She knew where the eight belonged on her number puzzle, and where the elephant went on her zoo puzzle, but her mind had trouble telling her hands how to make them fit. She kept trying, anyway.

She could be stubborn, and sometimes she demanded Tierney's attention with increasingly loud and intense calls—"mommy? . . . Mommy?! . . . MOMMY!! MOMM-EE!!!! MOMM-EEEEEE!!!!!" —until Tierney dropped whatever she was doing and focused on her. Naia was just as passionate when expressing her feelings. She hugged with abandon. She kissed with conviction. When Greg's father visited, he was a favorite target—"Kiss Paw-Paw!" she would yell before consenting to sleep. Bob was delighted by the attention.

Like most people with Down syndrome, Naia was small for her age. At her third birthday, she was two feet, ten-and-a-half inches tall, and weighed twenty-seven-and-a-half pounds. That translated as the seventy-fifth percentile for height and around the sixtieth percentile for weight among girls her age with Down syndrome. She was on the very low end of the growth chart for typically developing children, just as she had been at her first birthday.

Though she was petite, she had shed much of her baby pudge, and her facial features were defining themselves more clearly and adorably. Her hair was as silky and fine as it had been in infancy, but it had grown into the long, loose curls of a very young lady. Her looks drew people to her, and her countenance still favored Greg.

The characteristic features of Down syndrome were evident— around her eyes and the bridge of her nose, in particular—but they had remained subtle. Some people didn't realize she had the condition, while others spotted or suspected it right away. Another tip-off that something was different was the faint surgical scar down the center of her chest.

That was the only sign of the health problems that had dogged her early months. Dr. Lee Ellison's heart repairs had held up flawlessly. Naia's only health concerns were her frequent colds, which most likely resulted from her small respiratory passages, a common effect of Down syndrome. Other than that, she was hale and hardy.

"I am just joyful about Naia and her growth and development," Tierney said one afternoon when Naia was nearly three. "I have to temper myself and say, 'Tierney, just brace yourself, at some point that might change.' But that point hasn't happened, and Naia is just a delight."

The previous two years also had brought growth and changes to Naia's family, in ways both planned and unexpected. The changes echoed something Tierney had said shortly before Naia's birth, back when she and Greg had just purchased their new condo — the one that would later be ruined by fire. At the time, imagining what she thought lay ahead of them, Tierney had marveled: "We'll have a new place, a new baby, new everything."

The "new everything" had indeed happened, though it was different from what Tierney had envisioned. They now lived in a new city, and they had new jobs and a new home. They also had a new baby.

Some things hadn't changed, though. Greg and Tierney's intellectual fervor was as strong as ever, as were their ambitions for Naia and their reliance on faith, hard work, and each other to guide them through hard times.

The world around them had changed in those two years as well, in ways that promised to someday revolutionize treatment and possibly prevention of Down syndrome and almost every other disorder and disease.

Five months after Naia's first birthday, an international team of scientists announced that they had decoded the chemical formula spelled out in the DNA of the twenty-first chromosome. It was a breakthrough for research not just on Down syndrome, but also on epilepsy, Alzheimer's disease, and Lou Gehrig's disease, all of which had been linked to genes on chromosome 21.

With the code in hand, scientists redoubled efforts to explain why a third copy of the chromosome results in Down syndrome. Some prominent geneticists speculated that knowledge might eventually lead to treatments for the condition — drugs that could block or temper the unwanted effects of the extra chromosome. And unlike Nutrivene-D and Piracetam, those drugs would be based on hard science.

"Once we can find the genes that are important for learning problems, what we hope is that we'll be able to understand what those genes do, and somehow compensate for having an extra copy of the gene," said David Patterson, chair of the science advisory board of the

National Down Syndrome Society, who took part in the chromosome 21 mapping project as president of the Eleanor Roosevelt Institute in Denver.

Other scientists saw broader implications. Ralph Tanzi, a professor of neurology at Harvard Medical School, said the sequence of the twenty-first chromosome could help reveal why people with Down syndrome have relatively low rates of breast, lung, and gastrointestinal cancers. One theory is that the extra chromosome triggers a biological shield against tumors—a finding that, if proven, might suggest gene therapy treatments to suppress those cancers. "One can argue that an extra dose of a gene will usually be a bad thing. But—once in a while— it can be a good thing," Tanzi said.

No one suggested it would be easy to make the leap from decoding the chromosome to creating new treatments. One scientist described chromosome 21's DNA sequence as "a mess, a hornet's nest, a hodge-podge of duplications, altered sequences and arrangements that determine the health and welfare of our species."

Only seven weeks later, there was even bigger news on the gene-mapping front. Two formerly competing teams of scientists, one from government, one from the private sector, stood together at the White House to announce they had finished deciphering a first draft of the entire human genome—the genetic information contained on all twenty-three human chromosomes.

With British prime minister Tony Blair joining him via satellite, President Bill Clinton declared, "Today, we are learning the language in which God created life. . . . Without a doubt, this is the most important, most wondrous map ever produced by humankind." He continued: "Genome science will have a real impact on all our lives, and even more, on the lives of our children. It will revolutionize the diagnosis, prevention, and treatment of most, if not all, human diseases."

Some scientists felt compelled to tone down expectations for the raw DNA sequence. They cautioned that it would take decades to isolate the estimated thirty-five thousand or so individual human genes from the genome. One reason was that the decoded genome was roughly equivalent to a single sentence with 3.2 billion characters, one hundred thousand pages long, in a language made up of just four letters, with garble woven throughout and few evident rules. Researchers also needed to determine what proteins human cells were instructed to make from the different gene recipes, and how those proteins interacted to build the body and regulate its functions.

"We have the encyclopedia, but we don't have Hamlet," said Shirley Tilghman, a Princeton University geneticist.

Nevertheless, there was widespread agreement that the genome map would herald a new age of discovery. Dr. Francis Collins, head of the National Genome Research Institute and chief of the international Human Genome Project, predicted that tests would be available within a decade for predisposition to twenty-five major causes of illness and death. He didn't mention whether those tests might be available prenatally, though he did note the ethical considerations involved.

Collins understood that new tests didn't automatically mean new treatments. People might learn they had ticking bombs in their genetic code, or in the genetic code of the fetuses they carried, but they'd have no way to defuse them. It would mean more information, not necessarily more answers. Pregnant women would still have essentially two choices: continue or abort.

The potentially dark implications were immediately apparent. "The history of eugenics from early in the twentieth century to the Nazis and the more recent rage of 'ethnic cleansing' are certainly a warning that humanity may not be ready for the genetic knowledge we are coming to possess," wrote J. Craig Venter, head of the Maryland company that revolutionized gene mapping.

"Master-race efforts at 'genetic cleansing' may well be imaginable in the distant future and cannot be excluded," Venter wrote. "The immediate threat, however, is genetic discrimination. While we are just now beginning to identify the spelling errors in the genetic code associated with colon or breast cancer or Alzheimer's or Huntington's, there will be a gap of years, if not decades, between this discovery and a cure based on the targeted gene. In the meantime, individuals so diagnosed might well be discriminated against by insurance companies that will refuse to take them on, or employers who will refuse to hire them. Clearly, human rights and civil rights law will have to be updated to include this new class of diagnosed person. At this stage, one can only imagine the future potential of abuse."

Adding to the worries, Venter said he thought that so many cures and life-lengthening treatments might arise from the decoded genome that the resulting increase in human health might dangerously strain earth's resources. Venter didn't say so, but it was easy to imagine his arguments about limited resources and longer life spans being turned into justifications for just the thing Venter said he feared: a new age of eugenics.

A substantial portion of the American public seemed alert to those dangers. A CNN-*Time* poll released the morning of the White House announcement reported that 46 percent of Americans believed the Human Genome Project would have harmful effects, while only 40 percent thought the results would be positive. Nevertheless, fully 61 percent of those polled said they would want to know if they were predisposed to developing a genetic disease.

Two months later, as Naia neared her second birthday, a different kind of progress was evident on the national stage. At the 2000 Republican National Convention in Philadelphia, a twenty-six-year-old Tennessee woman named Windy Smith became the first person with Down syndrome to address a national political convention. She stood at the huge podium in First Union Center wearing a bright red dress and a shiny elephant pin, staring out at a crowd of delegates that had just named George W. Bush the GOP presidential nominee.

Months earlier, she had sent the Texas governor a letter rooting for him, along with twenty-five dollars she had earned at her job at a clothing manufacturer. She read part of the letter to the convention crowd and to millions of Americans watching on TV. "Remember the Alamo and remember why you want to be president!" she told Bush. The audience answered with a standing ovation.

Six months later, after Bush completed his tortuous path to the presidency, Windy Smith took a seat next to First Lady Laura Bush in the gallery of the House of Representatives. Together, they witnessed the new president's first speech to Congress.

But progress came in fits and starts. Ugly stereotypes die hard. The same month that Windy Smith sat proudly alongside the first lady, *Politically Incorrect* television host Bill Maher used his show to equate mentally retarded children with his dogs.

Maher: "I have two dogs. If I had two retarded children, I'd be a hero. And yet the dogs, which are pretty much the same thing—(audience reaction)—what? They're sweet. They're loving. They're kind. But they don't mentally advance at all."

One of his guests, Cynthia Garrett, a talk show host who trained as a lawyer, objected: "My nine-year-old nephew is retarded. I've never thought of him like a little dog."

Maher: "Well, maybe you should."

But it wasn't just late-night comedians. John Silber, the acerbic former president of Boston University, a man with a doctorate in philosophy, gave an interview in which he made a spirited case for a meritocracy in education based on equal opportunity. Some people, he suggested with scorn, wanted a system built on the premise that all students should show equal levels of achievement. Then he went a step further.

"The only time you have equality of achievement is if you cut everybody down to the lowest common denominator," Silber said. "We'll all get down to the level of Down syndrome. Is that what you want? That's equality? Or maybe it has to be worse than that. Maybe it has to be the equality of Alzheimer's."

When Tierney and Greg heard comments like those of Maher or Silber, their anger and revulsion was equaled only by a renewed resolve to do all they could to make the world hospitable for Naia.

"Some people ask, 'Are these kids worth it? Why are my tax dollars going to these people?'" Tierney said. "Are they really going to be able to make a meaningful contribution to society when other children—who may be gifted—are not getting all the resources they need?'"

"How do I answer them?" Tierney continued. "I think that any parent who has a child with special needs would immediately understand that it *is* worth it. And so, people have to make a leap of faith. They should want for these children the same thing they want for any child, for their child. When you leave behind a group of people who have a different set of abilities, or economic circumstances, or a different color skin, or ethnic background, that's when you start adding to the most difficult problems that we have to face in this country."

## CHAPTER 22 "YOU KIND OF KNOW YOU CAN LIVE THROUGH IT"

Six weeks after Naia's second birthday, the Fairchild family welcomed a new addition. Tierney gave birth to a son: Cole Christian Fairchild. He was a jovial, adorable, placid fellow who bore a strong resemblance to his big sister. But in addition to his gender, there were two major differences: Cole had a typical complement of forty-six chromosomes per cell, and his heart was free from defects.

Despite all they had been through, Tierney and Greg hadn't known whether Cole would be diseased or disabled—and hadn't tried to find out—until the day he was born. As much as they valued having learned about Naia's condition in advance, as much as it had prepared them for their future, as much as they were thankful that prenatal testing had allowed them to make a choice about the pregnancy with Naia, their thinking had shifted dramatically in regard to their need for such information.

During Tierney's pregnancy with Cole, her obstetrician, Michael Bourque, counseled her against undergoing a triple screen. In light of the false-negative result on that test with Naia, they'd never trust the results. So why bother? If they wanted information about possible problems with their second pregnancy, information ultrasound couldn't provide, Bourque urged them to get as close to 100 percent accuracy as possible. That meant amnio.

But their experience with Naia had changed Tierney and Greg. They didn't want the triple screen, and they didn't want amnio or any other invasive test that would count Cole's chromosomes. This time, there would be no wrenching decision to make, no back and forth, no uncertainty about whether to proceed or abort.

They firmly believed in abortion rights. But after their experience with Naia, they realized the only choice for them would be to continue a pregnancy. "We already had a child with Down syndrome," Tierney explained. "We knew what dealing with a child with special needs was like. Knowing what to expect had been one of our arguments in favor of testing the first time. That was the right thing to do, and we don't regret it. This time our rationale was that if God is going to bless us with another child with special needs, we weren't going to do anything about it—anything to stop it."

As it turned out, the ultrasound images of Cole swimming in Tierney's womb were unremarkable. All systems were go. Greg and Tierney never had to face the question of what to do in the event the ultrasound waves had picked up echoes of thick neck folds, or a heart defect, or a malformed spine, or some other sign of trouble. When they talked about it after Cole's birth, Tierney and Greg were confident that even if there had been ultrasound warning signs, they wouldn't have sought amnio or other, more definitive prenatal tests.

"You never know until you're in the situation. I acknowledge that," Greg said. "However, I think if even we had an ultrasound that showed some kind of marker, I don't think we would have had amnio. If an ultrasound had found a heart defect, we'd go to a cardiologist. And then we'd get a crew that's ready to deal with the heart defect. If the ultrasound found some other anomaly, we would have gotten the crew that deals with that anomaly. But knowing whether that anomaly is attached to Down syndrome wasn't going to do anything for me. We already know what to expect from Down syndrome. All it would do is answer the question—but it ain't going to fix the heart problem. . . . All it would have done is answer our curiosity."

"Or our fear," Tierney said.

"OK," Greg said, "yeah, our fear. The point is, there wasn't going to be any new information. And what was left, quite honestly, was the ego loss of, 'Oh boy, we're going to have two children with this problem.' And honestly, at this point in Naia's life, it has turned out to be not that big a deal. I'm not claiming this is all easy as pie. If it happened to be another child with Down syndrome, would I be disappointed? Sure. . . . But we'd be OK. You kind of know you can live through it."

"We are extremely cognizant of Naia's disability," Tierney added. "But we haven't felt a burden from Naia. It's who she is. We don't know what Cole's personality is going to be like yet, or what any other child we might have will be like. Whatever it is, we'll work on it together."

A few months after Cole's birth, Greg and Tierney reopened discussions on their original family plan of three children, one adopted. The demands of caring for two little ones, one of them disabled, as well as maintaining two high-powered jobs, made them decide to hold off any decision for at least a few more years. But there were signs that adoption had become less likely.

"When we think about adoption, we think there might be issues that we may not want to bring into our current set of complications, our life, our hectic life," Tierney said. "But I think in general we still believe that we can have three, biological or not, and I'm beginning to think that if we did, the time would be in the next couple of years, maybe the same distance apart as Naia and Cole, maybe even a little bit greater. Of course, that's adding the risk that I would be in my later thirties at the time of conception . . ." Her voice trailed off. She didn't need to explain the link between advanced maternal age and the heightened risk of Down syndrome.

Other big changes in their lives involved where they were living and working. Greg, Tierney, and Naia had remained at Joan's house for a full year after the condo fire. Then, a few months into Tierney's pregnancy with Cole, the family moved from Connecticut to Charlottesville, Virginia, a college community of fifty thousand people, some one hundred miles southwest of Washington, D.C.

Having completed his Ph.D. studies at Columbia, Greg joined the faculty of the University of Virginia, as an assistant professor at the Darden Graduate School of Business Administration. It was a homecoming: Tierney and Greg had both received degrees from Darden, and they had been married in UVA Chapel.

Tierney, meanwhile, had proved too valuable to United Technologies for her bosses to allow her to simply give notice and move to Virginia. There was an opening at the corporate office for a manager of executive education and development, so they offered it to her as an enticement to stay with the company. As a bonus, she could do the job largely from an office at the Darden School, where a majority of training courses were held for United Technologies' executives. Her office was a short walk from Greg's.

Tierney's new job required her to fly to Hartford once or twice a month for several days at a time. During those trips, Greg's father, Bob, made the ninety-minute drive north from Rustburg to keep Greg company and help with Naia. After a three-month maternity leave at home with Cole, Tierney usually brought her baby boy on those trips to Hartford; Joan was eager to help out and spend time getting to know her new grandson.

*       *       *

Along with their new jobs came a new house. As it turned out, they
never moved into the condo they had bought in Hartford. By the time
the post-fire renovations were complete—the building needed complete refurbishing—Greg and Tierney were making plans to move to
Charlottesville.

Greg and Tierney bought a newly built home just two miles from
the UVA campus, in a historic section of the city called Kellytown.
It was a red house with a peaked roof and white trim, with a front
porch and wide front stairs to welcome visitors. Within a few months,
they began exploring the possibility of also buying one of the smaller,
older homes in the neighborhood. They figured they could fix it up
and rent it to college students or young faculty members. And then,
someday, it could become a home for Naia, a place of her own—with
them nearby.

By coincidence, the Fairchilds' new hometown had been the starting
point of the U.S. Supreme Court's most notorious decision involving
mental disabilities. It began in 1924, when Virginia legislators passed a
eugenics law allowing for involuntary sterilizations of "defective persons" whose reproduction was considered "a menace to society."

The first target of the law was Carrie Buck, a seventeen-year-old
Charlottesville resident who bore a daughter out of wedlock. Showing
signs of being mentally disturbed or disabled, she and her baby daughter, Vivian, were committed to the Virginia Colony for the Epileptic
and the Feebleminded. Carrie's mother, Emma, was already a resident
of the same asylum. Taking note of the three family members in their
midst, asylum officials considered Carrie an ideal candidate for sterilization under the law, which boldly stated that "heredity plays an important part in the transmission of insanity, idiocy, imbecility, epilepsy and crime."

At a trial to test the law's constitutionality, the asylum's superintendent, Dr. Albert Priddy, testified about Carrie's family: "These people
belong to the shiftless, ignorant, and worthless class of anti-social
whites of the South." A sociologist came to court from the Eugenics
Record Office at Cold Spring Harbor, New York, the center of Ameri-

can eugenics research from 1910 to 1940. He testified that his examination of baby Vivian showed that she was "below average" and "not quite normal."

Based on those assertions, a Virginia judge ruled that Carrie should indeed be sterilized. The decision was quickly appealed to the U.S. Supreme Court, where it became known as *Buck v. Bell*. In 1927, the high court upheld the decision, eight to one, in a ruling written by Justice Oliver Wendell Holmes Jr., usually considered a great champion of individual rights. After recounting the supposed facts of the case, Holmes wrote: "It is better for all the world, if instead of waiting to execute degenerate offspring for crime, or to let them starve for their imbecility, society can prevent those who are manifestly unfit from continuing their kind."

With regard to Emma, Carrie, and Vivian Buck, Holmes added the now infamous phrase: "Three generations of imbeciles are enough."

As University of Virginia professor David O'Brien has explained, Holmes's reasoning was born of his own experiences: "Holmes's nasty language has to do with his acceptance of Darwinism. He was very cynical about mankind. He never had any children; he was an agnostic; and he was wounded in the Civil War. This prepared the way for his acceptance of Social Darwinism and the belief that only the strongest should survive."

Before its repeal, the Virginia law led to the sterilization of approximately eighty-three hundred people. Similar laws passed by more than two dozen other states resulted in the involuntary sterilization of an estimated sixty thousand Americans. Six years after *Buck v. Bell*, the German Nazi government adopted a law based on the same principles as the Virginia law. That law became the justification for the sterilization of more than three hundred fifty thousand people.

There was never a federal law in the United States allowing forced sterilization. The state laws were wiped off the books by 1960 in the wake of post–World War II revulsion toward eugenics and the widespread recognition that the laws were based on faulty science and false assumptions.

In a footnote to the sordid history of forced sterilization, scholars have shown that Carrie Buck's trial was rigged and the "facts" of the case were fiction. Carrie's lawyer had conspired against her with asylum officials. Moreover, Vivian's birth wasn't the result of teenage promiscuity, as had been claimed in evidence against her. Rather, it resulted from Carrie's rape by a relative of her foster parents, an assault that might well have contributed to Carrie's emotional problems. As for Vivian, she was hardly defective. Before she died of measles at age eight, Vivian was a "B" student in first grade. She received an "A" in deportment. She made the honor roll.

In May 2002, on the seventy-fifth anniversary of the *Buck v. Bell* decision, Governor Mark Warner apologized for Virginia's forced sterilization law. "The eugenics movement was a shameful effort in which state government should never have been involved," Warner said. The same day, a plaque was dedicated in Charlottesville honoring the memory of Carrie Buck. It stands a quarter-mile from Greg and Tierney's house.

## CHAPTER 23 "NAIA! COME BACK!"

A few weeks after Naia turned two, as her third Christmas approached, the Fairchild family went church shopping. They got a lesson they never bargained for.

Friends had suggested the Foursquare Gospel Church in Waynesboro, Virginia, about thirty miles from Charlottesville. Foursquare Gospel was a Bible-based, evangelical congregation whose motto was "Church with a Vision." Greg and Tierney thought it might be the right place for them to put down spiritual roots.

One benefit Greg and Tierney found at Foursquare Gospel was the babysitting offered during services. The youngest children were divided into three groups: infants and toddlers in one class; two- and three-year-olds in another; and four- and five-year-olds in a third. On their first two visits, Greg and Tierney left Naia in the room for two- and three-year-olds, and they thought she had done fine there.

Yet, after the second visit, Greg and Tierney's friends suggested that Naia might be happier in the room for younger children—the infants and toddlers. Their friends had a one-year-old daughter in that class. They also had a three-year-old son in the older class that Naia had previously attended. Tierney and Greg thought Naia might enjoy playing with their friends' daughter, so they agreed to move Naia to the room for younger children.

On their next visit, Tierney and Greg left Naia in the infant/toddler room and found seats among the worshippers. As it happened, it was the Sunday of the annual Christmas pageant. Rather than the traditional passion play, children from the church would act out a story of a girl who learned the true meanings of Christianity and Christmas.

Shortly before the show began, Tierney—who at the time was very pregnant with Cole—left her seat to use the bathroom and check on Naia. When she looked through a window into the infant/toddler room, Tierney saw Naia sitting alone in a playpen, eating Cheerios from a cup. The sight troubled her. Naia was clearly the oldest child in the room, and neither of the two adults supervising the children were paying attention to her. Also, the other children were roaming or crawling about freely. Naia, the oldest child in the room, was the only one confined to a playpen.

Tierney also noticed that the two- and three-year-olds in the next room, where Naia had been previously, were being fitted for costumes and lined up by their teachers. Upset, she went back into the sanctuary to find Greg. When Tierney told him what she had seen, Greg left his seat and went to the classroom.

"Why is she in the playpen?" Greg asked the young woman overseeing the children.

"She wouldn't listen," the woman answered. She said Naia had dropped some Cheerios on the floor then had picked them up and eaten them. The woman said she had asked Naia to stop, to no avail. So, she put Naia into the playpen. That way, if more Cheerios dropped, at least Naia wouldn't eat them off the floor.

Skeptical, but not wanting to overreact, Greg went to talk it over with Tierney. They would decide together how to respond, if at all. As they sat whispering, the Christmas pageant got under way. Tierney and Greg watched as the children from the two- and three-year-old classroom came rumbling into the sanctuary. The costumes Tierney had seen earlier were for the pageant. Parents grabbed their cameras and pointed out their little darlings.

Tierney and Greg immediately realized that Naia would have been among the shepherds and angels if she hadn't been placed among the younger children, only to be isolated further in a playpen. For the first time in her life, Naia had been excluded from an activity, separated from her peers. Tierney began to cry, as much in frustration as sadness. She and Greg rose from their seats. Greg turned to the friends who had urged them to join the church and said goodbye. They hustled to the classroom, plucked Naia from the playpen, and drove home.

In the hours that followed, they received sympathetic calls from their friends—who asked Tierney and Greg to pray with them for greater awareness of people with special needs—as well as from the church pastor.

"We're really sorry this happened," the pastor said. "We'd love you to come back." She said the church genuinely welcomed people like Naia—hadn't Tierney and Greg seen the teenagers with special needs who played Santa's helpers, ringing bells and walking through the aisles before the pageant?

Greg and Tierney had noticed them. But they had wondered why those children weren't integrated into the pageant, with speaking roles or even nonspeaking parts, rather than quickly paraded in and out of the church. The pastor explained that the special-needs class had been rehearsing for a separate concert. Having them walk through the church as Santa's helpers was a way to include them in the pageant without interrupting their other work. As for Naia, the pastor said, a volunteer could be assigned to her, so she could be in the class with her peers.

Greg and Tierney agreed to consider it—"Were we overly sensitive?" they wondered. Or, was this their first test, their maiden challenge in making sure that Naia was as fully included as possible, despite her delays. They talked it over without reaching a conclusion; Cole's birth two weeks later gave them something else to focus on. A decision about the church would wait.

A few months later, Greg and Tierney decided to visit Foursquare Gospel again, with Naia and Cole. But the fit didn't feel right anymore. They weren't sure it was because of what had happened at Christmas, and perhaps it was unrelated. But they knew they needed to keep looking for a new church to call their own.

The experience at Foursquare Gospel reinforced something Greg and Tierney had realized when they had first heard Naia's diagnosis. They would need to remain vigilant to ensure she was included wherever she went—in church, in school, on the playground, everywhere. And, someday, in her search for housing and employment.

Greg had declared as much when they were deciding whether to continue the pregnancy. "Tierney," he had said then, "we're going to have to go into our child's school, fighting with administrators, changing this and that. I'm going to have to make sure people aren't abusing my child, putting him in the back of the room or locking him in the closet. This is what we're going to have to do. But I'm mad about it."

As it turned out, the reality during Naia's first three years was not so dramatic, the church pageant and the Cheerios-in-the-playpen incident notwithstanding.

"For the most part, we haven't found that people want to keep Naia off on an island to herself," Greg said shortly before Naia's third birthday. "And it doesn't seem like people resent us, or we're in there fighting with people who don't want to admit our child somewhere. In other words, in contrast to what I said before Naia was born, it hasn't turned into a modern version of the old integration fights, with us sitting in administrators' offices trying to convince them to allow our daughter to walk through the door with the other kids."

Instead, some of the biggest challenges involved the subtle interactions of everyday life. "It's socially a bit of a balancing act because you don't want to be too out front the first time you talk to somebody," Greg said. "You know, 'Hi, I'm Greg, and I have a child with Down syndrome.' Nor do you want to be keeping the information out of the discussion when it's pertinent. So you're always trying to figure out when to tell people."

Added Tierney, "It's kind of like me telling someone I married someone black. Sometimes in certain situations, it would be really helpful if people knew. But you just never know the best time to introduce it. You have to really think about it."

Social issues also came up every time they fielded questions that reminded them how many people misunderstood the nature of Down syndrome—"So, which one of you carries the Down syndrome gene?" one MBA student had asked Greg. And it wasn't just adults. The more Naia ventured outside their house, the more Greg and Tierney found themselves trying to interpret the reactions of other children.

On a walk down their street, Greg and Naia came across a little girl holding a dog on a leash. Naia wanted to try holding the leash, too, and the little girl tried several times to teach her how. But Naia wasn't getting it.

"She doesn't really understand a lot, does she?" the girl asked Greg.

"No, she really doesn't. You're going to have to keep working with her."

Afterward, Greg wondered whether it was a typical reaction of a preschooler to a younger child. "Or, did she think a two-and-a-half-year-old should really catch on about this leash thing. Or, was it that her parents told her to be really nice to Naia because she's different and she doesn't understand everything. I don't know."

Whatever the case, Greg and Tierney grew more strident about making certain Naia was included to the extent her abilities allowed. "I want her in the most inclusive place she can be because I can see the benefits long term in her being with typically developing peers," Tierney explained. "She's going to get more out of it, and those are the kids who are in her neighborhood, who are in her school, who might otherwise be teasing her."

\*     \*     \*

Work toward the goal of inclusion had continued without interruption since Naia started early intervention therapies just a month after she was born. Even before they moved to Charlottesville, Tierney and Greg tapped into Virginia's version of Connecticut's Birth-to-Three program, called "Babies Can't Wait," to line up speech therapy and physical therapy for fine- and gross-motor skills.

"I've always been of the mind that these therapies are essential. I would call myself almost fanatical about making sure that I am giving Naia every opportunity," Tierney said. "I guess it could be a burden for some people, and I guess some people might tire of it, but I just made it part of our routine."

"Thank God she has a diagnosis," Tierney continued. "What if she didn't have a diagnosis? What if she didn't get early intervention services? With the advances made in education, adult learning, adult living, we are seeing more and more children with Down syndrome being able to get their drivers' licenses, hold down jobs, live in the community. I just look at it all and think of how fortunate we are."

Just as she had once kept a little brown book to keep track of Naia's medical needs, now Tierney recorded notes from therapy sessions and special education team meetings in a composition notebook with a black-and-white speckled cover. The entries read like a secret code of developmental goals and milestones: "Lateral rotation—on ball to promote balance." "Fine motor—emphasize completion, focused play; shape sorter needed." "Twenty-five percent discrepancy by age." "Brian asked about the frequency of collecting baseline data on Naia's attention span in various activities." "Karissa is working on pincer grasp and tripod." "Jenny case study."

Brian was Brian Boyd, Karissa was Karissa Gick Randall, and Jenny was Jenny Weinberg, all of them graduate students in special education at the University of Virginia's Curry School of Education. Tierney and Greg had arranged for them to serve as aides to Naia at the university's Malcolm W. Cole Child Care Center, where Naia was the first child with mental retardation enrolled in its twenty-year history.

"She's just a poster child for early intervention," said the daycare center's director, Karen Taylor. "It's been good for us to have her here."

The graduate students earned course credits for some of the time they spent with Naia, and some of the time earned them seven dollars an hour from Tierney and Greg. That cost was in addition to the one-hundred-fifty dollars a week they paid for Naia's full-time daycare at the center.

And those weren't the only costs. A typical month for Naia would include four meetings with a speech therapist, three with an occupational therapist, and one with a physical therapist, for which Greg and Tierney made copayments of ten dollars for each visit. They also paid about seventy dollars a month for a "special instructor" to make regular visits to the Cole Center, to help coordinate Naia's involvement in her class of typically developing toddlers and two-year-olds.

The money added up—it wasn't onerous, but it wasn't insignificant, either—though Tierney and Greg rarely gave it a second thought. It was worth whatever it cost to help Naia keep up or come close. "I know in my mind that with a developmental delay, at some point the learning curve could become too great for her. It could accelerate too fast," Tierney said. "The challenge for us is how we will help Naia stay on top of it without feeling overwhelmed."


Naia's therapy sessions cleverly combined work and play—the only method that would work with a stubborn toddler. Speech therapist Sandy Heitz let Naia blow bubbles to work on breath control. Physical therapist Mary Jane Pudhorodsky fitted her for a special tricycle that would allow her to keep up with the other kids. Heitz worked with other children Naia's age with Down syndrome who hadn't begun talking. Heitz credited early intervention for Naia's verbal skills and physical achievements.

As part of the therapies, Naia received regular evaluations of everything from her developmental milestones, to her speech and language skills, to her sociocultural and psychological conditions. The assessments generally focused on documenting Naia's delays—the better to target them for therapy—but there were encouraging surprises, as well.

When she was twenty-nine months old, Naia underwent a speech and language evaluation that found she had the skills of a typical child who was twenty-five months old, meaning her delays were virtually insignificant. "These scores show receptive and expressive language skills solidly within normal limits," wrote the tester, a speech therapist named Cherrie Waxman. "She has clearly done very well in her early intervention program, and is developing speech and language in a logical sequence."

Naia's moderate delays meant she could be a full-fledged member of the gang at her daycare center.

The Cole Center was a five-minute drive from Greg and Tierney's house, located in a modern, two-story brick building that could hold up to 170 children. The room where Naia spent her days was clean, bright, and filled with tiny chairs—each labeled "chair." Labels also were affixed to a mirror, a pencil box, and anything else that would hold still.

On a wall, labeled "wall," were pictures students had made by pasting leaves onto paper trees. Naia had glued six leaves onto her tree— more than some of her classmates, fewer than others. On a shelf, labeled "shelf," was a notebook where Naia's graduate student aides left daily progress notes for Tierney and Greg. "Naia had a great day today," one note read. "She said, 'I want more corn, please,' and 'I want peas, please' at lunch. We were so impressed with her two full sentences—mealtime definitely brings out her best!" "Naia is the little independent woman today," read another. "Naia danced and danced. . . . She loved the 'Grease' soundtrack."

But not all the notes were upbeat. "Naia had a rough day today," said one. "She wouldn't eat breakfast. And most of the day I spent trying to get her to play with the other children. . . . Is she going through a 'no' phase? Because that's all she was saying today."

Outside the building was a large play area with climbing structures, slides, and an oval track for tricycle riders. Best of all, as far as Naia was concerned, the yard was next to a rail line, where she could press up against the fence and watch CSX freight trains rumble past. Sometimes she'd even count the cars.

On a warm, fall day, Naia and her classmates spent much of their time outside. Her hair pulled back in a ponytail, Naia wore blue pants and a white shirt decorated with generous helpings of her lunch. She was shorter, less agile, and less verbal than most of her friends, but she was clearly a member of the group, subject to all the good and bad that went with it.

At one point, Naia was among several children playing in a sandbox, digging holes, making tunnels, and grabbing toys from each other's hands.

"Naia, you have to wait!" yelled a little girl named Hannah, keeping a tight grip on a yellow shovel.

"Wait," said Naia. And she did.

When she got bored of waiting, Naia climbed out of the sandbox. That didn't sit right with Hannah.

"Naia! Come back!" she called.

But Naia was already off to join a new group of friends playing with hula hoops. They were happy to see her.

"I gave Naia a hug," boasted a little boy named Bennie.

Naia's teachers, Donna Robinson and Pam Bryant, kept an extra eye on her, but they only occasionally needed to intervene as Naia made her way around the yard. "This is a first-time experience for me, working with a child like Naia," said Robinson, a warm, motherly woman who was a twelve-year veteran of the center. "I was unsure of myself in the beginning. I wondered, 'Am I going to be able to help this child?' What if I don't do the right things for her?' "

A year after Naia enrolled, those worries were gone. "The way I see it now, she is like any other child in this class. They are all different, and they all need to work on different things. This one might need help with social play, and that one might need work on language. We help them all."

Though she tried to treat all the children equally, it was clear Robinson had a special place in her heart for Naia. "Ooooh, I just love Naia," she said, her face brightening into a smile. "She is a wonderful little girl with a great personality. I can't say enough about her."

As Robinson spoke, Naia came over and looked up at her.

"Mommy?" she asked.

"Mommy's at work, Naia," Robinson said.

"Mommy work," Naia said, and moved on.

Naia gravitated toward some older, preschool children on the playground. One was a pretty little girl named Rachel in a red shirt with a picture of Winnie the Pooh. She was especially protective of Naia, like a big sister. Rachel helped Naia to find her footing on some climbing bars and made sure none of the other big kids bumped into her. Asked what she liked about Naia, Rachel explained: "She's so young and nice. I just like her. And, she has almost the same color skin as me." Then she was off, to make sure Naia found her place in line for the water fountain.

\*        \*        \*

Though Naia successfully integrated with her daycare classmates, Tierney and Greg knew that was only the first step. A bigger challenge awaited in the public school system, where the inclusion of children with disabilities was a relatively new phenomenon.

For more than two hundred years, most public schools had little or no room for children with serious mental or physical disorders. As recently as 1970, schools in the United States educated only one in five children with disabilities. Some states even had laws excluding children who were deaf, blind, emotionally disturbed, or mentally retarded.

If those children weren't in institutions, they were most often kept home, perhaps trained to do menial tasks like the young woman whom Tierney's father recalled doing chores at his family's New Hampshire farmhouse, or the cousin of John Mallin's who learned English by watching television.

The march toward including children with disabilities in public schools began in the 1960s, when grassroots advocates—mostly parents of children with physical and mental disabilities—borrowed slogans and concepts from the civil rights and women's rights movements to press for better educational opportunities.

Their efforts led to the 1975 passage of the federal Education for All Handicapped Children Act, which evolved into the 1990 Individuals with Disabilities Education Act (IDEA), the federal law at the heart of all special education programs. Its cornerstone was its promise of free, appropriate public education for all disabled children in the least restrictive environment. To translate that into classroom practice, each student who qualified for special education—whether mentally, physically, or psychologically impaired, or even learning disabled—would be evaluated and provided with an Individualized Education Program (IEP), that identified his or her needs and plotted the best approach to meeting them.

Naia received an IEP at twenty-nine months that described her "disabling conditions" as a developmental delay with speech and language impairment. The six-page form recounted evaluations of Naia's development and even her personality. "Naia is described as curious and interested in her surroundings, and very willing to please others," it said. "Naia wipes her own nose, demonstrates some interest in toilet training, removes her coat without assistance, puts possessions away when asked, and eats with a spoon independently."

Naia's IEP also outlined goals and objectives, from initiating play with other children to forming short sentences. Her IEP would be updated on a regular basis, all the way through age twenty-one or her graduation from high school, whichever came first.

In the early years of the federal special education law, the usual approach to fulfilling the promise of a free and appropriate education was "mainstreaming," which, despite its name, usually meant placing disabled children in classrooms separate from their nondisabled peers. Public schools created special education classes for children with disabilities. Children with special needs were selectively placed in one or more regular classes where they could demonstrate the ability to "keep up" with their typically developing classmates. As often as not, that meant nonacademic offerings like lunch or art.

By the 1980s, mainstreaming began to be replaced by "inclusion," which meant placing disabled students in the classrooms they otherwise would attend, even if they couldn't learn as well or as quickly as other students. Sometimes they'd be taken out of class for therapy or special instruction, but proponents of "full inclusion" preferred that support services such as teacher aides be provided to keep disabled children in their regular classrooms as much as possible.

Yet success for individual students was often elusive. President Gerald R. Ford, who signed the original law in 1975, warned at the time: "Unfortunately, this bill promises more than the federal government can deliver, and its good intentions could be thwarted by the many unwise provisions it contains. . . . Even the strongest supporters of this measure know that they are falsely raising the expectations of the groups affected." More than a quarter-century later, those criticisms were still heard.

One of the biggest problems was money. Although federal law prohibited schools from citing cost as a factor in deciding what kind of special education to offer, even affluent school districts struggled financially to meet disabled students' needs. The federal government promised in 1975 to pay 40 percent of the educational costs of disabled students, but it never paid up. By the year 2001, an estimated fifty-one billion dollars was being spent a year to educate the nation's disabled students, of which the federal government paid about six billion dollars, or about 12 percent. State and local governments were left to cover the balance.

The financial burden led some parents of nondisabled students—as well as some fiscally conservative commentators—to complain that a disproportionate share of resources was being devoted to six million children in special education, at the expense of the forty-four million typical and gifted children. They noted that although 12 percent of the nation's schoolchildren qualified for special education programs, they received an estimated 40 percent of new money invested in elementary and secondary education in the previous thirty years. Per pupil costs for special education students were on average sixteen thousand dollars a year, versus seven thousand dollars for typical students, but in one extreme case the cost was estimated at two hundred fifty thousand dollars a year for a single student.

None of that surprised advocates for the mentally retarded. Author Michael Bérubé, whose son, Jamie, has Down syndrome, explained it this way: "First of all, special ed *should* cost more than regular ed, particularly when severe physical disabilities are at issue: More vulnerable children need a greater degree of care." In his book *Life As We Know It: A Father, a Family, and an Exceptional Child,* Bérubé continues: "Second, the argument is incredibly disingenuous. *Every* area of American public education is scandalously underfunded, and blaming disabled children for shortfalls is a particularly nasty form of scapegoating —as if one were to blame the homeless for our nation's lack of low-income urban housing."

There also were frequent disagreements over what the law actually required—it doesn't mention mainstreaming or inclusion or any other specific approach. One principal's dream of a least restrictive environment was another's nightmare of classroom chaos and blown budgets. At the same time, some teachers were concerned whether they would be able to handle the needs of special education students while trying to meet demands for higher test scores and tougher curriculums.

As a result, the law was applied differently from school district to school district, often to the chagrin of parents of disabled children. For instance, while 72 percent of special education students in North Dakota were taught in regular classrooms, the same was true for only 8 percent in South Dakota, a state with nearly identical demographics, according to a 1993 study by *U.S. News and World Report.*

Even parents of special education students sometimes disagreed on general principles. Some fought when their children were placed in segregated special education classrooms, and some fought when their children were included in regular classrooms. "If he were in a regular classroom, he wouldn't get as much attention as he does now," the mother of a boy with physical disabilities told a group of researchers. Another mother, Sue Benes, said her son, Brett, who has Down syndrome, was at times ignored in an inclusion preschool but thrived in self-contained special education classes.

By contrast, there was Deanna Lesneski, a.k.a. Flagpole Mom. In 2000, Lesneski spent nineteen days lashed to a flagpole at her son's school near Pittsburgh. She was motivated by what she said was school administrators' failure to provide the resources they had promised for her son, Ryan, to be included in a regular class. Ryan has Down syndrome, asthma, and a hearing disability. Lesneski abandoned her protest only after the district agreed to hire an aide proficient in sign language and reversed a policy that had banned Ryan from carrying his own medications in school.

Because each child's needs had to be considered individually, and because of different interpretations of the law, battles over special education frequently ended up in court. The standards became clearer after a 1989 decision by the U.S. Fifth Circuit Court of Appeals, in a case involving a six-year-old boy with Down syndrome. The case, *Daniel R. R. v. State Board of Education,* laid out a series of tests that favored placement in regular classrooms. At the same time, the court required school systems to balance "whether the child will receive an educational benefit from regular education" against any perceived detrimental effect a child with a disability would have on the education of other students.

Since then, other courts have taken similar approaches, placing the burden largely on school systems to prove that they've tried everything possible to avoid separating special education students from their peers. It remained a school-by-school issue, with some districts embracing disabled children and others serving them begrudgingly.

The Venable Elementary School in Charlottesville is an impressive, three-story pile of red brick with four huge white pillars out front.

Opened in 1925, it was named for Colonel Charles Scott Venable, who served General Robert E. Lee during the Civil War and later taught at the University of Virginia, located a few blocks away. The school motto: "Each Child an Opportunity."

When Naia finished preschool, she would become one of the 275 children who attended kindergarten through fourth grade at Venable. When that happened, she would follow in the sneaker prints of an affectionate blond boy named Max Dreyfus, the first child with Down syndrome to embark on a program of full inclusion at Venable.

In addition to Down syndrome, Max and Naia had heart surgery in common. They were born with the same defect; Max's was corrected at fourteen months and, like Naia, he had no further signs of heart troubles. Coincidentally, both also had younger brothers who didn't have Down syndrome.

Max was a member of Laura Flickinger's kindergarten class, a collection of high-spirited boys and girls from a wide mix of racial and socioeconomic backgrounds. Max was seven, four years older than Naia and two years older than most of his classmates. It was Max's second year in kindergarten—after an extra year in preschool. His parents had urged the second kindergarten year on school officials to give Max a better chance at keeping up educationally and behaviorally with his classmates.

"He's always been headstrong—he gets that from his parents—and he tends to get frustrated easily, which is typical of kids with Down syndrome," explained his mother, Emily Dreyfus, a community education coordinator with the local Legal Aid Society. Max also had a tendency to use what teachers politely call "bathroom talk," and when he felt bored or disconnected, he sometimes expressed himself physically. He would swat classmates, or hug them too hard, or stick out his leg as they walked by, or urge a little girl to eat her pizza by putting some on her face. She cried.

Max's inappropriate behaviors were held in check by an impulse-control medication called Clonidine. Its success allowed Dreyfus and her husband, Neal Walters, a lawyer, to pursue the goal they shared with Tierney and Greg: keeping their child in a regular classroom. "I want him to learn to read, and I think that's something he can clearly do," said Dreyfus, who enlisted Tierney to serve with her on the local Special Education Advisory Committee. "By fourth grade I would love to have him reading paragraphs and comprehending. Being able to read a menu, follow basic directions. With math, I'm not at all sure what we can hope for. The concepts don't seem to speak to him at all.

"My other big goal for him is purely social," she added. "Any kid in the world, and especially a kid with a disability, needs to learn to function in the world with all sorts of people. The only way he can gather those skills is by being exposed to typical kids and having the variety of experiences of the kind that happen in a general education classroom."

School officials were willing to try. "It's been a learning experience for all of us," said Venable principal Ron Broadbent. "I think we've done something special here with this little boy, and it's great to see the successes he's starting to enjoy. From the outrageously gifted to the severely retarded, we need to build a program that says, 'This is what's best for your child.' Perhaps for another child this kind of inclusion wouldn't work. But clearly for Max it's in his best interest."

But, Broadbent cautioned, "no child has the right to deny another child the right to learn." For Max to remain in a regular classroom, he would have to abide by that rule. If not, he would be moved to one of Venable's "self-contained" classrooms for special education students deemed incapable of inclusion.

To give Max the best possible chance, the school system provided him with a full-time aide, Cereather Waller, a shy, caring woman who did everything from making sure he ate his peanut butter crackers at lunch to keeping him involved in class activities. He also received extra attention from the classroom resource teacher, Charlene Franck, and had near-daily visits with the school speech therapist, Claire Cline. In addition, Max's parents paid a tutor to work with him on reading development.

The school system never denied anything to Max because of costs, which Max's parents thought reflected genuine support for inclusion. It also revealed a sophisticated understanding that the federal IDEA law banned cost-based decisions about special education.

On a Thursday in late October, almost two months into the school year, Miss Flickinger's class gathered around her for story time. Flickinger had once been among them—she had attended Venable in the 1970s—and was in her tenth year as a kindergarten teacher. She was upbeat and articulate, with blond hair pulled back in a ponytail. She wore a simple black sweater and a long skirt beribboned with green, purple, and gold stripes. Waller and Franck were taking breaks, so for the moment Flickinger was the only teacher in the room.

The children knew it was story time because Flickinger had changed into her gold "story shoes" and settled into a rocking chair in the corner, near a cage that held the class pet, Stripey the guinea pig. They crowded around Flickinger on the floor, their bottoms on the carpet, except for Max. He sat on a wedge-shaped cushion that not only felt good, it helped him to sit still by defining the space he was supposed to occupy. But, on this day, the wedge wasn't working. It was becoming a diversion unto itself.

"If you throw your wedge again, Max, I will have to take it away," Flickinger warned. Max said nothing, and Flickinger returned to the book of the day, a fantasy story called *Tarzanna,* about a female Tarzan who captures a boy named Gerald who studies spiders. Max wasn't listening, but Flickinger kept trying.

"Max, can you see from there?" she asked.

"Max, keep your hands on your own body."

And, later, "Max, you'll like this one."

But none of it worked. "Max, we've got to make a decision about the wedge."

Flickinger interrupted her reading—and the other children moaned. "That's not fair! We want the story," said one girl.

"I know," the teacher said calmly as she took Max's cushion and sat him in a chair. Flickinger's patience reflected her conviction that the rest of the class wasn't harmed by the extra time and attention Max needed.

"It's good for him to be here. The more diversity you have, the more chance you have to say, 'Gosh, there are people in the world who look different than me, and act different, and we can still all get along,'" she said later. "Prejudice is a lack of education. If you're exposed to people who are differently abled, or a different color, or from different places, you're not going to develop stereotypes."

When the story continued, Max was soon off the chair and lying on the floor. He seemed ready to take a nap. Franck, the resource teacher, returned to the classroom and headed right for him.

"Let's go for a walk, Max. Outside," she said.

"We'll be learning stuff?" he asked.

"Yes," she said.

Franck took Max to the playground, where the fresh air seemed to revive him. He ran—looking back over his shoulder to call out, "Come on! Run!"

Max loved attention from other children—even their negative reactions when he wrestled too hard with them or made faces at them—and he tried to make connections where he could. But it wasn't easy. Max was not yet included on the "birthday party circuit," which pained his parents. The children around him got older, but invitations for cake and ice cream didn't arrive in Max's mailbox.

While prowling around the playground, Max spotted a pretty second-grader with long hair sitting on a low brick wall. He went over and sat next to her. She smiled shyly at him, and he took her hand.

Another girl yelled, "C'mon, you idiot."

Max looked up, following the sound with his eyes. Franck cringed. But it turned out the other girl wasn't talking to Max. She was issuing a standard schoolyard taunt to her friend, the pretty girl with long hair. The girl blushed. She let got of Max's hand and walked away.

Max hopped off the wall, unbothered. He found Franck, and they went back to class.

## CHAPTER 24 "YOUR FAMILY IS ALWAYS THERE FOR YOU"

Although life for the Fairchild family was moving smoothly ahead, a painful gap remained. Greg and Tierney didn't know whether Ernie would ever be part of their lives. At times, Tierney considered her father's treatment of Naia a reflection of her own tumultuous relationship with him. "Sometimes I think I push him to be somebody he's not going to be," she said once. But at other times, Tierney looked for ways to bring them closer together.

Tierney and Greg's frustration with Ernie came to a head during a phone conversation back when Naia was approaching her first birthday. Ernie's girlfriend casually mentioned that, at that very moment, Ernie was bouncing her young grandson on his knee. Why doesn't he do that with Naia, they wondered. He hadn't even held her.

A few weeks later, on Ernie's next trip through Hartford, Tierney took her father to dinner at a Bertucci's restaurant. After placing their orders, father and daughter fell into conversation about child-rearing philosophies. At first, they found common ground in their belief that some modern parents tended to be too lenient. Tierney saw an opening to move from abstract concepts to the reality of Naia.

"I just want to understand what you're willing to do, how involved you're willing to be, how you're going to interact with Naia," she said. "I want to know what your issues are with her."

"I thought they should have been apparent to you," Ernie answered flatly, as Tierney recalled afterward. It wasn't the Down syndrome, Ernie said. It was race—the fact that Naia's father was black. Tierney sat back in her chair, in stunned disbelief.

Her father hadn't changed since a decade earlier, when he spent a year giving Greg the silent treatment. Despite having abandoned that approach; despite having walked Tierney down the aisle at her wedding; despite his visits to their home and their visits to his; despite his friendship with Greg's parents, Ernie still disapproved of interracial marriage. Particularly his daughter's interracial marriage.

Ernie told Tierney that he respected people who were different from him, and he respected Greg and his family. He said he didn't believe in discrimination. But then he told Tierney he considered her marriage a betrayal of her "heritage" that clouded any relationship he might have with his granddaughter.

Ernie also said he thought mixing races might cause physical problems or "sickness," a comment Tierney interpreted to mean Down syndrome. Ernie said he could see himself playing some role—sending Naia gifts, perhaps, and acting as what he called "a passive supporter." But sitting there in Bertucci's, a half-eaten pizza before him, his youngest child across from him, Ernie said he couldn't see himself doing much more than that.

Tierney felt her cheeks grow red. She was shell-shocked, sickened. She kept her tone level and pointed out the illogic of his words, the hypocrisy of his behavior. She tried to use reason and scientific knowledge to contradict his points. But no matter what she said, she knew she wasn't convincing him. And, she decided, she'd rather be home with her family than spend another minute hearing her father's theories and rationalizations. She left the restaurant, exhausted and sad.

When he heard about the dinner, Greg was disgusted. Surprised, too—not just at Ernie, but also at himself for not realizing that Ernie had never changed his stripes. "This guy has done such a good act around me, my parents, that I thought maybe he had gotten over those views," Greg said. "I feel duped. I made the assumption that because there was a change in his behavior, there was a change in his views."

Ernie's comments reminded Greg of something he had learned many years earlier. "In America," Greg said, "it doesn't matter to a certain set of people what I and my family accomplish, who we are. It's always going to be a problem."

Greg remembered a routine he once heard by the comic Chris Rock. During a performance at Harlem's Apollo Theater, Rock yelled from the stage: "There's not a white man in this room that would change places with me. And I'm rich!" He said even a one-legged white busboy would pass up the chance to be Chris Rock, based on the rationale: "I'm gonna ride out this white thing, see where it takes me." The mostly black audience howled in recognition.

It occurred to Greg that his father-in-law was the one who had gone to college on a basketball scholarship—the stereotypical route for black advancement—while the Fairchild family had never used sports to get ahead. "My father's parents were both college-educated. One had a master's degree. My father is a colonel, senior vice president of a bank. I'm getting a Ph.D. And we don't cut it with him?"

Greg and Tierney realized there was an odd twist to Ernie's reasoning: Naia was a victim of garden-variety racial discrimination, not the more specialized discrimination based on disability, though the two had much in common and the same corrosive effect. It turned out that Ernie would reject any child of theirs, not just one who had the mental delays and physical characteristics of Down syndrome.

Several days later, Ernie called with an apology of sorts. He said he had been too blunt, cruel even, and the comments he had made over dinner didn't fully reflect how he felt. He might not agree with Tierney's choices, but he knew he couldn't change them. More important, he would respect them.

"Respect is absolute," Tierney responded. "It's black and white. It's not gray. If you want to have a relationship with us, what's most important is that you respect my child, and that you demonstrate that with your actions." Ernie said he understood.

Afterward, Tierney told Greg: "I'm willing to accept it as a starting point. But I can't say I won't be cautious."

Greg had nearly reached the point of telling Ernie to "hop off the train because we're going on without you." But he, too, would wait and see. "Time will tell," Greg said.

Tierney and Greg had little contact with Ernie in the eighteen months that followed. Any hope for rapprochement was diminished not long after the Bertucci's dinner, when a series of stories in the *Boston Globe* documented the experiences of Tierney, Greg, and Naia, covering the period from the discovery of Down syndrome through Naia's first birthday. The stories included an account of the conflicts with Ernie.

Ernie didn't dispute Greg and Tierney's version of events or their recollections of conversations with him. But he was angry they had shared his comments for public consumption, and the space between them widened.

Tierney was saddened by their estrangement, though not surprised. "It's natural to wish you could have a good relationship with your father, that he'd be involved and care for your children," she said. "It would be nice to even go back to how it was before. We'd see him, spend time together. Now we don't even have that."

Greg was sympathetic. He knew the situation was difficult for Tierney. But he was left cold by Ernie's complaints about his loss of privacy. "I'm supposed to feel bad for him?" Greg said. "He has these hidden feelings about his daughter having married me, and we're supposed to help him keep that secret? . . . If anyone thinks that I'm just so happy to have married into a white family that I'll keep quiet, maintain some kind of white wall of silence, well, I'm not that guy."

Months passed with little contact. Phone calls here or there, but no meetings, no family events, no discussion of the painful words spoken over pizza. Time, the move to Charlottesville, and Cole's birth did nothing to heal their wounds.

When Naia was two-and-a-half and Cole was nearly six months old, Ernie had yet to touch Naia or even set eyes on Cole. It was time, Tierney decided, to write him a letter. Working behind the scenes was Tara, who had encouraged Ernie to make amends and urged Tierney to reach out, understand, and forgive their father.

In a six-page letter to Ernie, Tierney recounted his comments and explained why they had hurt so much, even quoting back some of what Ernie had said at Bertucci's. In a plaintive tone, she asked if he realized how much she had needed him during Naia's difficult first year, and how hard it was not to have had that support. She wrote, "I do love you, Dad," and she urged him to help rebuild their relationship. She told him about Cole—"a healthy, happy boy"—and Naia—"a smart, energetic girl." She said she hoped he would get to know his grand-children.

Then Tierney asked her father three questions whose answers would determine what, if any, future they would have together: Do you think black people are inferior? Can you accept your mixed-race grandchildren? And, if we start seeing each other again, will you treat us with respect and acceptance, or should we expect endless replays of past battles?

A month passed with no reply. Tierney was bracing herself for the possibility they might never speak again. Father's Day approached, and Tierney picked out a card with a photo of Rodin's *Thinker* on the cover. Inside, it read: "Thinking of you on Father's Day." She thought it fit the bill—it would mark the day without getting all gushy. She looked at other cards, but she rejected the ubiquitous "You're the

Greatest Dad on Earth!" messages. Before she could mail her card, a letter arrived from Ernie. In it, he praised her for taking the initiative, and said it was wonderful to hear that her family was well. Then he got to the point:

> Without trying to recall any conversations with you and/or Greg, it would have been best if none of them had taken place. That said, and the conversations behind us, I regret having lost my senses of decency and objectivity at certain times responding to your concerns and perceptions, and I do sincerely apologize for having said anything that may have led to or caused any of the unrest between us.
>
> Getting to the chase, I do not believe any race to be inferior to any other in any way. . . . One thing I value very much is the freedom of choice. I can discriminate without challenge who I want to associate with and who I choose not to. . . . What does this mean to you? As my daughter, I always have deep feelings about your ongoing well-being. And for you and Greg, I sincerely respect who you are and your excellent stations in life, and wish you both Godspeed. The downside is simple in that I think I enjoy other activities more than your good company. That is not disrespectful and it is no different than associations anywhere you look.
>
> Sincere congratulations to both of you for Naia and Cole! . . . One final regret I have is that Mr. and Mrs. Fairchild have had to be exposed to the senselessness of my actions going out of control. I have a deep respect for them as stated in the past, and I apologize for any unrest the events may have caused them.
>
> In closing, it is my desire to let the past be history, untouched again. Endless discussions of any of the events will serve no objective purpose, certainly not as much as allowing them to pass quietly into oblivion. Take good care, as I know you will. The best of health to everyone and all, with my best regards.
>
> Dad

Tierney and Greg each read the letter several times. Some parts were hard to swallow, but they felt better after each reading. "This is an apology," Greg said, half-incredulous. "This is more than I ever expected out of this man. I admit I have some questions about the guy, but I forgive him."

But Greg wasn't completely ready to move on. He had a vivid memory of Ernie's silent treatment when his romance with Tierney was first revealed, and he regretted never having confronted Ernie about it after the thaw. "I'm still working on my degree of forgiveness," he said. "If he calls and says, 'I'm coming through Charlottesville, and I'd like to stop by,' I'm not sure I'm ready for that yet. I have to walk before I can run on this. But I do respect what he has done."

Greg hoped that, for Tierney's sake and the sake of their children, the letter would start a new chapter in their lives. Hard feelings might linger, but if Ernie could demonstrate that he accepted their family, if he accepted the mix of color and disability written in Naia's genes, perhaps anyone could. And if he did, they should accept him in return.

Tierney was torn between clear-eyed objectivity and raw emotion. Sometimes she focused on the harshest portion of the letter, the part about Ernie not enjoying their company. In a strange way, Tierney said, it was her favorite line. "It's refreshingly candid," she said. "We are just very different people, and for whatever reasons Dad wants to say, and whatever reasons we want to say, it's honest to admit that we really don't enjoy interacting with each other. That's OK. We don't have a problem with that."

At other times, the letter soothed Tierney like a warm bath. She allowed the words to touch her unprotected heart and salve hurts that dated to her childhood, when she suffered the slights of being low child on Ernie's totem pole. It was those times when she read the letter as a sincere and heartfelt apology, in whose text and subtext she could find a genuine, if awkward, expression of a gift she had longed for: her father's love and approval.

"I was very prepared for this to go the other way," she said one night, tears welling in her eyes. "I've of course been missing my Dad, and I've been sad for that loss. But I feel like I don't have to be sad anymore. I feel like he has taken great strides to understand and compliment me for who I am, even if I've caused him pain."

She paused and caught her breath. "I hope this was a cathartic experience for him. It was for me."


And yet, as more months passed, there were few signs the letter exchange would mark a new dawn. Despite continued efforts by Tara to bring together father and daughter, phone calls with Ernie remained brief and awkward. There were no face-to-face meetings.

By coincidence, Naia's third birthday fell on Thanksgiving Day. Tierney and Greg thought it would be an ideal opportunity to host their entire extended families, celebrating both happy occasions at once. Invitations went out, and Greg began experimenting with new turkey recipes.

A few weeks before the big day, they got a note from Ernie, politely declining to attend. He had plans elsewhere.

"I don't know what the future will be," Tierney said. The initial blush of emotions surrounding the letter had worn off. Her feelings about Ernie were tamped down, and her focus was on Greg and their children. She again wore a mask of detached resolve. "Someday, Naia and Cole will have these letters," she said, "and I think that will be a positive thing for them and our family. If nothing else, it will show our children the value of sticking to your core beliefs."

In contrast to their estrangement from Ernie, and their cordial relationships with George, Allison, and Greg's sister, Marla, Tierney and Greg continued to enjoy close ties with Tierney's mother and sister, and Greg's parents.

After the move to Virginia, Joan had filled her home with pictures of Naia, and later Cole, to ease her longing for them. "She is the star of my life. Having them here was a grace and a blessing for me," Joan said. Joan had never doubted that Tierney should continue the pregnancy, and everything that had happened since then only strengthened her belief.

"No one is without a gift. When you find it, that's where you belong. Naia will find hers, and she will give back to others. There's no question in my mind that anyone who touches her life will be blessed. There's nothing sad about Naia. The sad part of life is people who don't find their gift."

She knew about the tensions that separated her ex-husband from Tierney and her family, and she saw them as Ernie's loss. "It's sad to think about anyone who would turn their back on Naia," Joan said. "They're missing something. There's a wonderful beauty inside her that they're missing."

Tara, meanwhile, began building a family of her own. Not long after Naia's third birthday, she married an environmental engineer named Gary D'Oria, and together they began thinking about having children. When she looked back on Tierney and Greg's decision, and ahead to one she might someday face, Tara's evolution became clear.

"It's certainly possible that I would make a different decision from

Tierney, but now more than ever, I might feel less inclined to make that decision," she said. "Knowing Naia, I feel more secure with the issues, and I also feel more secure about my ability—and our ability as a couple—to handle those issues."

"I got a sense early on that Tierney and Greg's lives were going to be richer, that they were going to be rewarded. I think their courage said something important about them as people," Tara continued. "I realized that what they did can make the difference between an ordinary life and an extraordinary life."

Bob and Mary were the biggest beneficiaries of Tierney and Greg's move to Virginia. Bob regularly drove to Charlottesville to help with childcare and household chores—neighbors got used to the sight of him mowing Greg and Tierney's lawn. Mary, meanwhile, would take charge of Naia, Cole, or sometimes both when Greg or Tierney traveled for work, or even for weekend getaways to celebrate their anniversary or attend a conference. Bob and Mary often came together on weekends, for family dinners. Greg's parents also adopted Onyx the poodle when it became clear that the care and feeding of Naia and Cole meant the little dog wouldn't get the attention she craved.

When Bob visited Naia at the daycare center, he took note of how she fit so well with her nondisabled peers—a bit slower, a bit less agile, but not much. "I think Naia is going to be able to integrate and be part of the mainstream throughout her life," he said with grandfatherly pride. "She'll always require some additional assistance, but I think she'll be fine. She has a tremendous amount of potential. Who knows, she may go on to college and be just like most children."

Bob and Mary even took a sign language class to better understand Naia, and the results were apparent almost immediately. On a visit to their house, Naia said a word Mary couldn't make out. But at the same time, Naia made the sign for "cat." Mary recognized it and said the word out loud. The excitement of being understood swept across Naia's face.

"One of the reasons people say they don't want a handicapped child is that it's an awesome responsibility," Mary said. "If I'm going to take the position that I don't believe in abortion, then I should be a real asset, to say, 'I'm here to help you after this child is born.'"

Though generally optimistic, Mary worried about Naia's hard-to-understand speech and her social challenges. Mary told a story about playing with Cole one day. When Naia noticed, she tried to grab the spotlight. "She said, 'Look at Yaya!' and, 'See Yaya!'" Mary recalled. "I think about how that will be in the future. Girls she plays with now are going to move on. She might not feel like she's going forward, and she'll still want them to 'See Yaya.'"

Yet Mary remained upbeat. "That's where family comes in," she said. "That's your surety in life. Your family is always there for you, and so it will be for Naia."

# CHAPTER 25 "I THINK WE SHOULD TALK ABOUT IT MORE"

One fall night in a Boston restaurant, three people fell into a remarkable discussion about prenatal testing, abortion, and Down syndrome. The topics themselves weren't all that extraordinary. Abortion was always a hot subject, and the Human Genome Project and advances in prenatal diagnosis had recently been in the news. Plenty of people were wondering how those developments might affect them and their children.

What made the conversation remarkable was the unique, firsthand experience of the participants: a middle-aged couple and their adult daughter with Down syndrome, a young woman who defied nearly every stereotype about the condition.

She was Ashley Wolfe, the poised young woman who appeared in the Connecticut Down Syndrome Congress videotape that Tierney and Greg had watched three years earlier, when they were deciding whether to continue or abort. Tierney and Greg later met Ashley at a meeting of the Massachusetts Down Syndrome Congress, and they had been struck by her intelligence and poise.

At twenty-three, Ashley had a job at Harvard University and a budding career as an actress and motivational speaker. She was petite, barely five feet tall, with dark blond hair, blue eyes behind gold-rimmed glasses, and a soft, breathy voice. Her mother, Nancy Wolfe, was an acting coach who ran a summer arts program at Wesleyan University; her father, Stan Wolfe, was an oral and maxillofacial surgeon who was director of oral health for the Connecticut Department of Public Health.

In the four years since she appeared in the video, Ashley had become the first special education student in her high school's history to speak at graduation, a privilege granted in part because of the seven semesters she spent on the honor roll. Her speech brought down the house.

She also had acted opposite Farrah Fawcett in a television movie based on Bret Lott's book, *Jewel*. Fawcett played the title character and Ashley played Jewel's daughter, Brenda Kay. Ashley called Fawcett "amazing, extremely gracious, a cool, friendly person."

When Ashley first read the screenplay, however, she saw the word "mongoloid" and angrily threw her script across the room. She only agreed to continue after her mother explained that the story took place in the years before that word was deemed derogatory. Ashley's acting credits also included the role of a developmentally delayed girl whose boyfriend was accused of raping her, in an episode of the NBC television series *Third Watch*.

She was represented by a speakers' agency whose other clients included novelist Isabel Allende, basketball businessman Magic Johnson, civil rights legend Coretta Scott King, and Nobel Prize winner Derek Walcott. Ashley's speeches invariably began, "Hi. I'm Ashley Wolfe. I have Down syndrome and I have a wonderful life." Schooled in the tricks of public speech, she then went for a laugh line based on her appearance: "I'm twenty-three years old—I only look sixteen. . . . Lucky me!"

Her message in speeches, and life, was straightforward: "Never judge anybody, disability or not." She had an extra message for parents of children with Down syndrome, born of her own parents' approach: "Don't ever put limits on your child. And have hope."

After high school, Ashley had won admission to a two-year program at Lesley College in Cambridge, Massachusetts, for people with learning disabilities and special needs. She graduated with a certificate in business services.

On this night, Nancy and Stan had come to Boston from their home in Connecticut for one of their regular visits with Ashley. Before meeting Stan for dinner, Nancy and Ashley had attended a performance of Anton Chekhov's *Three Sisters,* a poignant play about hope, happiness, and despair. Ashley understood all those emotions, though the play was a bit difficult for her to follow.

Afterward, Ashley, Nancy, and Stan met at Bob the Chef's barbecue restaurant in Boston's South End. With a little prodding, they moved easily into conversation about the abortion decisions that sometimes follow prenatal testing. Stan and Nancy had never faced such a choice—Nancy was twenty-seven when Ashley was born, and she hadn't undergone amnio.

"If I had known that I was pregnant with a baby with Down syndrome," Nancy said, "I don't know what I would have done."

"But you would have made the right choice," Ashley insisted.

"There's every possibility," Stan said, "that we would have elected to have an abortion."

"But," said Nancy, gesturing toward Ashley, "look what we would have missed."

"Ha!" said Ashley.

"I tell you though, Ash," Nancy said, "having you makes me know I would never judge anyone who makes that choice, either way."

"I think it's a personal choice," Ashley said. "There's always the option of abortion. But for me, I don't see the point in that. You're ending a life. That is the fear, the insecurity of a person taking over. There are obstacles in life and you get through it."

"And yet," Stan said, "so many people with Down syndrome are so much more retarded than you."

"I understand that," Ashley said. "But I think that's making a judgment, putting a label on it, and I don't like that. . . . Everyone has potential. It's recognizing that. You can be severely handicapped, retarded, but you still have potential. You still have a future."

"Are you making the case that parents should not choose abortion?" Stan asked. "I wouldn't want to get into that."

Ashley thought about it a moment. "I wouldn't know what it feels like to be in that position," she said finally.

"I hope you never are," Nancy whispered.

The meal arrived, and the conversation moved on. Most people with Down syndrome could never participate so fully or articulately in such an abstract conversation; indeed, many twenty-three-year-old women likely couldn't do so with their parents, regardless of whether they had developmental delays. That was one of the reasons Ashley Wolfe was a role model for Tierney and Greg as they imagined their fondest wishes for Naia's future independence, intellectual engagement, and overall achievement.

"Until somebody tells me that Naia is not going to be like Ashley Wolfe, why wouldn't I continue to strive to give her absolutely everything to try to achieve that?" Tierney once said. "And if not, when and if I have to face that she will not be like Ashley, she deserves everything she can have to succeed, to be as independent as she can be, and to be as much a productive part of society as she can be."

On a typical day, Ashley would wake at 7:15 A.M., make herself breakfast of cereal or eggs, and dress in clothes she had picked out the night before, perhaps a flowered dress with a stylish white jacket, accented by pearl earrings. She'd pack herself a water bottle and a snack, and then leave her apartment to catch the Number 86 bus to Harvard Square.

She'd hop off the bus shortly before 9 A.M. and walk from the stop to her office, a nondescript second-floor room with bright, cream-colored walls, industrial gray carpet, and huge skylights. She'd spend the next four hours organizing batches of resumes and cover letters sent to the Harvard employment office by people seeking nonacademic jobs at the university. After Ashley logged them in and placed them in the proper order, another worker would scan them into a computer database. The previous year, the employment office received twenty-six thousand resumes, so the paperwork never stopped.

"Ashley is terrific to work with. She's extremely detail-oriented, which is exactly what's called for in this job," said Laura McNamara, her supervisor. McNamara also played the role of "second mom," in Ashley's words, bringing her home for dinner and generally watching out for her.

Ashley worked at Harvard about twelve hours a week—three days, four hours at a stretch—at about ten dollars an hour, without benefits. George White, manager of the employment office, was helping her look for other jobs at Harvard with more hours and health coverage. He had helped her set up informational interviews at the library and at the university's health services center. But Ashley was competing against people who had no developmental delays, and no job offers had surfaced.

"Most of the jobs here are pretty competitive, and some are frankly too advanced for Ashley," White said. "Harvard does make an outreach to the disabled community, but it also can be a very demanding place." Nevertheless, he remained optimistic that Ashley could find another job at Harvard, and he vowed to continue helping her.

In the meantime, Ashley also worked about fourteen hours a week during afternoons and evenings at a branch of the Somerville Public Library. She shelved books and helped at the front desk. The job also gave her the opportunity to indulge her interest in reading. She had recently checked out *Shackleton's Incredible Voyage,* by Alfred Lansing, about polar explorer Ernest Shackleton's survival for more than a year on ice-bound Antarctic seas.

"It took me a little bit to get into it, because it's different from what I usually read. But I liked it," Ashley said. "I'm more into books, for instance, like *Harry Potter*. I love that. I'm up to the third one in the series. It's a very good reading level for me. It's kind of like a novel, but it also has little illustrations that go along with each chapter, and that helps me because I need a visual. That way, when I'm reading the chapter I can draw pictures in my mind of what's happening."

After working at the library, Ashley might catch another bus back to Harvard Square to take an adult education class in jazz dance. Other nights she might go to a Bally's Fitness Club, where she worked out with free weights and exercise machines. "My goal is to strengthen and tone," she said. "Bally's does have a really nice lap pool, too, and I need to get back into that." Careful not to seem a braggart, she didn't mention that she had been a Special Olympics gold medalist in swimming.

After work, class, or a workout, Ashley would head home on the Number 87 bus, perhaps stopping first to pick up groceries. She'd settle into her apartment, which she shared with two other young women with developmental disabilities who also graduated from the Lesley College program. Ashley would neatly hang up her work clothes, freshen up, then get into something comfortable to cook dinner. She liked making stir-fried meals, tossing in turkey or chicken with the vegetables. Other nights she'd make pasta or homemade pizza.

"After dinner, I get ready for work the next day. Maybe do some housecleaning. And I would have dessert before going to bed. I don't watch a lot of TV, but I do have some favorites. I love *Buffy the Vampire Slayer*. I watch the show *Charmed*. I also like *Seventh Heaven* and *Angel*. Those are my main shows. But if I see the preview of the next show, I'll judge if the episode is worth seeing or a waste of time. And then, if it's a waste, I don't watch."

Twice a month, Ashley received a visit from Diane Wilcox, an adviser from the Lesley College program, whom Ashley's parents paid to continue working with her. Wilcox made sure she was balancing her checkbook, planning her meals, and handling any social issues that arose. "She is the best-case scenario of a kid with Down syndrome living independently," Wilcox said. Ashley's greatest need, Wilcox said, was help with money management. "She sometimes has written checks when she hasn't got the money to cover them. But that's something we're working on." Ashley also has difficulty with directions; she is unable to drive a car.

Though she had two roommates, Ashley spent little time with

them. "We get along OK," she explained. "We hardly fight. We have our own routines. We don't get into each other's faces. But that's it. On the down side, we have no relationship, no bond whatsoever."

Indeed, the social side of Ashley's life remained a source of pain. She often felt left out, struggling to connect. It wasn't the sting of overt discrimination, but the ache of loneliness. It was hard for her to find friends she could relate to. Most people with Down syndrome were unable to keep up with her, and Ashley couldn't quite manage a complete relationship with peers who weren't developmentally disabled. It wasn't so much that she was excluded from a social life; she just wasn't invited to join one.

"Down syndrome is only one part of me. There's so much more," she said. "People don't take the time to find out."

"We've always said Ashley lives in a gray area," her mother said. "She has Down syndrome, but she's smart enough to hurt about what happens to her. Sometimes she doesn't get the subtleties of social interaction. She's an incredibly social creature, but sometimes she would just withdraw rather than engage and feel comfortable."

Ashley was Stan and Nancy's second daughter. Ashley's big sister, Rebecca, two-and-a-half years her senior, graduated magna cum laude from Harvard. While there, Rebecca Wolfe wrote a story about Ashley for a student magazine. "I'd spent my elementary years terrified that someone would make fun of me for Ashley. I hated myself for feeling even a little ashamed of her, and dared them to try it," Rebecca wrote. "I will always have conflicting and confusing emotions of love, admiration, frustration, and sadness for her."

Rebecca also organized a book of photographs of Ashley, and helped Ashley write captions for the photos. One showed Ashley snuggled in Rebecca's lap, listening as her big sister read her a book. Under one photo, Ashley wrote: "I know I am different from other people because I have Down syndrome and it's OK to be different." On the last page, she wrote: "I talked a lot about how painful it is that I do have Down syndrome and all of the obsticles [sic]. I try not to let them take over me. I just can't."

Rebecca dedicated the book to Ashley, calling her by her pet name: "For Shley-shley, who has the courage to wake up every single day with the knowledge of the constant challenges and frustrations she will have to face. And who still gets out of bed."

Six years after they collaborated on the book, Ashley and Rebecca felt their relationship had matured and improved. They had grown closer during a period when they lived in nearby apartments after Rebecca graduated from Harvard and Ashley completed the Lesley College program. "We had every Sunday together to go to yoga or brunch or both," said Rebecca, who had since moved to California to pursue a Ph.D. in education policy at Stanford University. "We were able to enjoy each other on closer to a peer level. It was a lot more fun and a lot less work than our relationship had been in the past."

And yet, when she looked toward raising a family of her own, Rebecca was unsure whether she would continue a pregnancy knowing her child would have Down syndrome. "It's very difficult for me to say out loud, but I think I would have the abortion rather than face wanting to have a child who was as exceptional as Ashley but knowing in my heart she probably would not be," Rebecca said. "Part of the reason it's hard to say out loud is, to some extent, I would want to be the kind of person who would have that child, regardless."

"I don't think that negates the love I have for Ashley or who she is as a person," Rebecca added. "It's about choices."


Over dinner with her parents, Ashley talked about a romantic relationship that had gone sour and about her own dreams for the future. "I did have a boyfriend-girlfriend relationship. We were college sweethearts, but I broke up with him for good reasons," Ashley said. "It wasn't completely his fault. His disability was very physical. His speech and his thoughts weren't all there. But he did hurt me, enough that I had to break it off with him."

"So, you sucked him dry and threw him out," joked Stan Wolfe.

"Dad!" Ashley laughed.

It was less a kidding matter to her mother. "I wonder, is she cutting off a relationship that has some good potential?" Nancy Wolfe said. In an earlier conversation, Ashley had said she was confused about another young man. "Now it sounds like you've made a decision about him, too," Nancy said.

"Oh Ma, I'm still confused," Ashley said with mock exasperation. Ashley said she dreamed of marriage, and perhaps children, though she knew she wasn't ready for either.

In fact, many women with Down syndrome are believed to be capable of bearing children; by contrast, most men with Down syndrome are believed to be sterile. Complicating matters of reproduction, a child whose parent has Down syndrome has a much higher chance of inheriting the extra chromosome. In one study of twenty-six pregnant women with Down syndrome, ten delivered babies with Down syndrome, ten delivered healthy babies without Down syndrome, two aborted, one had a stillbirth, and the others had babies with various physical and mental problems. For many years, people with Down syndrome were subject to involuntary sterilization, under the same principle that had been applied to Carrie Buck in 1927, but by the end of the twentieth century that practice was almost entirely replaced by specially designed programs in sexual education.

For Ashley, the issue remained academic. "I'm still new to the whole dating thing. I'm too young now," she said. A few weeks later, though, Ashley told her mother she had begun dating not one, but two new suitors.

Her adviser, Diane Wilcox, was optimistic in the long run: "There's no reason to think she couldn't find a nice guy, end up married, and have a family of her own. That's sort of in the hands of the fates, just like my own life or anyone else's."

Another continuing challenge for Ashley was her health. As a girl, she underwent several surgeries for dislocated hips and spent the better part of two years in casts that extended from her waist to her toes. More recently, she was diagnosed with fibromyalgia, a painful muscle condition that sapped her strength. She also suffered from gastrointestinal problems. "Between the two of them, the fibromyalgia and the gastrointestinal, I'm dealing with an extreme amount of pain," Ashley said. "It drains me. I can't really deal with anything. I get extremely tired. I have my good days and bad days."

Sometimes, Ashley's energy flagged in the middle of a sentence. Her speech slurred, her shoulders slumped, and it seemed all she could do to keep from putting her head down on the table to rest. But she pushed forward.

She kept trying to make new friends, attending a social group for people with developmental disabilities. Like many young women her age, she tried to convince her parents to "back away, respect my space." She hoped for more hours and responsibilities at the Harvard employment center, or maybe a new and better job. She kept looking for acting jobs and eagerly awaited calls from her agent for speaking engagements.

"In my life now, I'm between feeling happy and content, and sad and concerned," Ashley said, sounding like many twenty-three-year-old women without Down syndrome. "I don't give myself enough credit. I don't give myself a break. I've gotten better at recognizing that I need help. The next step is asking for help. That's where I am right now."

Twenty years separated Ashley and Naia. To help Naia reach Ashley's level, or at least fulfill her potential, Tierney and Greg would need to challenge and protect her, struggle with and for her, love and comfort her. They would need to keep abreast of new treatments and new laws affecting the disabled. They would need to juggle work and home, friends and extended families, therapy sessions and team meetings, without overlooking Cole or each other.

Tierney would need to spend nights working with Emily Dreyfus on the Special Education Advisory Committee. Greg would need to attend meetings of the National Down Syndrome Congress, which had invited him onto its board of directors and made him its treasurer.

"This is the way we live. If it wasn't this, it might be something else," Tierney said. "This is our life. This is our family." They had struck that deal by choosing Naia.

One night a few weeks before Naia's third birthday, Greg brought Naia and Cole home from the daycare center. He plunked Cole down on a carpeted area next to the kitchen. Naia toddled around the living room holding her favorite doll, a modern-day Raggedy Ann called a Groovy Girl, with caramel skin and a funky wardrobe.

On one of her room-to-room circuits, Naia noticed her baby brother. "Hi, Cole!" she called out with a Scarlett O'Hara accent. He looked at her and burst into a two-tooth smile. When she walked away he grew sad, so she turned back. "Don't cry, Cole," she said—"Don' cra', Coe'"—and came over to pat him on the head. Later she would help feed him dinner, a messy affair that Cole and Naia both loved.

Tierney came home from work and Naia yelled, "Mommy!" Before Tierney had even put down her bag, she began negotiating with Naia over dinner.

"Cookie, Mommy!" Naia said.

"No way, big girl. No cookies here."

"Chicken. French fries," Naia countered.

"OK," Tierney said. "With corn or broccoli?"

"Broccoli."

While waiting for dinner, Naia watched a *Sesame Street* alphabet video, dancing and singing along with songs about letters. Tierney called from the kitchen: "What's after 'H'?"

"I!" Naia yelled.

"What's after 'O'?"

"P!"

Back to the video: "J, Joe, jeans, and jellybeans, let's sing a song about 'J!'"

After dinner it was upstairs for bath time. Next, Tierney read books to Naia and Cole. Then it was time for bed.

Greg came upstairs and said goodnight to his son, then his daughter.

"Night, Daddy," Naia said.

"Good night, big girl," Greg answered.

Tierney swept Naia up over the rail into her crib. But Naia wasn't quite ready to sleep.

"Pray," Naia said.

"You want to say your prayers, Naia?" asked Tierney.

"Yes."

Naia stood inside her crib, her palms pressed together in the steeple of prayer.

"OK," Tierney said, "who are we going to pray for?"

"Mommy!" Naia said.

"OK, Naia. God bless . . ." "Bless Mommy."

"Who else?"

"Daddy!"

"Who else?"

"Tissues."

"Tissues, Naia?"

"Yes."

"OK, tissues. Who else?"

"Naia . . . Cole . . . Ma-Ma . . . Paw-Paw . . . Baby Bop."

"Baby Bop? From *Barney*? OK, Baby Bop. Who else?"

"Ice cream."

"No, not ice cream. We're praying for all the people."

"Bennie . . . Donna . . . Pammie."

"Everybody from school?"

"Yes."

"OK, say it with me, Naia: Keep them safe and healthy."

"Healthy," Naia said.

"Say Amen."

"Amen, Mommy."

"Mommy loves you."

"Kisses, Mommy!"

Tierney leaned in for her goodnight kiss. She turned out the light and tiptoed from the room.

Her day complete, Naia lay down and went gently to sleep.


That same month, an expectant young couple walked into genetic counselor Alicia Craffey's office at the University of Connecticut Health Center. They had come seeking guidance.

They were both thirty-five and they already had a lifetime of history together. They dated in high school, but that ended when she broke up with him. A year after their breakup, he told her he was moving out West. To her surprise, she was devastated. But she didn't try to stop him. Three years passed and he returned to the small Connecticut town where they had both grown up and where she still lived with her parents.

One morning at 5 A.M., he stood, uninvited, at the foot of her bed, covered with dirt and grease. His car had broken down nearby and he had walked to her house. It was too early to ring the bell, so he had climbed through her window.

She woke up, startled, but she calmed when she realized it was him. She recognized him even before she could make out his features in the darkness. She knew by the smell, a good smell, one she had tucked away and remembered.

"Hi," he said. "I'm starving."

She took him downstairs to the kitchen. Her mother was so happy to see them together she didn't ask any questions. She just cooked him breakfast.

When they came into Craffey's office, they had been married for seven years. She was pretty, petite, with dirty blond hair and sparkling green eyes—a thoughtful, contemplative, well-spoken woman. He was nearly six feet tall with jet-black hair and warm brown eyes, a sweet smile, and a good sense of humor. They had bought an old farm, and she was working full-time getting it into shape to board horses. He was a salesman during the day and spent his off-hours helping to fix up the farm.

Craffey had counseled enough couples to know they were deeply in love. They had an easy banter between them and a mutual respect. They told her they were ready to add children to their lives, and this was her first pregnancy. She was eighteen weeks along.

After overcoming the fear of miscarriage, she had undergone a routine amnio because of her age. The results had come back the day before: the fetus she carried had forty-seven chromosomes in each cell, the signature of Down syndrome.

When their shock and denial faded, they focused on whether their child's mental retardation would be mild, moderate, or severe. Craffey gave her standard explanation that no one could know in advance, but most children with Down syndrome were in the mild to moderate range. They talked about abortion. They talked about keeping the baby. They talked about adoption. Craffey answered their questions. She consoled them.

They told her they didn't know how they would tell their families, no matter what they decided. Sad and confused, they ran out of things to say. They sat in Craffey's office, waiting for the other to speak.

Breaking the silence, Craffey asked, "What do you think?"

"Well," the man said finally. "I think I know what we should do."

"I'm not sure," his wife answered. "I think we should talk about it more."

## PUBLISHER'S NOTE ON PHOTOGRAPHS
## AND E-MAIL

A gallery of photographs of the Fairchild family is available for viewing on-line at www.beacon.org/naia. E-mail may be sent to the author at choosingnaia-@yahoo.com. Letters may be sent to the author in care of Beacon Press, 25 Beacon Street, Boston, Mass., 02108-2892.

# APPENDIX: DOWN SYNDROME, BIRTH DEFECTS, AND PRENATAL TESTING RESOURCES

National Down Syndrome Congress
7000 Peachtree-Dunwoody Road, N.E.
Lake Ridge 400 Office Park Building #5, Suite 100
Atlanta, Ga. 30328-1655
770-604-9500; 800-232-NDSC
www.ndsccenter.org

National Down Syndrome Society
666 Broadway
New York, N.Y. 10012
212-460-9330; 800-221-4602
www.ndss.org

Down Syndrome Health Issues
(Web site maintained by Dr. Len Leshin)
www.ds-health.com

National Association for Down Syndrome (NADS)
P.O. Box 4542
Oak Brook, Ill. 60522-4542
630-325-9112
www.nads.org

American Association on Mental Retardation
444 N. Capitol Street, N.W., Suite 846
Washington, D.C. 20001-1512
202-387-1968; 800-424-3688
www.aamr.org

The Arc of the United States
(a nonprofit group that helps people with mental retardation and similar developmental disabilities and their families)
1010 Wayne Avenue, Suite 650
Silver Spring, Md. 20910
301-565-3842
www.thearc.org

A Heartbreaking Choice
(a Web site for "parents who have interrupted their pregnancies after poor prenatal diagnosis and for the professionals who provide their care")
www.aheartbreakingchoice.com

National Society of Genetic Counselors
(a Web site providing information about genetic counseling and help finding
genetic counselors)
www.ngsc.org

Your Genes, Your Choices: Exploring the Issues Raised by Genetic Research
(a description of the Human Genome Project, the science behind it, and the
ethical, legal, and social issues that are raised by the project)
Written by Catherine Baker, part of the Science + Literacy for Health project of
the American Association for the Advancement of Science (AAAS) and funded
by the U.S. Department of Energy
ehrweb.aaas.org/ehr/books/index.html

Understanding Gene Testing
U.S. Department of Health and Human Services
Public Health Service, National Institutes of Health, National Cancer Institute
www.accessexcellence.org/AE/AEPC/NIH/index.html

March of Dimes Birth Defects Foundation
1275 Mamaroneck Avenue
White Plains, N.Y. 10605
888-MODIMES (663-4637)
www.modimes.org

# AUTHOR'S NOTE

I first spoke with Greg and Tierney in mid-August 1998, when their decision to continue Tierney's pregnancy was just days old. I was led to them by Alicia Craffey, their genetic counselor, who had seen a memo I posted on an Internet listserv for genetic counselors. The memo described my interest in finding a couple whose experiences I could document to reveal the human side of the prenatal information explosion.

Because it was impossible for me to be present at every scene described in this book, particularly during the period surrounding the initial diagnosis, I reconstructed events by relying on Greg and Tierney's remarkable memories, supplemented by the more than two thousand pages of Naia's medical and developmental records. I also conducted dozens of interviews with people involved in Naia's life and care. Those interviews took place as close in time to the actual events as practicable. The accounts of different participants rarely conflicted except in minor respects. None of those conflicts affected the story in a material way. All thoughts and feelings described in the narrative are based on the individuals' own recollections of what they were thinking or feeling.

To supplement my interviews, I drove the routes Greg and Tierney traveled, read certain books they read, watched videos they viewed, and visited places they did, at one point even lying down on the examination table in Ultrasound Room 1 at Saint Francis Hospital. I confess I drew the line at putting my feet up in the obstetrical stirrups.

It is a legitimate concern that the subjects of a book like this will alter or shade their behavior in the presence of a writer, or in their retelling of events at which the writer wasn't present. I believe the effects were mitigated in this case by several factors, among them Greg and Tierney's demonstrated commitment to truth telling; their willingness to reveal unflattering information about themselves; and the consistency with which their versions and interpretations of events matched those of others.

No names have been changed, and no events were staged for my benefit or for the benefit of photographs displayed at www.beacon.org/naia. I did not alter, compress, or otherwise manipulate events for the sake of the narrative. This isn't an hour-by-hour log of the Fairchilds' lives, and the omissions fall into two general categories: events that lacked relevance, and information I simply didn't possess. Though my interviews with Greg and Tierney formed the heart and soul of this book, any errors of commission or omission are mine alone.

Also for the record: Tierney's father, Ernie Temple, never consented to an interview, despite repeated requests. In a telephone conversation following publication of a *Boston Globe* series that served as the outline for this book, he acknowledged the accuracy of the quotes I had ascribed to him based on Tierney and Greg's recollections. I have tried to be as fair with him as I have with everyone else in this book.

On terminology: When the archaic and ill-founded terms "mongolism" and

"Mongolian idiocy" were banished from intelligent conversation, the common name of the condition became Down's Syndrome. That, in turn, evolved to Down syndrome. Trisomy 21 is the most accurate name of all, but it's struggling for popular acceptance, and I chose to use it primarily when dealing with the scientific nature of the condition. In most references to Naia's mental disabilities, I used the terms "mental retardation" and "mentally retarded," as opposed to the up-and-coming "developmentally disabled." I did so because I found no strong evidence that the term "mentally retarded" was on its face pejorative.

This book uses the sometimes awkward method of describing individuals with Naia's condition as "a child (or boy, girl, man, woman, etc.) with Down syndrome." That's the form favored by advocates for people with the condition, and it contrasts with the shorter and more colloquial "a Down (or Down's) child." Some might view this as political correctness, but "Down's child" puts the condition before the person, which seems backward to me. For similar reasons, I eschewed the word "normal" to describe the absence of Down syndrome.

Also, I didn't write that Naia is a "victim" of Down syndrome, is "afflicted" with it, or "suffers" from it. To call Naia a victim would be to suggest that she had been wronged by her parents when they continued the pregnancy. As for affliction and suffering, the physical disorders linked to the extra chromosome can indeed cause pain, and so can the necessary treatments for them. But there is nothing inherently painful about Down syndrome. Some advocates go to the opposite extreme, describing people as "blessed with" Down syndrome. I wouldn't go that far, but I understand what drives their rhetorical ardor. Consider the difference: "Down's sufferer Judith Scott, who is an artist" versus "Artist Judith Scott, who has Down syndrome."

Finally, the words "baby" or "unborn child" are occasionally used when embryo or fetus would be more scientifically accurate. This is not a political statement about the point at which life begins. Rather, it reflects the language used by Tierney and Greg (and Kim and Dino Bento, for that matter), as well as many of their family members, friends, doctors, nurses, and other health care providers.

# SOURCES

## CHAPTER 1 "DON'T WORRY, MOM, EVERYTHING WILL BE FINE"

R. Boostanfar and J. K. Jain, "Pregnancy Outcome and Clomiphene Citrate (Clomid) Dose," *Fertility and Sterility* 75 (April 2001) (4 supp. 1): S10.

David S. Newberger, "Down Syndrome: Prenatal Risk Assessment and Diagnosis," *American Family Physician* (August 15, 2000): 825–32.

National Center for Health Statistics, "Advance Report of Maternal and Infant Health Data from the Birth Certificate, 1991," *Monthly Vital Statistics Report* 42, no. 11 (1994 suppl.): 1–32.

Siegfried M. Pueschel, ed., *A Parent's Guide to Down Syndrome: Toward a Brighter Future*, 2nd ed. (Baltimore, Md.: Paul H. Brookes), particularly the discussion of triple screen on pages 29–39.

James F. X. Egan et al., "Efficacy of Screening for Fetal Down Syndrome in the United States from 1974 to 1997," *Obstetrics and Gynecology* 96, no. 6 (December 2000): 979–85.

Spina Bifida Association of America, "Facts about Spina Bifida," available on-line at www.sbaa.org.


## CHAPTER 2 "IF YOU ARE GOING TO CRY, YOU CRY LATER. IT BLINDS YOUR EYES"

Joseph Woo, "History of the Developments of Ultrasound in Obstetrics and Gynecology," available on-line at www.ob-ultrasound.net/history.html. Also, Joseph Woo, "Ultrasound Measurements for Down Syndrome," available on-line at www.ob-ultrasound.net/xdown.html.

Margaret B. McNay and John E. E. Fleming, "Forty Years of Obstetric Ultrasound," *Ultrasound in Medicine and Biology* 25 (1999): 3–56.

Angela Scioscia, Kenneth Lyons, and William I. Cohen, "Responding to Parental Concerns after a Prenatal Diagnosis of Trisomy 21," *Pediatrics* (April 1, 2001): 878–82.

E. B. Hook, "Chromosome Abnormalities and Spontaneous Fetal Death Following Amniocentesis: Further Data and Associations with Maternal Age," *American Journal of Human Genetics* 35 (1983): 110–16.

N. French et al., "Evaluation of the Health Belief Model and Decision-Making Regarding Amniocentesis in Women of Advanced Maternal Age," *Health Education Quarterly* 19 (1992): 177–86.

Frank Newport, David W. Moore, and Lydia Saad, "Long-Term Gallup Poll Trends: A Portrait of American Public Opinion through the Century," released by Gallup News Service, December 20, 1999, particularly the data on abortion rights percentages.

C. Mansfield, S. Hopfer, and T. M. Marteau, "Termination Rates after Prenatal Diagnosis of Down Syndrome, Spina Bifida, Anencephaly, and Turner and Klinefelter Syndromes: A Systematic Literature Review," *Prenatal Diagnosis* 19 (1999): 808–12, especially the information on decision-making after the diagnosis of a fetal abnormality.

## CHAPTER 3 "I'M JUST SO SICK OF HAVING TO DEAL WITH DISCRIMINATION"

Matt. 26:31–56.

J. Langdon H. Down, "Observations on an Ethnic Classification of Idiots," *London Hospital, Clinical Lectures and Reports,* no. 3 (1886): 259–62.

Stephen Jay Gould, *The Panda's Thumb: More Reflections in Natural History* (New York: W. W. Norton, 1980), 160–68.

Karen Stray-Gunderson, ed., *Babies with Down Syndrome: A New Parents' Guide* (Bethesda, Md.: Woodbine House, 1995).

C. P. Torfs and R. E. Christianson, "Anomalies in Down Syndrome Individuals in a Large Population-Based Registry," *American Journal of Medical Genetics* 77, no. 5 (June 1998): 431–38.

J. M. Friedman, "Racial Disparities in Median Age at Death of Persons with Down Syndrome—United States, 1968–1997," *Morbidity and Mortality Weekly Report,* U.S. Centers for Disease Control, June 8, 2001, 463–65.

John O'Neill, "Down Syndrome Life Spans Lengthen," *New York Times,* July 31, 2001, 6.

Mary Louise Buyse, ed., *Birth Defects Encyclopedia: The Comprehensive, Systematic, Illustrated Reference Source for the Diagnosis, Delineation, Etiology, Biodynamics, Occurrence, Prevention, and Treatment of Human Anomalies of Clinical Relevance,* 2 vols. (Oxford: Blackwell, 1990), 1: 841–43.

Molly A. Minnick, Kathleen J. Delp, and Mary C. Ciotti, *A Time to Decide, a Time to Heal: For Parents Making Difficult Decisions about Babies They Love,* 4th ed. (St. Johns, Minn.: Pineapple Press, 1996).

## CHAPTER 4 "THE MIRACLE YOU PRAY FOR MIGHT NOT BE THE MIRACLE YOU RECEIVE"

E. F. Fugger et al., "Births of Normal Daughters after Microsort Sperm Separation and Intrauterine Insemination, In-Vitro Fertilization, or Intracytoplasmic Sperm Injection," *Human Reproduction* 13, no. 9 (September 1998): 2,367–70.

Anne F. Thurston, "In a Chinese Orphanage," *Atlantic Monthly,* April 1996, 28–41.

K. Johnson, H. Banghan, and L. Wang, "Infant Abandonment and Adoption in China," *Population and Development Review* 24, no. 3 (1996): 469–510.

Sarah Lawrence College, Human Genetics Program, program of study publication.

## CHAPTER 5 "I'M REALLY SORRY TO HAVE TO TELL YOU THIS"

Lawrence Otis Graham, *Our Kind of People: Inside America's Black Upper Class* (New York: HarperCollins, 1999).

Robert C. Hayden and Karen E. Hayden, *African-Americans on Martha's Vineyard and Nantucket* (Boston: Select Publications, 1999).

## CHAPTER 6 "WHAT DO PEOPLE USUALLY DO?"

James J. Nortra, "Heart, Endocardial Cushion Defects," in *Birth Defects Encyclopedia: The Comprehensive, Systematic, Illustrated Reference Source for the Diagnosis, Delineation, Etiology, Biodynamics, Occurrence, Prevention, and Treatment of Human Anomalies of Clinical Relevance*, 2 vols., ed. Mary Louise Buyse (Oxford: Blackwell, 1990), 1: 841–43.

V. Alexi-Meskishvili et al., "Correction of Complete Atrioventricular Septal Defects with the Double-Patch Technique and Cleft Closure," *Annals of Thoracic Surgery* 62, no. 2 (August 1996): 519–25, discussion on 524–25.

G. Rizzoli et al., "Does Down Syndrome Affect Prognosis of Surgically Managed Atrioventricular Canal Defects?" *Journal of Thoracic and Cardiovascular Surgery* 104, no. 4 (October 1992): 945–53.

"Life with Down Syndrome," prod. and dir. Frank Barton, University of Connecticut Health Center Video Department, for the Connecticut Down Syndrome Congress, videotape, 1997.

## CHAPTER 7 "THIS CHILD WILL CAUSE TRAUMA AND TRAGEDY FROM THE FIRST BREATH"

Sam Howe Verhovek, "Tulsa to Observe Race Riot's Seventy-Fifth Anniversary after Long Cover-Up," *New York Times,* May 31, 1996, 12.

"Profile: Tulsa to Memorialize Losses of Black Community in Race Riot of 1921," transcript of National Public Radio story by reporter Wade Goodwyn, May 31, 1996, taken from "Weekly Edition, Best of NPR News," broadcast February 12, 2000.

*Loving v. Virginia,* 388 U.S. 1 (1967).

Paul J. Benke et al., "Risk and Recurrence of Down Syndrome," University of Miami School of Medicine, Miami, Fl., October 1995.

Siegfried M. Pueschel, ed., *A Parent's Guide to Down Syndrome: Toward a Brighter Future,* 2nd ed. (Baltimore, Md.: Paul H. Brookes), 24–26.

Karen Stray-Gunderson, ed., *Babies with Down Syndrome: A New Parents' Guide* (Bethesda, Md.: Woodbine House, 1995), 10–29.


## CHAPTER 8 "SO, YOU'RE JUST GOING TO GO WITH THE ABORTIONIST?"

B. J. Baty, B. L. Blackburn, and J. C. Carey, "Natural History of Trisomy 18 and Trisomy 13:I Growth, Physical Assessment, Medical Histories, Survival, and Recurrence Risk," *American Journal of Medical Genetics* 49 (1994): 175–88.

H. Goldstein and I. C. G. Nielsen, "Rates and Survival in Individuals with Trisomy 13 and 18," *Clinical Genetics* 34 (1988): 366–72.


## CHAPTER 9 "NO PROBLEM"

I spoke with Janet Marchese on several occasions, the most important of which was a 1999 interview to confirm Greg's account of their telephone call, which she did. I tried repeatedly to interview her further about her own experiences and past, but by then she had shut down the exchange and we never connected for a full interview. As a result, I relied on our earlier conversations and several published sources for accounts and quotes about her life and her involvement with adoptions of children with Down syndrome.

Lynn Ames, "Down Syndrome Proves No Match for Volunteers," *New York Times,* October 26, 1997, WP2.

Mary McGrory, "Finding Joy in Parenting 'Imperfect' Children," *Raleigh News & Observer,* February 4, 1991, A8.

Ray Weiss, "New Yorker Runs Nation's Best-Known Adoption Service for Down Syndrome Children," Gannett News Service, February 2, 1996.

Charmaine Crouse Yoest, "No Child Is Unadoptable," *Policy Review: The Journal of American Citizenship,* no. 81 (January-February 1997).

## CHAPTER 10 "THERE'S NOTHING TO BE SORRY ABOUT. I'M NOT SORRY"

J. Gordon Lambert, *Fetal Development,* Adam Medical Encyclopedia, U.S. National Library of Medicine, 8600 Rockville Pike, Bethesda, Md. 20894; available on-line at www.nlm.nih.gov/medlineplus/ency/article/002398.htm.

## CHAPTER 11 "I CAN'T REMEMBER THE LAST TIME THE BABY KICKED"

"Yale to Begin Clinical Trial for Test to Provide Earlier Detection of Down Syndrome," Yale University Press Release, December 7, 1999.

## CHAPTER 12 "WE DON'T HAVE MORE TIME"

Jane Eliot Sewell, *Caesarean Section—A Brief History,* for the American College of Obstetricians and Gynecologists in cooperation with the National Library of Medicine, (Bethesda, Md.: National Institutes of Health, Department of Health & Human Services, 1993).

Emily Martin, *The Woman in the Body: A Cultural Analysis of Reproduction* (Boston: Beacon Press, 1987).

Martin S. Pernick, *A Calculus of Suffering: Pain, Professionalism, and Anesthesia in Nineteenth-Century America* (New York: Columbia University Press, 1985).

Richard W. and Dorothy C. Wertz, *Lying-In: A History of Childbirth in America* (New Haven, Conn.: Yale University Press, 1989).

## CHAPTER 13 "HELLO, SWEET BABY. HELLO"

C. Everett Koop, *Koop: The Memoirs of America's Family Doctor* (New York: Random House, 1991).

Jason Morrow, "Making Mortal Decisions at the Beginning of Life: The Case of Impaired and Imperiled Infants," *Journal of the American Medical Association* 284 (2000): 1,146–47.

Martin S. Pernick, *The Black Stork: Eugenics and the Death of "Defective" Babies in American Medicine and Motion Pictures since 1915* (New York: Oxford University Press, 1996).

Steven Selden, *Inheriting Shame: The Story of Eugenics and Racism in America* (New York: Teachers College Press, 1999), citing M. Grant, *The Passing of the Great Race, or the Racial Basis of European History* (New York: Charles Scribners & Sons, 1921).

Laila Williamson, "Infanticide: An Anthropological Analysis," in *Infanticide and the Value of Life,* ed. Marvin Kohl (Buffalo, N.Y.: Prometheus Books, 1978), 61–75.

A. G. Campbell and R. S. Duff, "Deciding the Care of Severely Malformed or Dying Infants," *Journal of Medical Ethics* 5 (1979): 65–67.

Peter Singer, *Practical Ethics,* 2nd ed. (New York: Cambridge University Press, 1983), 185–88.

Transcript of debate between Peter Singer and Adrienne Asch, "Ethics, Health Care, and Disability," Princeton University, October 12, 1999.

Richard Brand, "Controversial Princeton Bioethicist Defends Views at Campus Debate," story moved on the Associated Press wire service, October 12, 1999.

Christopher Kliewer, "Issues Involved in Facilitated Communication and People with Down Syndrome," *Facilitated Communication Digest* 3, no. 1 (1994): 8–14.

## CHAPTER 14 "WE HAD TO GIVE HER THE CHANCE TO MAKE IT"

The letters of Jewel Lott were graciously provided by her grandson, the author Bret Lott.

Bret Lott, *Jewel* (New York: Pocket Books, 1999).

Marja Mills, "A Simple Index Card Keeps Life in Perspective for 'Jewel' Author," *Chicago Tribune,* April 6, 2000, D1.

Benjamin Spock, *The Pocket Book of Baby and Child Care* (New York: Pocket Books, 1946), 478.

Bernard Bard and Joseph Fletcher, "The Right to Die," *Atlantic Monthly,* April 1968, 59–64.

SOURCES

James W. Trent Jr., *Inventing the Feeble Mind: A History of Mental Retardation in the United States* (Berkeley: University of California Press, 1994).

Dorothy C. Wertz, "Families of Children with Mental Retardation and Developmental Disabilities: How Well Are They Doing?" *GeneLetter*, March 1, 1997, available on-line at www.geneletter.org/archives/mrndd.html.

John MacGregor, *Metamorphosis—The Fiber Art of Judith Scott: The Outsider Artist and the Experience of Down Syndrome* (Oakland, Calif.: Creative Growth Center, 1999).

Evelyn Nieves, "Artist Emerges with Works in a 'Private Language,'" *New York Times,* June 25, 2001, 10.

Michael O'Sullivan, "Wealth Beyond Measure," *Washington Post,* October 13, 2000, N59.


CHAPTER 15 "WHAT DO THE OTHER NINE PEOPLE KNOW THAT WE DON'T?"

American Academy of Pediatrics, Provisional Committee for Quality Improvement and Subcommittee on Hyperbilirubinemia, "Practice Parameter: Management of Hyperbilirubinemia in the Healthy Term Newborn," *Pediatrics* 94 (1994): 558–65.

T. B. Newman and M. J. Maisels, "Evaluation and Treatment of Jaundice in the Term Infant: A Kinder, Gentler Approach," *Pediatrics* 89 (1992): 809–18.

J. P. Spencer, "Practical Nutrition for the Healthy Term Infant," *American Family Physician* 54 (1996): 138–44.


CHAPTER 16 "SHE'S NOT PINK"

B. R. Rollnick and C. I. Kaye, "Hemifacial Microsomia and Variants: Pedigree Data," *American Journal of Medical Genetics* 15 (1983): 233–53.

P. J. Morrison et al., "Cardiovascular Abnormalities in the Oculo-Auriculo-Vertebral Spectrum (Goldenhar Syndrome)," *American Journal of Medical Genetics* 44 (1992): 425–28.

J. M. Connor and C. Fernandez, "Genetic Aspects of Hemifacial Microsomia," letter, *Human Genetics* 68 (1984): 349.

G. N. Wilson, "Cranial Defects in the Goldenhar Syndrome," *American Journal of Medical Genetics* 14 (1983): 435–43.

## CHAPTER 17 "I DIDN'T GET MY KISS FROM NAIA THIS MORNING"

A detailed description of Naia's open-heart surgery was contained in the surgical notes written by Dr. Lee Ellison and provided to the author. Ellison also elaborated on the notes in interviews.

Helen Buckler, *Daniel Hale Williams: Negro Surgeon* (New York: Pittman, 1954).

Harris B. Shumacker Jr., *A Dream of the Heart: The Life of John H. Gibbon, Father of the Heart-Lung Machine* (Santa Barbara, Calif.: Fithian Press, 1999).

Ruth Hubbard, "Eugenics: New Tools, Old Ideas," in *Women and Health: Embryos, Ethics, and Women's Rights: Exploring the New Reproductive Technologies,* ed. Elaine Hoffman Baruch et al. (New York: Harrington Park Press, 1987), 225–35.

## CHAPTER 18 "IT'S LIKE HER BIRTH, WHEN SHE DIDN'T CRY"

Nancy J. Lobaugh et al., "Piracetam Does Not Enhance Cognitive Abilities in Moderate- to High-Functioning Seven- to Thirteen Year-Old Children with Down Syndrome," *Archives of Pediatric and Adolescent Medicine* 155, no. 4 (2001): 442–48.

Information on Targeted Nutritional Intervention and Nutrivene-D is contained on a Web site affiliated with Dixie Lawrence Tafoya, see members.aol.com/TheRagans/.

Steven William Fowkes, "An Interview with Dixie Lawrence (Tafoya)," *Smart Drug News,* July 18, 1994, available on-line at www.ceri.com/dixie.htm.

Len Leshin, "Nutritional Supplements for Down Syndrome: What Happens When Hope Meets Hype," *Nutrition Forum* 15, no. 4 (July 18, 1998). Leshin also maintains the Web site "Down Syndrome Health Issues: News and Information for Parents and Professionals," at www.ds-health.com. He is a board-certified Texas pediatrician, a father of a son with Down syndrome, and a member of the Down Syndrome Medical Interest Group.

Transcript of CBS *48 Hours* show on Nutrivene-D and Piracetam, "Hype or Hope?" aired August 21, 1997.

Ani C. et al., "Nutritional Supplementation in Down Syndrome: Theoretical Considerations and Current Status," *Developmental Medicine and Child Neurology* 42 (2000): 207–13.

Siegfried M. Pueschel and Jeanette K. Pueschel, *Biomedical Concerns in Persons with Down Syndrome* (Baltimore, Md.: Paul H. Brookes), 39–46, 294–96.

SOURCES

Ira T. Lott and Ernest McCoy, *Down Syndrome: Advances in Medical Care* (New York: Wiley-Liss, 1992), 88–90.

Mark Selikowitz, "Controversial Treatments" in *Down Syndrome, The Facts* (New York: Oxford University Press, 1990), 180–87.

Paul T. Rogers and Mary Coleman, *Medical Care in Down Syndrome: A Preventive Medicine Approach* (New York: Marcel Dekker, 1992), 275.


CHAPTER 19 "NAIA IS A MIRACLE JUST AS SHE IS"

Len Leshin, "Plastic Surgery in Children with Down Syndrome," available on-line at www.ds-health.com.

R. R. Olbrisch, "Plastic and Aesthetic Surgery on Children with Down's Syndrome," *Aesthetic Plastic Surgery* 9 (1985): 241–48.

R. B. Jones, "Parental Consent to Cosmetic Facial Surgery in Down's Syndrome," *Journal of Medical Ethics* 26 (2000): 101–42.

Jane Southward, "Helping to Face a Cruel Society," *Sun Herald* (Sydney, Australia), June 29, 1997, 56.

S. M. Pueschel, L. A. Montiero, and M. Erickson, "Parents' and Physicians' Perceptions of Facial Plastic Surgery in Children with Down Syndrome," *Journal of Mental Deficiency Research* 30 (1986): 71–79.

Cate Terwilliger, "Down Syndrome Families Find a Role Model," (Colorado Springs) *Gazette Telegraph,* November 20, 1989, D1.

Policy statement of the Australian Society of Plastic Surgeons on procedures for children and adults with Down syndrome, available on-line at www.asps.asn.au/downsyn/.

"Hearing Parental Voices: An Opinion Survey on the Use of Plastic Surgery for Children with Down Syndrome," an unpublished survey, conducted in 2000 by Marcie Lewis, graduate student at Brandeis University.

[no byline], "Fire Destroys Warehouse in Hartford," Associated Press, moved on regional wires June 23, 1999.

"After the Fire," editorial, (Hartford) *Courant,* June 25, 1999, A20.


CHAPTER 20 "DA-DA!"

Individuals with Disabilities Education Act, Title 20 U.S.C., Chapter 33.

Chris Borthwick, "Racism, IQ, and Down's Syndrome," *Disability and Society* 11, no. 3 (1996): 403–10.

## CHAPTER 21 "WE HAVE THE ENCYCLOPEDIA, BUT WE DON'T HAVE *HAMLET*"

Rick Callahan, "Scientists Map Human Chromosome Associated with Down Syndrome," story moved on the Associated Press wires, May 9, 2000.

M. Hattori et al., "The DNA Sequence of Human Chromosome 21," *Nature* 405 (2000): 311–19.

Remarks by the president on the completion of the first survey of the entire human genome. Issued by the Office of the White House Press Secretary on June 30, 2000.

Richard Saltus, "Scientists Plot Road Map of Human DNA," also headlined "Decoding of Genome Declared; Rivals Present Rough Findings," *Boston Globe,* June 27, 2000, 1.

Craig Venter and Cohen Daniel, "Genome Research: Out of the Frying Pan or into the Fire? Potential Benefits Are Legion, but Abuses and Downsides May Make Us Rue the Day We Could Grow Wings on a Man," *Los Angeles Times,* June 26, 2000, B9.

CNN Staff Reports, "Genome Announcement a Milestone, but Only a Beginning," available on-line at www.CNN.com, posted June 26, 2000. (CNN-*Time* poll results included in Web story.)

Tom Humphrey, "Farragut Woman Reads Letter at Convention," (Knoxville) *News-Sentinel,* August 3, 2000, 1.

"Politically Incorrect" transcript, from episode airing January 11, 2001, provided by the National Down Syndrome Society. (Original transcript was removed from ABC's Web site.)

Sam Allis, "Conversation with Silber: 'Anybody Who Leads People and Has Ideas Is Going to Scare Some People,'" *Boston Globe,* December 12, 1999, 1.

## CHAPTER 22 "YOU KIND OF KNOW YOU CAN LIVE THROUGH IT"

Interview with Mrs. Laura Robinson, conducted by Mohini Shapero and Bjorn Schuman, October 9, 1995, as part of the Kellytown Oral History Project, under the auspices of the University of Virginia School of Architecture and the Curry School of Education.

*Buck v. Bell,* 247 U.S. 200 (1927).

Interview with Professor David O'Brien of the University of Virginia, by Sarah Salwen, available on-line at www.people.virginia.edu/mol3r/buck.html.

## CHAPTER 23 "NAIA! COME BACK!"

William A. Rieck and Donna E. Dugger-Wadsworth, "Inclusion: Administrative Headache or Opportunity?" *NASSP Bulletin,* October 1, 2000, 56–62.

Terry G. Cronis and David N. Ellis, "Issues Facing Special Educators in the New Millennium," *Education,* June 6, 2000, 639–48.

James Kauffman, "Today's Special Education and Its Messages for Tomorrow," *Journal of Special Education* 244 (December 1999): 244–54.

Michael Bérubé, *Life as We Know It: A Father, a Family, and an Exceptional Child* (New York: Vintage, 1998), 217.

Joseph P. Shapiro et al., "Separate and Unequal: America's Special Education System Was Intended to Give Disabled Kids an Edge. But It Is Cheating Many—and Costing the Rest of Us Billions," *U.S. News and World Report,* December 13, 1993, 46–60.

Michael A. Fletcher, "Bush Administration Gears up to Revamp Special Education," *Washington Post,* October 5, 2001, A3.

Marci J. Hanson et al., "After Preschool Inclusion: Children's Educational Pathways over the Early School Years," *Exceptional Children,* October 1, 2001, 65–83.

Lon Grahnke, "Experts View Merits, Risks of Including Disabled Children in Classroom," story moved on the Associated Press wires, February 28, 1999.

Janice Crompton, "Flagpole Mom Ends Her Protest; Agreement Reached for Schooling of Son," (Pittsburgh) *Post-Gazette,* September 20, 2000, B1.


## CHAPTER 25 "I THINK WE SHOULD TALK ABOUT IT MORE"

Don Van Dyke, Dianne McBrien, and Andrea Sherbondy, "Issues of Sexuality in Down Syndrome," reprint of article originally published in *Down Syndrome Research and Practice* 3, no. 2 (1995).

L. Bovicelli et al., "Reproduction in Down Syndrome," *Obstetrics and Gynecology* 59 (1982): 13S-17S.

Jason Kingsley and Mitchell Levitz, *Count Us In: Growing up with Down Syndrome* (San Diego, Calif.: Harcourt Brace & Company, 1994).

Siegfried M. Pueschel, ed., *A Parent's Guide to Down Syndrome: Toward a Brighter Future,* 2nd ed. (Baltimore, Md.: Paul H. Brookes), 237–46.

# SELECTED BIBLIOGRAPHY

Asch, Adrienne. 1999. "Prenatal Diagnosis and Selective Abortion: A Challenge to Practice and Policy." *American Journal of Public Health* 89, no. 11, 1,649–57.

Bakely, Donald C. 1997. *Bethy and the Mouse: A Father Remembers His Children with Disabilities*. Cambridge, Mass.: Brookline Books.

Beck, Martha. 1999. *Expecting Adam: A True Story of Birth, Rebirth, and Everyday Magic*. New York: Times Books.

Belkin, Lisa. 2001. "The Made-to-Order Savior: Producing a Perfect Baby Sibling," *New York Times Sunday Magazine*, July 1, 36–43, 48, 62–63.

Benjamin, Peggy H. 1991. *Andy: A Biography of a Boy with Down's Syndrome*. Lincoln, Nebr.: Midgard Press.

Bérubé, Michael. 1998. *Life as We Know It: A Father, a Family, and an Exceptional Child*. New York: Vintage.

Boston, Sarah. 1994. *Too Deep for Tears: Eighteen Years after the Death of Will, My Son*. London: Rivers Oram Press.

Brill, Marlene Targ. 1993. *Keys to Parenting a Child with Down Syndrome*. Hauppauge, N.Y.: Barron's Educational Series.

Bruni, Maryanne. 1998. *Fine Motor Skills in Children with Down Syndrome: A Guide for Parents and Professionals*. Bethesda, Md.: Woodbine House.

Buyse, Mary Louise, ed. 1990. *Birth Defects Encyclopedia: The Comprehensive, Systematic, Illustrated Reference Source for the Diagnosis, Delineation, Etiology, Biodynamics, Occurrence, Prevention, and Treatment of Human Anomalies of Clinical Relevance*. Oxford: Blackwell Science.

Cairo, Shelly, et al. 1991. *Our Brother Has Down's Syndrome: An Introduction for Children*. Toronto: Annick Press.

Cloud, Harriet H., and J. E. Drews. 1996. *Nutrition and Fitness for Children with Down Syndrome: A Guide for Parents*. Bethesda, Md.: Woodbine House.

Dmitriev, Valentine. 2000. *Time to Begin: Early Education for Children with Down Syndrome*. 2nd edition, revised. Austin, Tex.: Pro-Ed.

Fadiman, Anne. 1997. *The Spirit Catches You and You Fall Down: A Hmong Child, Her American Doctors, and the Collision of Two Cultures*. New York: Farrar, Straus and Giroux.

Geraghty, Helen Monsoon, with J. Callahan and L. Lewis, designers. 1995. *Chris Burke: The Young Actor Who Has Down Syndrome*. New York: Chelsea House.

# SELECTED BIBLIOGRAPHY

Gill, B. 1997. *Changed by a Child: Companion Notes for Parents of a Child with a Disability*. Garden City, N.Y.: Doubleday.

Gosden, Roger. 1999. *Designing Babies: The Brave New World of Reproductive Technology*. New York: W. H. Freeman.

Gould, Stephen Jay. 1980. *The Panda's Thumb: More Reflections in Natural History*. New York: W. W. Norton.

Graham, Lawrence Otis. 1999. *Our Kind of People: Inside America's Black Upper Class*. New York: HarperCollins.

Hassold, T. J., and D. Patterson, eds. 1999. *Down Syndrome: A Promising Future Together*. New York: John Wiley & Sons.

Hayden, Robert C., and Karen E. Hayden. 1999. *African-Americans on Martha's Vineyard and Nantucket*. Boston: Select Publications.

Hubbard, Ruth. 1993. *Exploding the Gene Myth*. Boston: Beacon Press.

Hunt, Nigel. 1967. *The World of Nigel Hunt: The Diary of a Mongoloid Youth*. New York: Taplinger.

Italia, B. 1992. *Chris Burke: Star of Life Goes on (Reaching for the Stars)*. Edina, Minn.: Abdo & Daughters.

Jablow, Martha Moragham. 1983. *Cara: Growing with a Retarded Child*. Philadelphia, Pa.: Temple University Press.

Josephson, Gretchen. 1997. *Bus Girl: Poems*. Cambridge, Mass.: Brookline Books.

Kingsley, Jason, and Mitchell Levitz. 1994. *Count Us In: Growing up with Down Syndrome*. San Diego, Calif.: Harcourt Brace.

Koop, C. Everett. 1991. *Koop: The Memoirs of America's Family Doctor*. New York: Random House.

Krantz, Hazel. 1990. *For the Love of Jeremy*. New York: Dutton.

Kumin, Libby. 2001. *Classroom Language Skills for Children with Down Syndrome: A Guide for Parents and Teachers*. Bethesda, Md.: Woodbine House.

Larson, Edward J. 1996. *Sex, Race, and Science: Eugenics in the Deep South*. Baltimore, Md.: Johns Hopkins University Press.

Lewontin, Richard. 2001. *It Ain't Necessarily So: The Dream of the Human Genome and Other Illusions*. 2nd edition. New York: New York Review Books.

Lott, Bret. 1999. *Jewel*. New York: Pocket Books.

Lott, Ira T., and Ernest McCoy. 1992. *Down Syndrome: Advances in Medical Care*. New York: Wiley-Liss.

MacGregor, J. M., with L. A. Borensztein, photographer. 1999. *Metamorphosis: The Fiber Art of Judith Scott. The Outsider Artist and the Experience of Down's Syndrome.* Oakland, Calif.: Creative Growth Center.

Marino, B., and S. M. Pueschel, eds. 1996. *Heart Disease in Persons with Down Syndrome.* Baltimore, Md.: Paul H. Brookes.

Martin, Emily. 1987. *The Woman in the Body: A Cultural Analysis of Reproduction.* Boston: Beacon Press.

McDaniel, J. B., and Christopher Burke. 1993. *A Special Kind of Hero.* Reprint edition. New York: Dell.

McDermott, Jeanne. 2000. *Babyface: A Story of Heart and Bones.* Bethesda, Md.: Woodbine House.

Melberg, K., and D. Hingsburger. 1997. *Sexuality, Relationships, and Down's Syndrome: A Guide for Parents of Children, Juveniles, and Adults.* Baltimore, Md.: Paul H. Brookes.

Miller, G. Wayne. 1993. *The Work of Human Hands: Hardy Hendren and Surgical Wonder at Children's Hospital.* New York: Random House.

Minnick, Molly A., Kathleen J. Delp, and Mary C. Ciotti. 1996. *A Time to Decide, a Time to Heal: For Parents Making Difficult Decisions about Babies They Love.* 4th edition. St. Johns, Mich.: Pineapple Press.

Noble, V. 1993. *Down Is up for Aaron Eagle: A Mother's Spiritual Journey with Down Syndrome.* New York: HarperCollins.

Pernick, Martin S. 1996. *The Black Stork: Eugenics and the Death of "Defective" Babies in American Medicine and Motion Pictures since 1915.* New York: Oxford University Press.

———. 1985. *A Calculus of Suffering: Pain, Professionalism, and Anesthesia in Nineteenth-Century America.* New York: Columbia University Press.

Pueschel, Siegfried M., ed. 2000. *A Parent's Guide to Down Syndrome: Toward a Brighter Future.* 2nd edition. Baltimore, Md.: Paul H. Brookes.

———. 1988. *The Young Person with Down Syndrome: Transition from Adolescence to Adulthood.* Baltimore, Md.: Paul H. Brookes.

Pueschel, Siegfried M., and Lynn Steiberg. 1980. *Down's Syndrome: A Comprehensive Bibliography.* New York: Garland STPM Press.

Rickert, J. E., and P. McGahan, photographer. 2000. *Russ and the Almost Perfect Day.* Bethesda, Md.: Woodbine House.

Ridley, Matt. 1999. *Genome: The Autobiography of a Species in Twenty-three Chapters.* New York: HarperCollins.

Rogers, Dale Evans. 1992. *Angel Unaware.* Reprint edition. Tarrytown, N.Y.: Fleming H. Revell.

Rothman, Barbara Katz. 2000. *The Book of Life: A Personal and Ethical Guide to Race, Normality, and the Implications of the Human Genome Project.* Boston: Beacon Press.

———. 1986. *The Tentative Pregnancy.* New York: Penguin Books.

Schwier, K. M. 1996. *Sexuality, Relationships, and Down Syndrome: A Guide for Parents of Children, Juveniles.* Bethesda, Md.: Woodbine House.

Selden, Steven. 1999. *Inheriting Shame: The Story of Eugenics and Racism in America.* New York: Teachers College Press.

Selikowitz, Mark. 1997. *Down Syndrome: The Facts.* New York: Oxford University Press.

Shonkoff, J. P., and E. Yatchmink. 1995. "Helping Families Deal with Bad News." In *Behavioral and Developmental Pediatrics: A Handbook for Primary Care.* S. Parker and B. Zuckerman, eds. Boston: Little, Brown.

Shriver, Maria. 2001. *What's Wrong with Timmy?* Boston: Little, Brown.

Stallings, Gene, and Sally Cook. 1997. *Another Season: A Coach's Story of Raising an Exceptional Son.* Boston: Little, Brown.

Stray-Gundersen, K., ed. 1995. *Babies with Down Syndrome: A New Parents Guide.* 2nd edition. Bethesda, Md.: Woodbine House.

Stuve-Bodeeen, Stephanie, and Pam Devito. 1998. *We'll Paint the Octopus Red.* Bethesda, Md.: Woodbine House.

Suskind, Ron. 1998. *A Hope in the Unseen: An American Odyssey from the Inner City to the Ivy League.* New York: Broadway Books.

Trent, James W., Jr. 1994. *Inventing the Feeble Mind: A History of Mental Retardation in the United States.* Berkeley: University of California Press.

Unruh, J. F. 1994. *Down Syndrome: Successful Parenting of Children with Down Syndrome.* Eugene, Oreg.: Fern Ridge Press.

Van Dyke, D. C., et al., eds. 1995. *Medical and Surgical Care for Children with Down Syndrome. A Guide for Parents.* Bethesda, Md.: Woodbine House.

Wertz, Richard W., and Dorothy C. Wertz. 1989. *Lying-In: A History of Childbirth in America.* New Haven, Conn.: Yale University Press.

Winders, Patricia C. 1997. *Gross Motor Skills in Children with Down Syndrome: A Guide for Parents and Professionals.* Bethesda, Md.: Woodbine House.

Wingerson, Lois. 1999. *Unnatural Selection: The Promise and the Power of Human Gene Research.* New York: Bantam Books.

# ACKNOWLEDGMENTS

My deepest thanks to Greg and Tierney Fairchild, two remarkable, courageous people. They were unfailingly gracious throughout the hundreds of hours we spent together in person and on the phone during the past four years. That was true even when they were sad or uncertain, even when they knew the information they were sharing or the events I was witnessing didn't cast them or their loved ones in the best light.

People often asked me why Tierney and Greg would open their lives to a stranger, submitting to a process that even I had to admit was something of a journalistic proctology exam. They provided the answer the first time we met: they believed that if people knew they had chosen to have this child, she and others like her would have a better chance for full and happy lives. That commitment never wavered.

I am equally grateful to Naia, a delightful girl who sorely tested my efforts to be an impartial, largely unseen observer. Her flirty games of peek-a-boo were nearly my undoing. She has been confounding expectations since birth, and I expect she'll do so her entire life. I'll be rooting for her, and watching. Thanks also to Cole, an adorable guy who never seemed unhappy about sharing the spotlight with his beloved big sister.

I owe a dept of gratitude to the Temple and Fairchild families, especially Bob and Mary Fairchild, Joan Temple, and Tara Temple. They welcomed me in every way and provided invaluable help in understanding the forces that have shaped Tierney and Greg.

My friend and *Boston Globe* colleague Dick Lehr believed from the start that *Choosing Naia* should be a book. He backed up his words by reading this manuscript in draft form and talking me down from rhetorical ledges over burgers and beers. Former *Globe* Spotlight Team editor Gerry O'Neill taught me the pleasures of digging to the bottom of every story, then digging some more. I admire him greatly.

I am indebted to Ben Bradlee Jr., who did a great job editing the *Globe* stories that formed the outline of this book. When I proposed a narrative series on prenatal choices, I had just spent three years as an investigative reporter. Hearing my idea, Ben cracked, "Zuckoff, are you going soft on me?" Then he put his shoulder down and cleared a path.

My friends and family have listened to me discuss this project endlessly, and I thank them for their patience and encouragement: Jeff Feigelson, Brian McGrory, Naftali Bendavid, Steve Bailey, Marjorie Pritchard, Joann Muller, Bill Rapai, Joe Kahn, Kate Shaplen, Richard Brackett, Jim Kreiter, Debby Kreiter, Reita Ennis, Bonnie Gorscak, Paul Kreiter, Satomi Kreiter, Jo Kreiter, Josef Norris, and my nephews, Lex, Andy, Austin, and Arthur.

Christopher Callahan, assistant dean of journalism at the University of Maryland, has provided me with nearly two decades of excellent advice and even better friendship.

# ACKNOWLEDGMENTS

I've spent thirteen years as a reporter for the *Globe,* and I'm deeply grateful for the friendship and support I've found there. Marty Nolan sponsored me, Stephen Kurkjian believed in me, and Michael Larkin and John Burke hired me. All remain true friends. Matt Storin gave me the freedom and encouragement to follow Naia. I've also had the great pleasure of working for and with editors Jack Driscoll, Helen Donovan, Greg Moore, Al Larkin, Tom Mulvoy, Mark Morrow, Louisa Williams, John Yemma, Tom Ashbrook, Don Skwar, Mary Jane Wilkinson, Ellen Clegg, Lucy Bartholomay, and Ann Scales. Special thanks to *Globe* friends Linda Hunt, Doug Bailey, Ande Zellman, Wil Haygood, Maureen Dezell, Anthony Flint, Larry Tye, Bruce Butterfield, Stan Grossfeld, Eileen McNamara, Wendy Fox, Joanne Rathe Strohmeyer, Eileen Peart, Ann Green, Barbara McDonough, Rose Devine, Margaret Murray, Don Norton, Steve Pena, Jack Thomas, Ellen Goodman, and Jon Albano of Bingham Dana & Gould. I'm indebted to Streett Jacobs for scaring his mother, Sally, and setting me on this path. Thanks also to publisher Richard Gilman and his predecessors, Ben Taylor and Bill Taylor.

Former *Globe* designer Janet Michaud used her formidable gifts to make the *Globe* series shine. Photo editor Leann Burden and copy editor George Patista treated the work with the care of journalistic NICU nurses. Thanks also to *Globe* librarians Lisa Tuite, Marc Shechtman, Bill Boles, Betty Grillo, Kathleen Hennrikus, Wanda Joseph-Rollins, Charlie Smiley, and Richard Pennington.

The Foundation for Child Development gave me a generous fellowship, and I appreciate the kindness of Carol Guensburg and Mary Crane at the University of Maryland School of Journalism.

The journey from newspaper series to book began when narrative journalism guru Mark Kramer invited me to speak at his annual conference. He introduced me to Helene Atwan, director of Beacon Press. That makes Mark godfather and friend. I can't fully express my gratitude to Helene, who as editor and publisher is godmother and midwife. She's a writer's dream. I am also grateful to the entire Beacon team, notably David Coen, Tom Hallock, Pam MacColl, Amy Smith Bell, Christopher Vyce, and Sara Eisenman, for their remarkable efforts.

Wilbur Doctor, emeritus dean of journalism at the University of Rhode Island, taught me everything. Leland Schwartz of States News Service rescued me. Bret Lott provided encouragement and generously shared his grandmother's letters. Dr. Allen Crocker was the first person outside the *Globe* with whom I discussed this idea. His devotion to people with Down syndrome is unsurpassed, and he helped me to believe in the value of this work.

Jo Ann Simons of the National Down Syndrome Congress offered steadfast support. Myra Madnick of the National Down Syndrome Society was an enormous help. Judith Tsipis at Brandeis University posted my "Wanted" memo on the Internet listserv for genetic counselors. That led me to Alicia Craffey, who led me to Tierney and Greg. Alicia's help meant the world to me. Several times, she playfully suggested that this book was really about her. Alicia, here's a secret: You were right. And yes, Julia Roberts should play you in the movie.

Numerous doctors and nurses allowed me to get in the way and pester them about what they were doing to and for Naia. Thanks to the staffs of Saint Francis Hospital, Connecticut Children's Medical Center, and Hartford Hospital, especially Drs. Lee Ellison, Michael Bourque, Seth Lapuk, Hank Leopold, and James F. X. Egan, nurses Karen Mazzarella and Cookie Eckel, and public relations pros Pete Mobilia and Tom Hanley.

Dr. Len Leshin's research and suggestions were a great help and much appreciated.

Special thanks to the Mallin, Bento, Dreyfus-Walters, and Wolfe families, for trusting me with their stories. Thanks also to the couple whose story ends this book.

My parents, Sid and Gerry Zuckoff, taught me to value hard work, to believe in myself, and to have empathy for others. I was born lucky. My brother, Allan Zuckoff, became a published author first and, as always, gave me something to shoot for.

This book is dedicated to my daughters, Isabel and Eve, who inspire and delight me. Without them, I wouldn't have understood the issues this story raised. They tolerate my devotion to work and, I hope, know it could never rival my devotion to them.

The hardest person to thank is my wife, Suzanne Kreiter, because there is so much to thank her for and no way to do so adequately, though I suspect she has a few ideas. We conceived this project together, and her contributions are on every page. Her photographs of the Fairchild family enlightened me. Her editing amazed me. She sustains me.